For Colton and Pierce

*May you realize all your dreams and goals
and find great happiness along the way.
I hope your lives are filled with
significance and success, good
health, lasting friendships,
and most of all, love.*

*With Love,
Dad*

FORWARD

NOW IS ONE of the greatest times on earth to be alive. This is one of the best books you can read to make the most of your future.

Bill Townsend? Never heard of him. That's because you've just begun to question how to become successful.

This is no armchair chat. Bill Townsend has been there–done that. Now he shares hard learned secrets for anyone willing to get off the couch and get into the action of the 21st century. In a world where everything is changing, opportunity is everywhere. You just need to know how to jump in.

These simple, well thought, timeless pages will change the way you think about what to do with your future "next"–no matter who you are –no matter where you come from.

I've been a lot of places on hundreds of successful journeys in business, show-business and life. If I'd known Bill and had this book 20 years ago, there would have been a lot more "WOW!" and a lot less "ouch" along the way. You've got a big advantage. You can put Bill's knowledge to work in your own life right now.

So who's Bill Townsend? He's a kid from the coal mining, steel mills towns of Western Pennsylvania who wound up becoming a leader in the monetization of the Internet. He's started companies with a few hundred dollars and turned them into multi-million dollar ventures with global impact.

Everyone Bill knows wanted the stories and the secrets. So here it is. Straight, simple, no added sugar, no trans-fats. In *"Yes You Can,"* Townsend shares what he's learned from building some of the biggest names on the Internet including Lycos, Deja.com (now Google and eBay), GeoCitics (now Yahoo!), sixdegrees.com (now LinkedIn) and more.

Sorry, Harvard, you don't need an MBA to rock the world.

"Yes You Can" is more than a "look what I did" memoir or an ego trip about business. Don't let the simplicity of Bill's presentation fool you. Buy the ticket. Take the journey.

You'll travel through Bill's experience and discover stories of others who have created successful lives, careers, and relationships. No matter who you are, you can use these pages to take control of your life and become more successful immediately.

Here's the director's advice. Own your own future. Take two chapters a day and change your life.

You're the next great story. Get started living it. Ready? OK. And, Action!

James Kellahin
Los Angeles, California

James Kellahin is an multi-award winning television director/producer/writer who began as an original advertising Mad Man. You can find him on Google, IMDB or LinkedIn to learn more.

WHAT AWAITS YOU

PROLOGUE

Yes You Can: How To Be A Success No Matter Who You Are Or Where You're From

THE BOOK YOU are about to read is for any person of any age who believes there is more to life than sitting on the sidelines and watching the game go by. It is for people who believe that the world holds something better for them, but perhaps they don't know where to begin to make that something a reality. It is for those of you who believe that success is something you can achieve regardless of your background, handicaps, or self-imposed limitations.

Every person reading this has undeveloped potential. Potential is defined as existing in possibility but not in actuality. It's the things you can do if you are just given a road map to help you do them. You have powerful abilities on the inside of you right now that may not be in use. This book may be the jumpstart you need to activate those skills and realize your dreams.

Within these pages, I hope to provide you with knowledge you can use to turn your hopes, dreams and ideas into golden opportunities that will define your way of life forever.

This book is unlike the numerous business books with their MBA terminology that fill the shelves of the local bookstore. This one doesn't profess to teach you how to master accounting, read a balance sheet, determine net present value, or develop an organizational plan for managing a Fortune 500 company. No, this book is written to give you the push you need to make positive changes in your life, beginning immediately. It is a tool for you to use as you begin life as a *successful person*. As you'll see, success doesn't have to relate to money alone. In fact, money is often simply a derivation of success.

A book alone cannot guarantee success, but it can be used to inspire your own creative genius. A book can provide you with suggestions, rules and guidelines; but only you can turn your dreams into realities. You must seek success and be absolutely dedicated to making your life the best it can be. It's not as hard as you may believe. It only requires that you be open to making your life better tomorrow than it was today.

Whether you wish to become a successful entrepreneur, successful friend, successful spouse, successful parent, or successful employee, if you strive to become successful, you can. You've probably heard the old saying, *"It's up to you";* well truth be known, it is up to you. Nobody can make changes in your life the way you can. Nobody can force you to be successful, but you sure can try to be. It is my hope that these pages will give you the motivation you need to take life by the horns and ride it 'round the corral to its fullest extent.

There are millions of people who have dreams that they keep bottled up for fear of failure. Perhaps they don't even know where to begin to turn their dreams into action. I hope as you read this book you will gain enough knowledge, enthusiasm, and direction to go out into the world and take action.

My motives in writing this book are to provide you with an easy-to-read guide to help you realize that success is possible no matter your situation. There are dozens of former and current employees who have encouraged me to share my thoughts on what it takes to succeed. Many of these people have experienced success, and while some would say I've taught them how to be successful, the truth is, they've taught themselves, by being mentally ready to receive success and make it happen and by opening their lives and being prepared for opportunity when it presents itself.

One last thought before you turn the page: Don't read this book because you have nothing else to do or because you think it will make a great addition to your bookcase. You'd be better off driving to a fast food restaurant and saturating your arteries with animal fat. Read this book with the goal of gaining practical knowledge that you can use in your daily activities and then act on what you've learned. Read it with the understanding that with every page you turn, you get one step closer to your goal. Read it knowing that tomorrow will be better than today and the next day even better than tomorrow. Be positive. Be open. Then you'll be on to the start of something big.

Now, let's get on to the good stuff.

Note: Some people prefer not to have their name included in a book and I have respected their request for anonymity by changing their names. This in no way decreases the value of validity of their stories, but does, at their request, protect their identities. In compiling information for this book, I have used my best efforts to ensure names, dates, and other information is correct. If I got something wrong, please forgive me. Even if the data is slightly incorrect, the gist of the story will still have relevance to finding your significance.

CHAPTER 1

Yes You Can: Pave Your Own Way

If you'll teach me everything you know about advertising,
I'll work here for free.

FOLLOWING MY SENIOR YEAR at the College of Wooster in Wooster, Ohio, I moved to Lexington, Kentucky to take a job with a harness racing magazine. It was a fulltime job offering a paycheck and since recruiters weren't knocking on my door to hire an art major from Pittsburgh, I took it with a bit of excitement mixed with trepidation. I wasn't sure publishing was for me but, like a few million other college graduates that year, I needed a job. This one paid $17,000 a year and I was excited to be entering the publishing industry. The job lasted five weeks. I couldn't stand the political infighting, the monotony of the position, and I simply knew it wasn't the way I wanted to spend the next few years of my young life. My employer and I parted ways and I left with $367 in my pocket and 10 months left on my apartment lease.

I had a serious decision to make. Where would I look for another job? Would I bartend somewhere? Would I move back to Pittsburgh and start over? All I knew was that I had $367 and owed $4,000 on my apartment lease. I also owed $253 a month on my car payment, $110 a month for insurance, $80 a month minimum credit card payment, plus miscellaneous expenses like electricity, water, and food. Something had to give. I spent the next few days trying to decide on a plan of action. I began interviewing, going through a list of companies in the phone book. Nothing panned out, yet I decided to stick with it and began asking friends for help in finding a new career.

You see, after leaving the magazine I decided I needed a career, not a job. There is a big difference. A job is something you go to each day and someone gives you a paycheck every two weeks. A career is something you do because you love it. It's all you can think about. It consumes you in such positive ways that you can't imagine doing anything else. That's how I wanted to spend my time and what I suggest you focus on too.

Determine Your Career Path

I began figuring out what I wanted to do with my life by making a list of every skill I had. I could draw and illustrate. I was a good photographer. I enjoyed creative endeavors. I loved television and movies. I had no formal business training but I could write a headline that would make you want to buy something. About this time my father bought me David Ogilvy's hallmark book, *Ogilvy on Advertising*, and I read it from cover to cover in one night. Working for a magazine wasn't a career for me, but perhaps being on the creative side of advertising was. Yes, this would be the path I would follow. I felt this is what I wanted to do. I would be an advertising man!

I set out to interview at all the local advertising agencies and began with the letter A in the phone book. It was a company called Ad-Success. I called the co-owner, Paul Scanlon, and set up an appointment to meet with him. A few days later I arrived in my khakis and neatly pressed shirt. Paul and I had what I thought was a very positive interview that covered what his agency did, what I wanted in a job, and whether there was a fit between the two. Well, I didn't get the job, but Paul gave me a few words of advice that I never forgot. He said, "Buy yourself a tie. Dress for the job you want, not the job you have." Would you believe I went to a job interview without a tie or jacket? It sounds like a simple mistake, but it's one that thousands of job seekers make every day. So you see, even though I didn't get the job, I learned something that would help me on my road to success. Now you have too.

"Dress for the job you want, not the job you have." Eleven words that can help you make a positive first impression in any situation. Taking a plane trip? Dress for the job you want, not the job you have. You never know who you might be sitting next to. Attending a Chamber of Commerce meeting to network? Dress for the job you want, not the job you have. Show professionalism and you'll garner more respect.

A few weeks after my interview with Paul Scanlon I had interviewed at more than 15 agencies in Central Kentucky. Nobody would hire me because I didn't have experience. And I couldn't get experience because nobody would hire me. I was caught in the same Catch-22 situation that millions of young people find themselves in after college or high school.

My family had been raising horses for many years and I had come to peripherally know a man by the name of Art Zubrod. Art is the manager of Brittany Farms in Versailles, Kentucky and is one of the nicest, most genuine people you could ever meet. Besides knowing everything about horse racing and breeding, he knows everyone in the horse industry. Once I told Art I was hoping to work in the advertising business, he suggested I visit the ad agency he used, which was called b.todd advertising.

b.todd advertising was listed under the T's in the phone book's listing of advertising agencies. They were the last listing shown and as fate would have it, I had just finished meeting with the agencies that began with M through S the previous week; all to no avail. b.todd advertising held the final opportunity I had to break into advertising and start my career.

Bruce Todd was the president of the agency. He proudly ran a small advertising business, and along with his wife, Nancy, built the firm to about $1,000,000 in revenue. Bruce's firm handled the advertising for three Pepsi-Cola bottlers, which made up 90% of his business and was interested in growing it beyond soft drinks. Because his was a small business, he wasn't in the position to hire someone, but as I sat across from him I knew this was my opportunity to move toward becoming a success.

As I listened to Bruce and his dissertation on the state of advertising, and admired the many awards on his wall, it struck me that the only way I was going to break into advertising was to make an offer that Bruce couldn't afford to pass up.

"If you'll teach me everything you know about advertising, I'll work here for free," I blurted out. Whoa! Did I just say that? The look on Bruce's face was priceless. He must have been thinking, "I must be crazy! Did I hear that right? Did this kid just offer to work for free?"

Perhaps he thought I said something else. So I repeated the offer. He looked at me as if I had just pronounced that in a previous life I was the King of England. After a few seconds of awkward silence he said, "Let me see what I can do." We concluded our meeting and went our separate ways. As I drove back to my apartment I feared I had appeared too desperate, but I hadn't any other means of breaking into an industry I thought I would enjoy working in day after day.

Three days later Bruce called to ask if my offer still stood and whether I could come to the office the next day. I replied with a resounding, "Yes I can!" I started work at 8 a.m. the next morning. My first ad was a design for a billboard for Pepsi-Cola with a large 2-liter bottle half obscured in ice with the simply headline, "Thirsty?" That afternoon I wrote my first radio spot. The next day I created a two-page advertisement for P.J. Baugh's Almahurst Farm and a series of T-shirts for WKQQ radio. These were followed by another Pepsi ad; then a television commercial for a local car dealer. One week on the job and I had created a 30-second commercial that would soon air on television. And all with no formal training in advertising science. I began absorbing everything Bruce could teach me about the advertising business. I read dozens of books. I joined the local ad club. I associated with other advertising professionals, who I attempted to learn as much from as possible. I wasn't in a job, I was starting a career and I loved it! The ad business was fun!

Within two months, Bruce decided I was of such value to his ad agency that he began writing me a weekly paycheck. All of a sudden my financial worries were taken care of and I could *really* focus on learning the advertising business; which I did. Within three years I was given the title Vice President, Creative Director, and working for clients such as Pepsi-Cola, Jeep, and a bevy of others, including one of the leading horse racing and breeding operation in the country, Brittany Farms. Bruce challenged me to approach what was a staid industry and push harness horse marketing to new levels, and the work I did for Brittany Farms and other horse breeding operations won several awards. This ad business was the most exciting thing to which I had ever been exposed, and the more I taught myself about the business, the better I got at figuring out how to connect with customers in ways that moved my clients' products.

Soon more television spots I created were airing on TV stations. Ads I wrote and designed appeared in national newspapers and magazines. I won a couple more awards. Then a few more. Within a couple years more than 30 advertising awards graced my walls and bookshelf. My first steps toward success had been taken to great effect.

I had overcome a common Catch-22 situation and was now on my way to making more money, enjoying my new career, and building a future in advertising.

You may think you can't afford to work for free. I certainly didn't think about the financial consequences when I blurted out that line, but I was ready to wait tables, tend bar, mow grass, do anything and work any number of hours in order to break into the advertising business. I would work my advertising job for free but work another job at night to pay my expenses.

If you want something enough that you are willing to moonlight to get it, then by all means do so. I know people who have taken positions with firms on a part-time basis at a reduced wage or even a non-paid internship, in order to gain experience critical to their careers. A part-time position gives you the freedom to work a second job to support yourself while you build up the skills needed to move into your preferred role full-time.

A former employee of mine started by interning three afternoons a week, working in a restaurant the rest of the time. After four months she had learned enough in her internship to know that she wanted to pursue a career in advertising. She then transitioned to working three days for the agency and three at the restaurant. Within a few more months, she quit the $6 an hour restaurant job and joined the agency full time, earning $28 an hour. The point of all this is that if you really want to become successful, then sometimes you have to take a chance to make your dreams come true. When I look back on my time at b.todd advertising, I can't believe how fortunate I was: not only was advertising exciting and fun, but also because Bruce really did teach me everything he knew about the business, which has helped me in every business situation since.

Because of that one line, "If you'll teach me everything you know about advertising, I'll work here for free," my journey through the door of opportunity began.

What Did You Learn?

1. Dress for the job you want, not the job you have. Show people you are serious about your career and they will notice.
2. Sometimes you have to take a risk to achieve what you want. Don't be afraid to stick your toe out and take that first step.
3. Things won't be handed to you on a silver platter. Create an opportunity in order to get on the path you seek.
4. Be willing to work for free – for a little while. That may open the door to some of your greatest opportunities.
5. When the door to opportunity opens, learn as much about your job and the jobs of others so you become indispensable.

CHAPTER 2

Yes You Can: Decide to be Successful

If opportunity knocks, will you put down the
remote control and answer the door?

AMERICA IS THE land of opportunity, and with the exception of rare instances, there is nothing stopping you from excelling in life and fulfilling your dreams. There are more opportunities available today than ever before in the history of mankind. Read that again. *There are more opportunities today than ever before.* Do you believe this? I do. There are no barriers to success, but there are plenty of excuses. If you believe you will be a success, and you believe it with all your heart, then you are well on your way toward success, as you've never imagined.

There are no short cuts to success. Very few people win the lottery. Few inherit millions of dollars. Becoming a success may be the hardest thing you ever do, but the rewards are definitely worth any amount of pain or difficulty you have to endure. You must be willing to work hard and give up everything that stands in the way of achieving your goals. You must find the things you do well and make sure you exploit them for your continued personal benefit. This sounds like it isn't much fun, but trust me, it will be the most fun you'll ever have.

David Ogilvy, the founder of Ogilvy & Mather, one of the world's largest advertising agencies, once told me, "Not everyone can make it as a business owner. Some people prefer the security of working for a big corporation and that's fine for them, but realistically, there are always limits to success when you work for someone else." Your lifestyle may be comfortable, but you must adjust to the fact that you can only rise so high up the corporate ladder. Big decisions will always be handed down from above and you will never be fully in control. And therefore, you will not and cannot control your destiny.

Think about that for a moment. Do you want to have a faceless corporation control your life like a puppeteer controls his puppets, or do you want to set your own course, take responsibility for your actions, and reap the success that awaits you?

You Don't Need An MBA

"Well, I'm not able to start a business," you say. "I don't know what to do." Or, "I don't have the money." That attitude gets in the way of what you *can* do. All you need to do is learn how to take the first few steps toward becoming successful. You will learn how to run your business while you're doing so. It's called *on the job training* and it's more valuable than any college class you'll ever take. You don't need an MBA to run a business. You can pick up the basics of an MBA through books like *The Ten Day MBA* by Steven Silbiger or *The Portable MBA in Entrepreneurship* by William Bygrave. If you want to get started right away, save the $50,000 an MBA will cost you and invest $50-$100 in a handful of well written books that will help you run your business.

Quit worrying about not having the education to manage your own business. You'll learn what you need to know as you go along. For now, the thing you have to do is make up your mind that *you're going to become successful.*

There is tremendous benefit in waking up and taking the first couple minutes of each day to put yourself in a positive mental attitude. There is a lot of research that shows that people who think positively, act positively. The Law of Attraction says people's thoughts (both conscious and unconscious) dictate the reality of their lives, whether or not they're aware of it. Essentially, "if you really want something and believe it is possible, you'll probably get it." Of course, the opposite also holds true: that putting a lot of attention and thought onto something you don't want means you'll probably get that too. So you must avoid negative thoughts and focus on the positive. And focus not on what you want, but think about what you want in terms of already having it. Wake up each morning and say to yourself, aloud, "I am in charge of my thoughts. I am happy, healthy and wise. Money comes easily to me. I am a multi-millionaire. I own two homes. I drive the car I want. I can get whatever I desire. I am a success." Even if you aren't a millionaire and you don't drive the car you want, you must start thinking in these terms. State the goals you want; don't just use my words. Focus your thoughts upon the things you desire with great feeling and enthusiasm. Feel and behave as if the object of one's desire is already acquired. Be open to receiving it.

If you wake up and feel grumpy or irritated, it is likely going to manifest itself into other things that make you grumpy or irritated. It's OK to wake up and feel this way (Lord knows I do a lot), but when this happens, immediately sit up, close your eyes, and think about something that makes you happy. Smile to yourself for 30 seconds. Tell yourself the things you envision yourself becoming. Put negative thoughts out of your mind and fill it with positive thoughts about your success.

You can get whatever you want out of life. You have the ability to make the changes necessary to put yourself in the positive mental state that is needed to receive success. Nobody can do it for you, but the great news is that you can do it for yourself and you should do it for yourself.

Think about the person working in a large corporation, spending each day doing the same task, over and over again. Are you that person? Are you tired of the same day-to-day activities that seem to get you nowhere? Of course, you are free to change jobs and try to move into more responsible or rewarding positions. There is absolutely nothing wrong with that. But for some people, security and a steady income just aren't enough to satisfy their core belief that they are destined for something better. These are the people who should be out on their own. They want more from life and there is no reason for them not to try to get it. Notice I said "not to try": you have the right to try to get whatever you want. It won't come easy and nobody will give it to you without effort, but you definitely have every right – in fact, you deserve – to get what you want out of life.

Believe In Yourself

Successful people don't let things like education, background, or obstacles get in their way. They make things happen based on their belief that they are going to be successful. In other words, you've got to have a plan to be a success. You've got to make a conscious decision that you will succeed and nothing will stop you. Your potential is not just going to magically appear out of nowhere. You have got to do your part and act so that you can begin to develop skills to help you achieve your goals. Soon you'll discover talents that you never knew you had. You'll start looking at the world as yours to conquer. Doors to opportunity will open. Nothing will get in your way.

I met the great Pittsburgh Steeler running back Rocky Blier when I was 14 years old and his life story inspired me. Blier, who suffered a knee injury his senior season with Notre Dame, was selected in the 16th round of the NFL draft and few thought he'd make the Pittsburgh Steelers' roster, but he did. He missed the next season because of military service in Vietnam. While serving his country, Blier was shot in the left leg and had a grenade explode under his right foot. He spent 1970 on the injured reserve list rehabilitating from his wounds. In 1971 he played in only six games. In 1972-73 he played mostly on special teams. But in 1974, six years after being drafted, Blier won a job as the team's starting fullback and remained at the position until he retired in the early 80s, collecting four Super Bowl rings along the way. Rocky Blier faced unbelievable adversity while pursuing his goal to become a success on the field yet he persevered where so many others would have failed.

My great uncle, Delvin Miller, was a horse trainer and driver who competed over a span of eight decades and whose career culminated with his being named the Goodwill Ambassador of Harness Racing and election to the Hall of Fame. Not bad for a man who was raised on a family farm in Avella, Pennsylvania, graduated from a small country school, served his country in World War II, losing a brother in combat, and pursued a career in a sport he loved. It was through him that I had the opportunity to meet many other professional athletes. Uncle Delvin introduced me to great horsemen like Stanley Dancer, Howard Beissinger, Billy Houghton, celebrities like Stan Musial and Jay Silverheels (TV's Tonto), and most of the great Pittsburgh Steelers team members of the 1970s championship years. All of these people possessed a terrific sense of self-worth and positive outlook that brought success their way.

I recall Rocky Blier as someone who had this intense spirit inside himself. In fact, Franco Harris, Mel Blount, Terry Bradshaw, Lynn Swann, Jack Lambert, and the other Steelers of the 1970s that I had the pleasure of meeting also had it. Most of us have it. You have it. Perhaps yours is lying dormant, waiting to be unleashed. It's your job to find it. You have to want to win the same way Terry Bradshaw, down by two touchdowns in the fourth quarter, would pull the huddle together and say to his teammates, "We're going to win this game, let's make it happen." The spirit in you will motivate you to success. Start talking to it. Start demanding more of yourself. Start facing each day with the attitude that nothing is going to stop you from succeeding. If you aren't satisfied with the routine of working for others and want to be your own boss then nothing should stand in your way. Age, gender, race, handicaps, lack of education and so on are only false barriers that people hold up as reasons not to succeed. They are excuses. The only real barriers are lack of goals, lack of desire, laziness, and fear. Overcome them and nothing will keep you from success.

There Are No Excuses

My friend Sylvia grew up in rural Western Pennsylvania with a father who never encouraged her. Her only brother was killed in a tragic boating accident. Her family was so poor that by the time she graduated from high school her front teeth were mottled with decay. She couldn't afford to attend a 4-year college, but did manage to enroll in a local business school and soon thereafter applied for a job with a local company. She was told she wasn't the first choice, but when the first choice didn't accept the job offer, she was offered the position and gladly accepted. She worked her way up through the organization, surviving three different owners and eventually running a multi-million dollar division of the firm. She is now Director of Operations for a leading online company and is a perfect example of overcoming your obstacles to become successful.

Sylvia took a chance and it paid off. Imagine being told "Well, you're not our first choice, but here's the job if you want it." Many people would turn it down. Would you? Sylvia didn't. She turned a job opportunity into a successful career.

The success of America's free enterprise system depends on people like Sylvia who are willing to take risks in order to compete in the system. Free enterprise offers endless opportunities to individuals who aren't afraid to strive to be better. Richard Florida wrote a book called The *Rise of the Creative Class* that outlines a new social class, separate from the industrial and service industries, which has changed the way Americans work and live. The creative class is made up of creative individuals who now comprise over 30% of the U.S. workforce and who lead the nation in innovation, excellence, and not surprisingly, income. These people are not afraid to stick their necks out in order to reach their goals. They are not afraid to pack their bags and move to where the jobs are located. They succeed by doing, not wishing they were. You can be part of this if you set your mind to do so. Find the career you want and go after it. Launch the company you want and make it profitable. Be the person you want to be and live each day to its fullest.

There will always be better products. There will always be better services. And there will always be people willing to pay for those products and services. But the only way to reap the rewards of the system is to jump right in and ignore the fear of failure. To become successful you need to have a vision of what it means to be successful and you must be willing to go out on a limb to pursue that vision. Without vision, there would be no progress and without progress, you cannot become successful.

The only way to generate wealth is through productivity, and the person who is willing to take risks to attain his or her goals has the best opportunity to gain great wealth. Yes, this wealth includes money. Often times, it includes lots of it. Wealth also means accomplishment to oneself and the satisfaction of knowing that you alone are responsible for your success. Nothing is more rewarding that making it on your own. Nothing feels better than to know that you are a part of something that is successful. Nothing will give you a kick more than seeing a check come into your company knowing that you were richly rewarded for a job well done. There is no way to describe the feeling of buying your dream car or new house, with cash, because you can.

And there is no more rewarding feeling than being financially able to give away your money because you want to help others reach their goals. For those who are blessed much is required. The ability to help others realize their potential can be one of the most fulfilling endeavors one can undertake.

Be In A Position To Help Others

I recall riding New York subway's #6 train one day several years ago and looking at the Wall Street Journal's listing of the stock price of my company. That particular day my personal holdings in the company were worth more than $15 million. I thought to myself, "Isn't it amazing that a company started the year before with a couple thousand dollars and an idea would now be worth millions of dollars?" I was feeling so good about what my hard work had resulted in that upon arriving home that night, I grabbed my checkbook and wrote out nearly two dozen checks to various nonprofit organizations that I thought deserved my support: The Watchful Shepherd, World Wildlife Federation, United Way, women's abuse shelters, child development centers, and churches. I wanted to give them money because that was important to me. And I gave them a lot. God had shown favor on me and I wanted to pass that good fortune on to others. Had I worked as a cog in a much larger a company, I would have never had the chance to do something like this. But because I wasn't afraid to fail, I was able to overcome my fears and start a business that put me in the position to help others which was always an important part of my core beliefs.

You may start to become successful and feel that every dollar you earn is yours and yours alone. After all, you earned it. But let me offer this piece of advice: when you earn money you are in a position to help others. Whether you tithe 10% through your church or decide to support a local charity or simply stop and take a homeless person to lunch, your ability to give back will be returned to you ten-fold. Some people call it karma. Some say it's the work of God. I don't know what driving force it is, but it works. The more you give of yourself, the more that is returned to you.

There is no better feeling than watching the people who work for you become successful, either through personal success such as buying their first home, or professional success from making career goals or starting their own business – even if it competes with yours.

Mike Nelson was a radio salesman for many years before we met at the Dallas airport in the fall of 1995. I was immediately struck by Mike's "can do" attitude, and within a few weeks he was working for me at Lycos, running the southwest advertising sales efforts. Mike excelled at online sales and when Yahoo! recruited him away from us, I knew it was an opportunity he shouldn't pass up. He moved to Yahoo!, built a world class team of sales professionals, and after a few years retired with many millions in the bank. Today he is busy pursuing a longtime dream of his, designing and building custom homes.

If you know that you want more out of life than you already have, take my advice and become an entrepreneur. If you would rather not take the risk and work for someone else, that is all right too, just commit yourself to becoming successful at your job. If you fall into the latter, don't stop reading this book; it will give you guidelines to become the most successful and invaluable employee your boss has ever hired.

Hopefully, you are now fired up enough to begin your research into the ways in which you can become successful. Start by tuning out all the noise in your life. Turn off the television. Forget about having to keep up with the Joneses. Concentrate on your goals, for you can get anything from life that you want, but you must be prepared to work for it. Take a hard look at yourself, but don't dwell on past mistakes. Learn from them. Change your behavior to insure you're on the path to success.

Now is the time to make your dreams come true.

What Did You Learn?

1. Make up your mind that you are going to be successful.
2. Successful people don't let things like education, background, or obstacles get in their way. They make things happen based on their belief that they are going to be successful.
3. Becoming successful is most easily accomplished by starting your own business, but if you don't want to pursue that route, build your success in your current job or seek one that gives you the opportunity to succeed.
4. Make a decision to give back to your community be it through cash donations, volunteering your time, or other means.

CHAPTER 3

Yes You Can: Turn Deficits into Opportunities

Success isn't just about the Benjamins

A YOUNG GUY from Texas moves to California and goes to a big "everything under one roof" store looking for a job.

The manager asks, "Do you have any sales experience?"

The kid says, "Yeah, I was a salesman back home in Texas."

The boss liked the kid's attitude so he gave him the job. "You can start 8am tomorrow morning," he said, "I'll come down after we close and see how you did."

His first day on the job was rough but he got through it. After the store was locked up, the boss pulled his new employee aside. "How many sales did you make today?"

The kid says, "One."

The boss says, "Just one? Son, that's not good enough. Our sales people average 20 or 30 sales a day. How much was the sale for?"

The kid replies, "$102,647.00."

The boss, shocked, says, "$102,647.00? What the heck did you sell?"

The kid says, "First I sold him a small fish hook. Then I sold him a medium fish hook. Then I sold him a larger fish hook. Then I sold him a new fishing rod. Then I asked him where he was going fishing and he said down at the coast, so I told him he was gonna need a boat, so we went down to the boat department and I sold him that 20-foot Bassmaster. Then he said he didn't think his Honda Civic would pull it, so I took him down to the automotive department and sold him a 4X4 pickup."

In shock, the boss says, "A guy came in here to buy a fish hook and you sold him a boat and truck?"

So the kid replies, "No, he came in here to buy a box of tampons for his wife and I said, 'Well, your weekend's shot, you might as well go fishing.'"

YOU NEVER KNOW what opportunity you'll be presented with; how will you respond when you're face to face with it?

As an American, seventy-five percent of the world's population already considers you wealthy. You may be a cashier at the mall, a sanitation worker, or a security guard. But ask the citizens of Africa, Columbia, Peru, Thailand, or any number of other countries if they would consider you wealthy and they'd answer, "yes." Three out of four people in the world would consider a person making $8.00 an hour wealthy. The majority of Americans are already better off than most of the world's population. It's like running the 100 yard dash and you get to start at the 75 yard line. You don't have to go far. Isn't America great?

Most Americans believe that becoming successful means you have earned a fortune and you'll never need to worry about money again. There's an old saying, "Fortune smiles on he who waits." Let me tell you: Don't believe it! Fortune smiles on the person who is *success oriented*. Fortune smiles on those who make fortune happen. Fortune will smile on you if you reach out and grab opportunity. But don't just grab and hang on, shake it, tear it apart and improve on it. If you are eager and ready to dedicate your time and life to becoming successful, then do it. Take a chance and grab that opportunity. Don't wait and don't hesitate. Don't make excuses. The difference between successful and unsuccessful people isn't about money, where you went to college, or who your Daddy knows. It's about what you do with the opportunities that are present in your life and how you position yourself to make new ones.

Live Joyfully and Have Fun

The joy of living comes from finding joy in doing whatever it is you do, rather than going through life with your eyes half closed, and, at the end of your lifetime, having regrets at never fulfilling your dreams.

I have met too many 40, 50, and 60 year old people who look back on their lives and wish they had taken more chances, explored more opportunities, and reached for more goals. They tell me they simply didn't think they had the time, money, skills, knowledge, or initiative to make changes in their lives. They say they were scared to chase their dreams. And here they are 30 years later, wondering why life isn't more fulfilling. It's really rather sad and something I hope you never deal with.

Here's how I approach life and make it fun.

Each day I give myself a test: find something and look at it a different way. I try to think of the world is one big defect and my goal each day is to figure out how to fix or improve one thing. Why does the water bucket always spill when I carry it across the backyard and how can I fix it? Why do we board planes from the rear forward when it would make more sense to board form the outside seats into the aisle? How can we fix music education in America and expose thousands of children and teenagers to the arts while shoring up the fortunes of local orchestras? Why can't I search the Internet for the information I want and not get 10,000 search results that don't matter to me?

After a while this becomes a game that is quite fun. If you want to try this in action, go sit in your car with a video camera and tape everything you'd change about your car. Hate the buttons on the radio? Videotape it and describe how you would change the design. Don't like the way the steering wheel tilts? Videotape it and describe how you'd fix it. Don't care for the way the seat belt holder squeaks against the leather seats? You guessed it: videotape it and describe how you'd fix it. Go ahead, look around the car and tell the camera what is wrong. You're bound to find something you don't like. When you're done, watch the video and look at all the items you found. You may be surprised with the number of "defects" you came up with. Now picture doing this every day. Just find one item that you think you can improve upon. Perhaps something will even jump out at you that will form the basis of a patent or a product or an entire business.

This exercise will help you develop problem solving skills and increase your creativity. It will help you gain insight into how things work. Best of all, it will expose you to new ways of thinking, for as everyone else lives with the status quo, you'll begin thinking outside the box, continuously seeking new ways to accomplish things. You can't help but become more entrepreneurial in your thinking when you view things as being defective and needing your special skills to fix them.

Now I don't expect you to take every defect and create a business around it, but there may just be one or two that could lead you to success. What is it that you know that seems painfully obvious to you, but that others ignore? Perhaps there is a business there. I recently started a company that documents home inventory because I found a better way of doing something that I knew most people didn't want to take the time to do.

Here's a tip: if you determine that one of the defects you found can form a business, you'll probably enjoy building that business because the seed – the core idea – came from you.

With so many defects in the world, I believe that every day has the potential for success and achievement. I am constantly open to new ideas and opportunities. Fortune continues to smile on me because I am still hard at work on every aspect of my life, seeking opportunities wherever they may hide. My life is filled with work, but I make it fun. My career is work, but I enjoy it because I know every challenge I undertake leads to my definition of success; which in turn makes it fun. My love life is work, but she and I make it fun. When we have to deal with things like maintaining the house or figuring out how to get some alone time together, we view it as a great opportunity instead of an obstacle. My children are work, but the gleam in my sons' eyes when I walk into the room makes it fun.

You too can have a life filled with fun. Think of it this way: if you have a dream and a goal and you are heading toward that goal, even the most treacherous and cataclysmic roadblocks can be fun if you focus on overcoming them and learning from them. Then you can look back on those roadblocks knowing that each one you tackled and managed to overcome put you one inch closer to your goal.

In the months immediately following my graduation from college, I decided to write a magazine article (a short-term goal) about how the Amish community of Wayne County, Ohio uses retired harness horses. I pitched the idea and received a freelance contract from *HoofBeats* magazine. Then I bought a couple dozen rolls of film, a notepad, and put a full tank of gas in my car. I found a contact in the Amish community who not only bought retired horses, but bred and raised them as well. I was ready to go out and take a swing at becoming a photojournalist. I had just one problem, one hurdle that seemed impossible to overcome. You see, the Amish religious beliefs prevent them from engaging in "graven images." They don't have mirrors and they certainly don't have photographs. To believe for a minute that a 21-year-old college kid, wearing a Ted Nugent t-shirt and jeans and driving a black Honda Prelude with tinted windows and chrome wheels was going to come into their community and photograph them was preposterous. What an insurmountable challenge this posed! But let me share something with you. I knew I had to gain the trust of my subjects. I met with community leaders, attended church services, shared my writings with families, and built that trust. I was honest with them and they sensed my sincerity. I explained how they would not have to see the photographs I would take, and that I'd only use pictures that were important to the story and portrayed their community and its standards in a positive light. I ended up with hundreds of great pictures, the magazine ran a multi-page story, and my work won the top Photojournalism Award from the American Horse Council in 1986. Had I let a roadblock get in my way of my goal, I wouldn't have won that award and I wouldn't have made longtime friends in the Amish community whom I still visit when I travel through central Ohio.

I hope you are beginning to see a pattern here of how I define success. For me, it isn't just about money. Money is simply the by-product of being successful. Success is what I accomplish in my career, my life, and with my family. It's about learning new things. It's about having an idea and doing something with it. It's about whom I meet along the way and how I maintain those relationships.

As I mentioned in the last chapter, there are no excuses for lack of success: not education, money, handicaps or any other barrier you can think of. I have approached success throughout my life by understanding that if I want something bad enough, I can get it. I earned my first money when I was nine years old and I started out with little formal education and no capital funds. I simply had a fierce desire to obtain something I wanted, probably a toy that is long gone, but I wanted it and I got it. I opened for business at 1046 East Beau Street and by the end of my first and last day in business I had grossed $12.50. My lemonade stand was the vehicle that helped me reach that early goal. Success!

Like most young people I held a variety of jobs growing up: stock boy, busboy, maintenance worker, lawn cutter, paperboy. Little do any of us realize but all these jobs teach us about running our own businesses. We learn people skills, customer relations, knowledge of finance, sales tactics, marketing, operations and more. We learn commitment and living up to our responsibilities. Combined, these skills set the stage for future success.

"But Bill," you say, "That's a rinky-dink lemonade stand, not a real business." I argue it is. When you think of running your own business, the day-to-day operations are just like that little lemonade stand, only bigger. My *cost of goods* (lemonade, cups, and water) was about $1.50. My *ad budget* was 40 cents (two sheets of poster board and a marker). My *labor costs* were nil because I was the sole proprietor. I *priced* my *product* at 25 cents a cup which meant at the end of the day, I had operated my business at an 80% *profit* margin. My *customers* were my neighbors and those passing by who had a thirst to quench and I just happened to be selling the best tasting lemonade on that block. All the basic elements of running a business were present in that little lemonade stand.

A business is as basic as five elements that flow from one to another: *PRODUCT, COST, PRICING, SALES, and PROFIT.* Together they may seem like a lot to comprehend, but taken individually, it is easy to understand how to create your business. The *PRODUCT* is what you sell. The *COST* is what you pay to be able to provide it to a customer. *PRICING* is your cost plus your desired profit which leads you to the total price of your product. *SALES* is the act of getting customers to buy your product. *PROFIT* is what you take home at the end of the day. Put together, they form the basis of what every entrepreneur must know about running a successful business.

Have a Simple Business Model

I enjoyed working for Bruce Todd at his advertising agency, but I knew I would never be president of his firm and would never enjoy the definition of success that I had in my mind if I worked for someone else. It was not an easy decision for me to make when I quit at age 24 from what was a great job to strike out on my own. Like most people, I had a rent payment, car payment, insurance, mounting credit card debt and other monthly bills. What made the decision even more difficult was that with no money, no steady income and no accounts receivable, I was going to start my own ad agency in Pittsburgh, Pennsylvania, 300 miles from where all my current clients were located.

I was barely able to afford the two-hundred twenty-five dollars a month office rent, credit card payment from buying desks, drafting tables and all the other necessities, plus my personal debts.

In December 1989 I hung a shingle on the door of Townsend Advertising Corporation and began looking for clients. My *product* was advertising. My *cost* of conducting business was office space, computers, and other overhead that I estimated was going to cost me $30 per hour. I also wanted to earn $30 an hour, figuring if I could bill clients 1500 hours of my time each year, I could take home a $45,000 salary. Thus, my *pricing* was $60 an hour (my costs + salary) plus a built in profit of $40 an hour for a total of $100 an hour.

Townsend Advertising Corporation's business model looked as simple as this:

	Revenues	Costs	Profit/Hour
Overhead	$30	($30)	$0
Salary	$30	($30)	$0
Profit/Hr.	$40	($0)	$40
Total	$100	($60)	$40

At the end of the first year, through carefully watching my spending, overhead came in under the $30 per hour rate and I billed 1540 hours so my company's financials looked like this:

	Revenues	Costs	Profit
Overhead	$46,200	($28,211)	$17,989
Salary	$46,200	($45,000)	$1,200
Profit/Hr.	$61,600	$0	$61,600
Total	$154,000	($73,211)	$80,789

By watching my costs, I was able to net an additional $17,989 in profit (estimated overhead billed at $30 an hour minus actual overhead of $28,211) and by beating my goal of 1500 billable hours, I was able to realize additional salary ($1,200) and profit levels ($61,600) which carried over into my second year of operations.

To be honest, I was flying by the seat of my pants. I didn't know if my overhead/salary/profit formula would work or not, but I drew a line in the sand and made that my business model. It may seem simplistic, but for someone just getting started in business, simple is better. There's an old adage of "KISS" which stands for *"Keep It Simple, Stupid"* and it really makes sense. The more simplistic your business model, the easier it is to reach your goals.

Write Down Your Goals and Read Them Often

How did I lower my costs? When I started the advertising agency I had a list of five clients that I desperately wanted to represent. That's a pretty easy goal, don't you think? I wrote this list on a piece of paper the same size as a dollar bill and I kept in my wallet next to any cash I had. Each time I'd reach in to pull out a few dollars I'd see it. It became a constant reminder of my goal. It also had the unintended effect of making me question why I was going to blow $20 on some silly expenditure that I really didn't need. I looked at that piece of paper so many times that it eventually became so ratty I had to replace it. I replaced it three times over the next four years, but my firm eventually represented all five of the targeted companies, plus 31 more.

So how did I go about getting clients? Just prior to opening the agency, I devised a strategy to create a bimonthly newsletter about advertising and mail it to a list of 200 prospects. Since I loved reading about what works in advertising, I figured others would too. My newsletter was a marketing piece for the firm and researching the newsletter's content kept me current on advertising trends, consumer studies, effective design, and other pieces of information critical to the success of my company. In a way, I took what was normally considered homework – researching the industry – and turned it into something fun that I could share with prospects and clients.

Within each newsletter I would purposefully mispel a word. I held a monthly contest where the first five recipients to locate a typographic error would win a subscription to *Success* magazine. Every two months I spent $256 on printing and mailing a newsletter and purchasing five subscriptions to Success. Why would I do this? Imagine the ease of getting to speak with one of my prospects when a month later I'd call and say, "Jill, it's Bill Townsend at Townsend Advertising Corp. I was calling to make sure your subscription to *Success* magazine had reached you." This is a much better way to begin a conversation with a prospect than simply calling to see if you can do business with them. I had dozens of prospects each year that helped me open their own door by responding to my contest. (By the way, did you catch the misspelled word in the last paragraph?)

To be honest, the success of the newsletter surprised me. I believe it was well received because it wasn't a sales pitch about my firm, but instead focused on informing the reader about a topic that was of interest to them. Prospects want to know what you can do for them, what you can offer to make them more successful or profitable, or perhaps just how you can simplify their job. My company's name, address, and phone number were on it so the reader wouldn't forget who was smart enough to share this information with them.

After the first newsletter was mailed I had three calls, and after three phone discussions I had my first appointment. Two days later I was driving to Cleveland to meet the president of a small manufacturing company. I drove four hours to the client's offices and met with my prospect for a little over an hour. I spent 15 minutes talking about my company and 55 minutes asking about his. After all, I needed to learn as much about his business and its challenges in order to know what to pitch him. After the meeting I drove four hours home, for a total of 8 hours of driving in a single day. My reason for not staying over was quite simple: I couldn't afford a hotel room. I wrote a 22-page marketing proposal and submitted it a few days later. I didn't get the business. It turned out the prospect appreciated my take on his business but felt my company wasn't large enough to support his goals. Well, this obstacle was unacceptable to me. I sent him an 11 x 17 inch flier with pictures of the 8 people on my staff:

President: me

Creative Director: me

Art Director: me

Copywriter: me

Media Planner: me

Media Buyer: me

Account Supervisor: me

Receptionist: me

It didn't change his mind and he awarded his business to another firm. But an interesting thing happened about four months later, when I received a call from another company looking for a firm to create a series of brochures. The president of the company I pitched in Cleveland had referred me to them. He was so impressed with my creative response to his rejection that he had enthusiastically referred me to several of his business acquaintances, telling them I was "a real go-getter." Over the next five years I created seven different brochures for this new client, who spent over $100,000 with my company. All this was possible because of my attempt to overcome an obstacle that was in my path to success.

My advertising agency grew to represent 36 clients in all areas of industry with an emphasis on law, technology, and healthcare. In my first year of business I made a profit. I was living high on the hog. Not financially, but emotionally. You see, my first vision of success was to create a profitable company, which I did. My second vision of success was to do great work, which I did. My third vision of success was to take home a paycheck to pay my personal bills, which I did.

Through hard and industrious work, I found myself succeeding where others said I'd fail. I attribute this to one thing: keeping focused on my definition of success. I looked for business everywhere. I'd meet people at the gas station and give them my card. I'd attend Chamber of Commerce meetings in order to network with other business owners. I sent direct mail out to every company I wanted to work for, even companies like Alcoa, Aristech Chemical, Bethlehem Steel, and Heinz, which in reality had no use for a small ad agency like mine (although I did get a noteworthy direct marketing project from Aristech in my third year of business in which we mailed pine tree seedlings to their customers as a way of reminding them of Aristech's commitment to the environment).

I was always looking for ways to get my name in front of prospects. Once, as I was looking through my college's alumni magazine, I spotted the name of the director of public relations at The Washington Hospital that was the largest healthcare provider in my hometown and one of the five target clients I wanted. I made an appointment to meet her and we instantly struck up a rapport based on our attending the same college. I sent her a thank you note for her time and added her to my newsletter list. A few months later she called, offering me the chance to create a physician's directory for the hospital. I quoted a price of $6,000 and delivered it for just over $5,400, saving my new client almost 10%. That led to another job and yet another and still another. Townsend Advertising represented the hospital for five years.

This brings up another item that I believe is important for the entrepreneur. If you quote a job and deliver it under the quote, pass the savings on to your client. They'll appreciate it and you'll sleep better. Plus, if you ever under-quote a project, your client may be much more willing to help cover the higher costs knowing you had saved them money in the past.

In the early days of my business a young woman came to me looking for a job. Wendy Petronka was a recent graduate of Syracuse University with a degree in Advertising and Psychology. I couldn't afford to hire her at the time, but thinking back to the opportunity Bruce Todd gave me, I suggested I'd teach her what I knew. She could work with me and any business she brought in she'd run and profit from. She jumped at the opportunity, starting the following week. She worked for me not only at the ad agency, but in two other jobs as well. When I campaigned for a seat in the United States Congress she became my campaign's treasurer and de facto day-to-day manager. When Lycos was founded I hired her to run the advertising technology and traffic system, where she excelled. All this was due to her willingness to jump a hurdle (my inability to pay her) to gain practical experience to help her reach her goals.

Could Wendy have known when she first knocked on my agency's front door that a few years later she'd be working for Lycos and sitting on stock options worth thousands of dollars? Absolutely not. But by taking the first step to reach her goals, she opened the door to opportunity.

I was a guest at a women's networking event sponsored by The Indus Entrepreneurs, a networking organization focused on entrepreneurship. The guest speaker, Donna Dubinsky, former CEO of technology innovator Palm, Inc., was asked by a participant what women can do to make advances in the workplace. Her response? "Do good work. Do great work. You will be noticed."

In 1990 I read an article in a business journal where Ed Smalis of Smalis Corporation wrote: "Smalis will fund any individual having the capabilities and qualities of becoming an entrepreneur. Smalis will provide funding for operations. Smalis will provide funding for inventory. Smalis will provide the capital to interested parties desiring to establish themselves in New Stanton, Pennsylvania. The above are but a few of the opportunities that exist today and are far greater than for those who crossed the Allegheny's in covered wagons."

I was so intrigued by these statements that I immediately called Mr. Smalis and set out to visit him. I learned that he had been a successful salesman to the mining industry and in his 60s decided to try to help anyone with a marketable idea. In an effort to discover the thinking, background, and business prospects of a potential entrepreneur, Ed would hold lengthy interviews with many potential entrepreneurs. As we discussed his efforts I learned that despite his offer to help entrepreneurs, the one problem he most encountered was the lack of real desire on the part of the prospect. Often people have a great idea, but they aren't willing to work hard to make it a success. They expect everything to be given to them. Sometimes they start a business but don't have the passion to work hard at it, developing new customers, serving those customers, and making their business successful. They expect customers to come to them. Passion is about desire. Desire, coupled with hard work, is what turns motivation into success. Ed had interests in everything from bulldozers to mailboxes. Some things he made money from and some he didn't, but he never knew which would pay off until he worked hard at it. I left that day with much admiration for this gentleman…and a new client for my agency.

Over the next couple years, Ed would share stories of how he overcame great odds to become successful. He would often preach "you must be willing to dedicate yourself to your business and to making money. To do this, you must possess all the qualities of an entrepreneur. Golf, cocktail parties, membership organizations and hobbies are of secondary importance. You can't allow interference from family or friends. You can't be distracted by time off, by so-called "free" evenings, weekends or vacations. Goals are not achieved on the golf course, at cocktail parties, through travel or by attending conventions." If you are into all of the above, you will only be working part-time and no successful business was ever built on part-time work."

I suggested that the highly motivated, hard-driving individual he was searching for no longer exists. "Hogwash!!" he barked back, "He or she is out there and I'll find that person! I found you, didn't I?"

I don't believe Ed was saying that you have to work 100 hours a week to be successful. I think he was trying to say that if you want to be successful, you have to be dedicated to that pursuit. It may take 40 hours a week or it may take 80 or it may take 100. You won't know how much effort or how many hours you'll have to dedicate to reaching your goals, until you try. But keeping in mind that balancing work, family, recreation, fitness, and other factors of living is important to a person's overall success, it is important to stress that being committed to your career is just as important as being committed to your spouse. You will find the right balance so don't worry about becoming a slave to work. Focus instead on working smartly and accomplishing steps along the road to success and eventually, you'll not only reach your goal, but charge right past it toward another one.

One weekend, Ed invited me to join him and his female companion in Deep Creek, Maryland. We spent hours discussing his background, what worked in business, and how he overcame obstacles. A wealthy man who lived in one of the most luxurious residences in Pittsburgh, he did something during that trip that forever stuck with me. Ed wanted to purchase a camping lantern, and he found the perfect Coleman lantern in a local hardware store. It cost $39. As I offered to carry it to the cashier he told me to wait a moment while he talked to the manager. I figured he was going to ask questions about the operation of the lantern, but in no time I realized he was inquiring as to the wholesale price and working to get a discount on this relatively inexpensive item. This haggling went back and forth for a couple minutes, and we left with a $39 lantern discounted to $28 including tax. In the car I asked him why he'd spend the effort to get an $11 discount on such a minor item. He responded by saying that the money wasn't the issue; he wanted to find out if the manager was focused on his goal. "You see," he said, "that manager's goal is to become successful and the only way he does that is if he sells products. I wasn't going to pay $39 for that lantern and I let him know it, but he wanted to make the sale so badly he dropped the price. Because that sale gets him closer to his goal."

On the way out of town the following day I stopped at the hardware store to ask the manager why he lowered the lantern's price. His reply? "I have to support my family and the only way I do that is to sell goods. I may never see that man again, but I believe he's now a satisfied customer and will come back here in the future for his hardware needs." This goal-oriented store manager gave up $11 in profit, yet still makes money because the lantern cost him only $18, netting him about $10. In effect, he made $10 while acquiring a new customer thus putting himself closer to his own goals. If you ask me, that's not a bad way to conduct business.

Whenever you are in business for yourself you begin to see people in a different light. Before owning my own company I would meet people but never really got to know what motivated them or what they did in their professional lives. Once I owned my ad agency and the monthly bills only got paid if I brought in business, all those two-legged humanoids marching around the malls, movie theaters, restaurants, sporting events and bars became prospects. I saw each person I'd come in contact with as a potential client or someone who knew a client. I wanted to know as much about someone and who they knew as I could.

Ask For Help

Many years later, one of my companies owned a web site called sixdegrees.com. The concept behind Six Degrees was that you could connect to any person in the world through one to six degrees of separation. It was based off the award-winning play (and later movie) by John, Guare, "Six Degress of Seperation." You know Doug. Doug knows Matt. Matt knows Dean. Dean knows Kevin and you want to know Kevin. The concept works well and can be applied to your own networking to introduce you to the people who can help make you successful. I happen to know a Doug who knows a Matt who knows a Dean who knows a Kevin who I'm helping investigate a new business in the solar powered water purification field.

Don't be afraid to ask people who they know. I am convinced that roughly 90% of the reason people don't succeed is because they don't ask for help. Perhaps they're afraid of rejection. Perhaps they just don't know how to ask. I gladly offer assistance to people who are trying to improve their lot in life. I know dozens, perhaps as many as 100 successful people who will try to assist someone who proves to be ambitious, courteous, and seeks advice. Or, as it says in the Bible, "Ask and ye shall receive." Or as the Law of Attraction simply says, you attract into your life whatever you think about. It's true, and the successful entrepreneur knows it works.

The worst thing that can happen when you ask someone for something is they will say "no". Oh my, the sky is falling! They said NO! Capital N. Capital O. Two big, huge scary letters that when combined form a word that millions are afraid to hear. "No." Did I scare you? "No, no, no, no, no, no, no!" I hope you are still standing and have not died of a massive coronary from hearing "no" so often. My point here is that most people I meet are afraid to ask for help because they're afraid of being rejected. But rejection isn't going to kill you. Perhaps the person you asked doesn't have an answer for you. Perhaps they don't know anyone who wants your product or service. Perhaps they are having a bad day because his wife said "no" the night before or her husband is an idiot who refuses to put the toilet seat down. Who knows? All I know is that when someone says "no," it just means you have to move on until you find someone who says "yes."

The Japanese have a saying, "A nail that sticks up will be hammered down." In their culture, standing out isn't viewed as a positive trait. But in our culture, standing out – reaching out – asking for help – is the perfect way to meet the types of people who can help make you successful. Perhaps the saying should really be, "A nail that sticks up, stands out".

You have to want so badly to succeed that you live, breathe, sleep and eat your vision of success. If you are lazy, neither this book nor any other book can help you. If you make every excuse known to mankind, you'll never succeed. However, if you're willing to focus on succeeding and tune out all the rubbish in your life in order to attain your goals, then you are ten steps ahead of everyone else who chooses to watch life pass them by. If you need help, ask for it. The worst that someone can say is "no," but I'll bet you'll be surprised at how many people respond by saying, "yes."

Repeat that again, *the worst that someone can say is 'no'*. "N" and "O": two simple letters that don't have to be scary. "N" and "O": the opposite of "Yes". See? There is nothing to be afraid of.

By the way, that company called sixdegrees.com? It was the intellectual property behind the formation of another successful company called LinkedIn.

What Did You Learn?

1. If you are eager and ready to dedicate your time and life to becoming successful, then take a chance and do it.
2. By identifying everyday defects you will begin to train yourself

to think like an entrepreneur, and may even uncover the "million dollar idea" in which to base a business around.

3. Your business model doesn't have to be complicated. In fact, the simpler, the better.

4. Begin networking with people to expand your circle of prospects. Ask for help and don't be discouraged if people say "no." A "yes" may be right around the corner.

BILL TOWNSEND

CHAPTER 4

Yes You Can: Succeed through Failure

The Art of Failure

IF YOU ARE in business for yourself there is always a risk. The successful business owners are those who aren't afraid of failure, but who are willing to take the risk. Failure and mistakes are the greatest teachers you will find. People who are blessed with easy successes often find that when the going gets tough, they lack the skills to overcome hurdles. Those who have learned through past mistakes often understand exactly what is required of them to turn a bad situation into a winning solution. I've made more mistakes than I'd care to admit, but each time I stumble I learn what not to do the next time. Even with the greatest ideas, there is still a degree of trial and error.

Life's real failure is when you don't realize how close you were to success when you gave up.

In the early days of Townsend Advertising, I created a direct mail piece that featured a picture of a goldfish, in his bowl, on top of the tallest building in my hometown. The photo was taken from the top down so you saw this little fish and the side of the building all the way down to the street. The headline read, "If you don't call me to make an appointment to discuss your advertising, Cleo, my goldfish, will jump from the tallest building in town." A few weeks later I got hate mail from two people, one of which was active in the local ASPCA. So the next time I took a picture with my feet on the ledge and changed the headline to read that I would jump. No hate mail this time. Maybe your first idea doesn't always work but something else comes about to replace or improve it. Or maybe those two people were hoping I'd really do it.

Another time I was trying to close a very large advertising client. I had the best cost structure, could deliver the larger audience, and had the best technology to deliver a highly targeted campaign. I also had a flawed understanding of the client's market. Whereas I thought the client was focused on selling to men, it turned out that their male-oriented product was actually purchased most often by women. Their $2 million ad budget went to a rival. In failing, I learned to ask questions and take the time to interview prospects so I could be confident in delivering a solution that accurately addresses their problem.

Learn From Your Failures

The point of this is that even in failure you can often find a positive element. Joseph Hardy started his first lumber company and named it Green Hills Lumber Company. He began selling lumber to contractors and soon found himself having difficulty getting the contractors to pay. Invoices were being paid late and sometimes not at all. On top of this, the company name was terrible! No contractor wants to buy lumber that is "green."

As the company was struggling, Joe came up with a new plan. He had a building in the small town of Eighty Four, Pennsylvania that was alongside a railroad track; the perfect location for receiving large quantities of lumber. He devised a new business strategy to provide lumber to contractors on a "cash and carry" basis, meaning, if you don't bring cash, you're not carrying any lumber out of the store. This eliminated his previous problem of late, slow, and non-existent payments. He underpriced all the other lumber companies in the marketplace. His prices were so attractive that contractors and the public would gladly pay him cash for the discounted price. He made the customer the number one focus of the business, and to this day, 84 Lumber Company is one of the largest lumber providers in America, with over 400 stores coast to coast. Joe lives life to the fullest, has often appeared on Fortune magazine's list of wealthiest Americans, and is one of the most successful people I've ever met.

Failure often opens the door to other opportunities. One of my employees at Lycos turned out to be a terrible salesperson. The guy was afraid to pick up the phone and make a cold call. Rejection loomed on the horizon of everything he did. Sometimes we were amazed he could even buy subway tokens! Even though he knew the product well, he would fumble for words and couldn't bring himself to expound on the benefits of advertising on Lycos.com. He lacked self-confidence, which meant he wasn't good in front of prospects, and that meant he didn't close much business. On the other hand, when he did get lucky and write a contract he would service his client like there was no tomorrow. He was a whiz at customer service. Unfortunately, if you're in sales and you're not bringing in the contracts, you won't last on the sales team. When it came time to release him we discussed his weaknesses and strengths. He explained that in the job prior to Lycos he worked with a team that included a lead salesperson and him. He really just supported the salesperson and handled the backend paperwork, which was a much different story than he told us when he was interviewing. I suggested he might want to consider getting out of sales altogether and go to work for a company that had a dedicated customer service staff. We parted on good terms and about 2 years later he called me to tell me he that after Lycos had taken a job with a financial services company and was recently promoted to Director of Customer Service for their Western region. The best part was this comment, "This is so much more than just a job, Bill, I think I've found my career. If you hadn't made me realize I was such a crummy salesman, I would still be trying to make a living in sales." Failure teaches; learn from it.

Kemmons Wilson was a high school dropout who at age 17 convinced a local movie theater manager to let him set up a popcorn concession stand inside the theater. It became so successful that the theater manager bought him out. He used that money to buy pinball machines and used those profits to buy a house. After financing a jukebox distributorship by borrowing against his home's value Wilson realized that the real money was in real estate. He soon became one of the biggest builders in Memphis, Tennessee. Wilson's best-known business is one that he started after traveling from his home in Memphis with his wife and five children, on a trip to Washington. Having stopped at several hotels on the way to Washington, D.C., Wilson was annoyed with the inconsistency of the accommodations. Some were clean, others filthy. Some had pools, others didn't. And most charged extra for children. Wilson devised a strategy to open a motel featuring nice accommodations, a clean restaurant, and best of all, no extra fees for children. His creation? Holiday Inn. By the late 1960s, the Holiday Inn chain had more than 200,000 rooms nationwide and was opening a new motel every three days.

Yet for all his success, Kemmons Wilson also made mistakes. When he loaned his friend Sam Phillips $25,000 to start a radio station in Memphis, he took 50% ownership in the venture. Phillips owned Sun Records and had a young singer under contract. When Phillips asked Wilson if he should sell the singer's contract for $35,000, Wilson said he should, even commenting that he didn't think the singer was very professional or would catch on with the listening public. That singer's name? Elvis Presley.

After his parents divorced, "R.P." was raised in a foster home in New York before moving to Florida to live with his grandparents. At age 16, and living in Chicago, he took a job selling products through department stores such as Sears and Walgreens, as well as on the Chicago fair circuit. Selling directly to consumers, he learned how to discuss product attributes and hone in on the unique selling points of each product. In the 1950s he invested $500 to create a couple television commercials in order to market a garden hose nozzle that allowed the user to add fertilizer, soap, weed killer and other products directly to the water stream. He built his company up from there but due to an inability to repay a bank loan, filed for bankruptcy in 1987. A few years later, with the bank about to auction off the assets of the company, he bought it out of bankruptcy. You've probably seen this man on your television screen reminding you to "Just set it and forget it!" A consummate entrepreneur, Ron Popeil is famous for his Showtime Rotisserie BBQ, the Pocket Fisherman, Dial-O-Matic food slicer, Popeil's Pasta Maker, and Food Dehydrator to name a few. His company, Ronco, has grossed more than $2 billion while making Popeil a multi-millionaire many times over. Says Popeil, "When I create something, I believe in it, and I'm very passionate about it." Get passionate about your life and believe in yourself.

Sol Linowitz was the United States' Ambassador to the Organization of American States appointed by President Johnson. Under President Carter, he served as co-negotiator of the Panama Canal Treaties and as the personal representative of the president to the Middle East peace negotiations. He was previously chairman of the Board of the Xerox Corporation, sat on the board of directors of Time Inc. and Mutual Life Insurance Co. of New York, and most recently was senior counsel of the international law firm Coudert Brothers. He was also awarded the Presidential Medal of Freedom, the highest civilian honor bestowed by our government. Sol is a fairly successful guy. I asked Sol if he had ever failed, and his reply was telling: "Yes, of course. Every week there is something at which one can fail. But you have to learn from these failures so you don't make the same mistake twice." Follow his advice and you'll turn out OK.

Another fellow, who shall remain nameless for now, lost his mother at age 9. He had no formal education and worked in a store, as a surveyor and in the local post office. He took an interest in politics and ran for office but lost the election. He didn't give up though. He ran again and was elected to the Illinois legislature. He ran three more times and won all those elections. In his spare time he studied to become a lawyer. He ran for U.S. House of Representatives and won. He campaigned for U.S. Senate and lost. He ran for President and won. What was the name of this man who faced so many failures early in his career? Abraham Lincoln. Honestly, if Abe can overcome a lack of education and become President, surely you can overcome your failures to become a success.

In 1990, I was watching the Super Bowl with a group of friends. With the San Francisco 49ers blowing out the Denver Broncos, the conversation soon turned away from football toward business. The group of us, ages 25-27, were all working and facing many of the issues that young adults face as they move into their careers. We worried about job security, health insurance, paying bills. The few of us who had our own businesses complained about paperwork and tax filing requirements. I was particularly vocal when my friend Doug shouted back, "Why don't you do something about it?" My response was immediate and made a lot of sense. I told him you have to be elected to the United States Senate or House of Representatives to be in a position to change the laws. "Well," said Doug, eager to return to watching the game, "Then do that!"

I brushed the conversation off, but over the next several months it struck me that there was nothing preventing me from running for Congress. All I needed to do was figure out what the issues were, determine my own plan of action for representing the 550,000 people in my district, and try to win an election. I pulled friends together, and over the course of 18 months we organized a campaign that had mobilized over 2,000 volunteers in five counties in Western Pennsylvania. We had little money and were outspent by my opponent 6 to 1, so we focused on knocking on over 23,000 doors, standing on corners with signs, and getting the message out through the media.

I was 27 years old at the time and the youngest Congressional candidate in the country, running against a 16-year Democrat incumbent in an area where Democrats outnumbered Republicans 4 to 1. I was flying by the seat of my pants, but as we went into election night, I found myself winning by the slightest margin. I was excited that all our hard work was going to pay off. At 11:05pm, with me leading the election results by 3,000 votes, a computer system went down in one of the more rural counties. There was silence in campaign headquarters as we nervously waited for it to be fixed so the counting could continue. Fifteen minutes went by. Then 30. Then 45. Finally the system was back online and the next news report showed the tide had turned and I was now losing by 3,000 votes. In the end, I lost the election by 1½%. I only needed 1,500 people to change their vote from and I would have been on my way to Washington, D.C.

Now some would say I failed, and it is true that I failed to win the general election. But I gained so many contacts and met so many people during my 18 months of campaigning that I never viewed my decision to run for Congress as a failure. It was one of the greatest learning experiences of my life. I gained extreme confidence in my speaking abilities. I learned that even when a door was slammed in my face, the next one may very well be open wide. Even though I didn't get the honor of serving my country, everything I was exposed to during the campaign served to my benefit because I learned from the experience.

Don't be afraid of failure; welcome it. For in failure you will learn a great deal about yourself, what you did wrong, and how to make it right.

What Did You Learn?

1. Don't be afraid of failure; it can be the best path to learning what works.
2. The darkest clouds often have a silver lining. Step back, examine the facts, and figure out what you could have changed to avoid failing.
3. The only way you fail to learn from failure is if you fail to attempt something in the first place.

CHAPTER 5

Yes You Can: Determine What You Can Change Now

Take those first steps.

THERE ARE SEVERAL STEPS for you to take as you begin to build a better life for yourself. I can't take them for you, but I can offer wisdom gleaned from years of experience. They come from personal successes and failures, from what others have taught me, and from what I've observed of the people who've worked for me. Lest you think I've cruised through all my ventures, you should know that the road hasn't always been easy for me, but an important lesson I learned long ago is that failures or setbacks do not justify giving up. Learn from your mistakes. Laugh if you want, but get right back up and try it again. Spit in failure's face and charge full speed ahead.

I challenge you to use the contents of these pages to take the first steps to build your new life. But unless you, and you alone, are willing to do whatever is necessary to help yourself, then all you are holding in your hands is a book of words that you might as well tear up and use for toilet tissue. I can give you the words and roadmap, but the driving is up to you.

A good starting point is to begin making a close analysis of yourself and your present life situation. Be brutally honest with yourself about who you are. What are your deficits? What are the things about you that you want to change? What might others want you to change? Try to look at yourself as others see you, whether this is from the point of view of your boss, co-workers, spouse, friends or whomever. Ask those closest to you to give you an honest evaluation of your skills. Call former bosses and get their opinions. Make a list of all the things you are good at and all the things you don't like about yourself and work on eliminating the "don't likes."

Let's look at deficits for a moment. The federal government is not the only one with deficits. You have them, I have them, and so do companies, world leaders, doctors, lawyers, writers, teachers and so forth. No one is perfect. There is no shame in recognizing your deficits; the shame is in ignoring them. The failure or refusal to acknowledge your weak spots and the refusal to do something positive to correct them will keep you pigeonholed in your current predicament.

Keep a Positive Attitude About Yourself

When you begin your own self-examination, remember that it is counter-productive to allow yourself to be depressed or discouraged by what you find. On the contrary, it is going to open your eyes to the things that you can immediately begin to change so that nobody ever again says bad things about you. Remember to keep a positive attitude. Be positive even if it hurts. One of my biggest deficits is always seeking perfection in everything I do. Not everything can be done with 100%

accuracy. For years I took it as a personal affront if an employee of mine failed because somehow, as their manager, I had failed them. I wanted the perfect staff. I now recognize that this will never happen and that my need for perfection is a challenge I must overcome. If I didn't stop myself, I would probably edit this book so many times that it would end up being ten words: "life is full of options, find relevance in all you do," but I've already committed myself to edit it only once. For a perfectionist, this is quite a difficult goal to meet, but I had to set this goal because it helps me overcome a deficit.

Of course, you won't like everything you learn about yourself when you shed your illusions and take a good look at your deficits. Nobody likes to admit that they have problems. But you will never succeed without doing all that you can to become a better person, let alone a better businessperson.

Identify Your Shortcomings and Adapt

One of the most demanding bosses I ever worked for was Jim Ficco at Ketchum Communications. Jim was the classic Type-A personality: extremely driven, and always working, giving everything to the company. What made Jim such a good boss was his dedication to succeed. What made him a great boss was that he eventually recognized that not all of the agency's employees shared his personality traits. Jim was driven and he expected his employees to be driven as well. But he understood that not everyone could focus their energies and become singularly focused like he was. He gave employees enough rope to hang themselves, but would be there to support them before the noose got too tight. While Jim was singularly focused on his job, I watched him adapt his interaction with others as he learned through his employees that people's priorities were oftentimes different than his own. Some wanted to come to work for 40 hours and leave the advertising business at the office. Some wanted to immerse themselves in creativity and live and breathe advertising seven days a week. Some wanted to work elsewhere but held onto their jobs because they were afraid to take that very important step of moving into their life's true purpose. As Jim identified what drove people, he became a better boss because he understood what motivated each person in the firm. He adapted himself to better communicate with each type of person and this led to his being able to alter what he admitted was a deficit—his Type-A personality—and use it to an advantage to push people to become better employees.

On the other side of the spectrum, I was an investor in a company where the President suffered from what I call "analysis paralysis". He couldn't make a decision to save his life. He had spent much of his career in the military and had orders handed down to him. He was adept at executing those orders, but couldn't make the leap to the corporate world where he had to originate the orders. He tried to take everything on himself, did not understand the importance of utilizing employee strengths, and did not have a grasp of basic business principles. Customers would ask how much something cost and he couldn't tell them. His standard reply would be, "Well, we'll have to look into what works." He couldn't step back and see his own shortcomings. When some of the investors tried to help him he turned us away, proceeding on his own merry path which ultimately led to bankruptcy. Let me give you some advice, if a customer asks what something costs, tell them! They are ready to buy. And before they can respond, tell them how quickly you can deliver it to them. Then tell them how you'll service them once you've sold it to them, so that they go beyond being satisfied customers and become fanatical about how great you are and how you deliver on your promises.

You may find that you are unable to accurately see your shortcomings or that it is confusing or difficult to muster the honesty and immunity to pain required to take a good, hard look at yourself. Even when you try to be honest, it's only human that your own self-protective instincts will take over and blind you to seeing your own problem areas.

Ask Your Colleagues for Personal Feedback

One very easy way to learn to identify your deficits is simply to ask someone. My partner loves to tell me about my deficits! But seriously, asking a colleague for personal feedback is a surefire means to gain valuable information, and I promise that if you ask, you will receive. People are very likely to respond to your request, especially if you explain you are trying to learn how to improve upon your deficiencies in order to become better at your career. They will probably be impressed at your honesty and flattered that you value their opinions. People are and will be willing to offer help and give you suggestions on how you might improve yourself or your work. Of course, you may get that one smart-alecky friend who walks in with a stack of 300 sheets of paper and proudly announces, "I jotted down a few of your faults." If that happens, tell them you would prefer to have everything input into a spreadsheet so you can cross-reference your faults with their annoying jokes!

But seriously, the people you should ask for help are basically those in a position to know you, to have seen your performance at work or elsewhere, and those likely to give sound criticism. You may not know whether your ex-boss or fellow office worker or past girlfriend or boyfriend will have anything constructive to say about you. This doesn't matter because you will never know the answers until you ask for them. There is never any harm in asking. *"Tell me about working with me. What was most difficult for you?"* You aren't obligated to listen to their advice if you think it's worthless. For instance, someone may tell you that the only thing wrong with you is your hairstyle. Now, a haircut is an easy thing to change if necessary but advice on haircuts is not what you are after in this process. What you are looking for are the biggies: **skills, creativity,** and **attitude.** You can worry about "dressing for success" later, and there are plenty of books to help you do so. Right now, you want to work on the *inside.* How many people do you know who spend more time working on maintaining their automobile than on maintaining themselves? You need to start by fixing your engine first and worry about your paint job later.

Ask for candid feedback on how your skills match up against others in your company. Do people think you have the skills to be in business for yourself? If not, what skills are you lacking? Ask about how you are viewed. Are you seen as creative in your approach to work, finding new and better ways to meet goals, or are you seen as someone who must be driven by a manager, pushed until you accomplish what is asked of you? Is your attitude such that you take criticism well, or are you defensive and look to blame outside influences for your own deficits? Find out what people think about the enthusiasm you bring (or don't bring) to work each day. Learn as much about yourself as you can so that you can begin to change these traits.

This is a difficult task to undertake because we don't like to hear bad comments about ourselves, but you must do it. These will be the best conversations you may ever have because if those you interview are honest with you, they will identify the areas you need to work on to become more successful. Make the calls. Learn about yourself. Then go to work fixing your engine.

In a survey of several dozen human resource directors, I found that the most common issues facing employee self-improvement are centered within three key areas: job skills, engagement, and communication skills. Let's look at each to learn ways to improve deficiencies. Perhaps you'll find a few of these insights worthwhile with regard to fixing your self-improvement issues.

Job skills represent the area that is easiest to fix. If you don't know how to accomplish a task you have three choices: 1) ignore the problem and hope it goes away; 2) blame the problem on others and try to distance yourself from it; or 3) figure out how to gain the skills you need to solve the problem. Since you're reading this book you probably realize the futility in taking the first two approaches, so let's look at how to gain the skills you need to broaden your abilities.

Many people lack the skills they need to be more successful. Whether you need help learning Microsoft Excel, running a tractor, understanding the retail business, becoming a real estate agent, or training to be an emergency medical technician, the good news is there are multiple avenues to learn the skills you need. The Internet gives you access to millions of often free resources that can help you learn about an industry or job function or skill. The local bookstore provides publications on virtually every area of business. Community colleges often offer skills enhancement programs such as how to learn Microsoft Excel or how to write a business plan. And industry trade associations often provide seminars and free information on their industries.

After giving a lecture at the Digital Hollywood conference in Los Angeles, I was approached by a young woman who was by profession the receptionist for a small accounting firm. She wanted to improve her understanding of marketing but was embarrassed to ask for help from her boss. I suggested she start at the library and look for books on marketing that addressed the areas she was interested in. I also suggested she pick up the easy-to-read paperback book, *Marketing for*

Dummies, by Alexander Hiam. Finally, I said she should go online to find links to industry associations such as the American Marketing Association. She thanked me for the suggestions and walked away.

I often wondered what she did with these tips. Two years later she answered my question when an e-mail arrived describing how she bought *Marketing for Dummies* and found it so interesting that she sought out several additional books at the library that dealt with statistical analysis of marketing campaigns, an area in which she felt particularly drawn. This led to her enrolling in a $65 adult continuing education course in statistics at her local community college. She joined the American Marketing Association and posted her resume on the jobs section of the site and was soon employed as a research analyst at a mid-sized marketing and promotions firm in a neighboring town. She is now making $29,000 more a year and found herself in a career that engaged her. This leads us to the next point.

Be Enthusiastic and Engaged

Engagement is an area where many people find themselves lacking. Are you engaged in what you do? If you are, is your engagement infectious, resulting in those around you becoming enthused about the work at hand? Or are you disengaged from work and unconsciously spreading a wave of negativism to everyone you touch?

In talking with the human resource directors, I learned that engagement really boils down to attitude. As the famous inspirational author Norman Vincent Peale once wrote, "The person who sends out positive thoughts activates the world around him positively and draws back to himself positive results." Melissa Ravenscroft has been working with The Amati Foundation in a development role. She has the arduous task of working with major corporations to sponsor our events and promotional vehicles, asking for $150,000 to $5,000,000 at a time. There is a project we have created that requires an endowment fund of $27,000,000, yet Melissa is so positive and enthusiastic about the prospect of landing sponsors that you can't help but get excited for her. Faster than you can say "Avian Flu," Melissa's positive thoughts infect everyone around her, making people want to see her succeed.

Attitude is about the way you view life and whether or not you let little things bother you, or like water beading on a duck's back, they let it roll off you. A positive attitude helps to cope more easily with the daily affairs of life. It generates optimism and makes it easier to avoid worry and negative thinking. If you adopt positive thinking as a way of life, it will bring constructive changes that will spread to those around you. With a positive attitude you see the best that life offers, become optimistic, and expect the best to happen. Even in work. With this attitude comes constructive thinking, creative thinking, motivation to accomplish tasks, and inspiration to achieve goals. It is certainly a state of mind that is well worth developing and strengthening.

You can wake up tomorrow and choose to be engaged. You can wake up choosing to believe in yourself and your abilities. You can view failure and problems as blessings in disguise, giving you the opportunity to learn and thus, improve yourself. You can go to work looking for solutions, seeing opportunities, and infecting those around you with your great attitude. Attitude makes you engaged. And if you are engaged, it becomes contagious.

Turn Your Negative Thoughts into Positive Ones

Maybe you are asking yourself, "well, it is fine and dandy to say wake up with a positive attitude and become engaged, but realistically, how do I do that?" There are many ways to start on your path to engagement. Self-help books, audio cassettes, and Internet sites are some of the tools that can help give insight into reaching your potential. Let me share with you two exercises that I have found worthwhile. You can even undertake them concurrently.

Divide a sheet of paper into two columns and, for a few days, jot down in the left column all the negative thoughts that come into your head. After the first three to five days, rewrite each thought in a positive way in the right column. The idea is to turn what you perceive as a negative into a mental image that is positive and reinforces the energy you put toward the task. By beginning to write the negative thoughts and their positive counterparts down, you will train your mind to make this a habit. For example, you may write, "I'll never get this finished by the end of the day," which could be rewritten as, "I will probably get most of this finished by the end of the day." You might write, "How will I get this promotion and make more money if I don't understand how to operate this machinery?" which may become, "If I seek out training on this machinery, I can line myself up for a promotion and the resulting increase in pay." One of my sales representatives at YouthStream Media Networks conducted this exercise and wrote, "How am I going I meet my monthly sales quota?" and responded in the right column by positively stating, "If I make three more calls a day, I'll meet quota. If I make five calls, I'll exceed it." Guess what happened the following month? He beat his quota. In fact, he beat it every month thereafter!

For the second part of this exercise, take five white index cards and write each of the sayings below on individual cards:

1. Today is going to be a great day.

2. If I think I can do it, I can. If I believe I can do it, I will. If I trust I can do it, nothing will stop me.

3. I can accomplish anything I want. I will open the door and

achieve success!

4. On the road to success, I'm behind the steering wheel.

5. Today I am completely engaged in my career. Nothing can stop me from becoming successful.

Use a blue marker to write the sentences. With a yellow highlighter, underline each sentence. The color is important, as blue will subconsciously relay feelings of loyalty and yellow imparts positive impressions. It may sound corny, but color theory has proven this out. It's one of the reasons I always paint my offices a light shade of yellow. Hey, every little bit helps, right?

Next, tape card #1 to your bathroom mirror where you'll see it first thing in the morning as you brush your teeth. If you follow the rule that you brush for 60 seconds, you can read this card perhaps 20 times, continually reinforcing that *Today is going to be a great day.*

Tape card #2 on the wall across from your toilet. When you're sitting on the porcelain throne each morning you'll read about how you can accomplish things.

Card #3 gets taped to the back of your door. As you leave the house on your way to work, this should be the thought you read.

Card #4 gets taped to the dashboard of your car where you'll see it each time you drive someplace.

Finally, tape card #5 to your computer monitor or place it in a small frame in a highly visible spot at your desk or cubicle at work. Or tape it to your iPad or tablet computer. Just put it somewhere you'll see it day after day. Take the time to read it at least three times a day.

This exercise may seem silly, but you will find that each card becomes a positive reinforcement that is similar to having a personal career coach telling you what a great day you are going to have and engaging you into a positive attitude.

Learn Top-Notch Communication Skills

The third common area of self-improvement is communication. In today's complex and global business world, learning to communicate is essential to success. It helps you stand out from the crowd, handle difficult situations with dignity, and maximize your interaction with others. Nothing is worse than feeling something you cannot express, or expressing something imprecisely. When you engage in conversation with another person, or sit down to write a letter or draft an e-mail, you want to present yourself in the best possible manner. In business settings, keep things formal. Corporate communications are no place for winks, Internet abbreviations or profanity. While internet chat rooms and personal e-mail may allow such shortcuts as IMHO, TTYL, or RTM, they shouldn't be used in a business setting as they instantly convey a lack of professionalism. Imagine the following e-mails sent to the president of a company whose business you want. The first is the actual e-mail delivered to a professional acquaintance of mine and the second is a more professional rewrite avoiding slang and more clearly articulating the message:

The original:

Mr. Slaven,

IMHO I think the best way to reach your goals is to get employees to RTM and sit in on live demos of our software. Let's set up a time to do this ASAP. ☺

TTYL, Jeff.

The revised e-mail:

Dear Mr. Slaven,

In my opinion, the most effective way to reach your department's goals is to have your employees read the manual and then review the software via a live demonstration. Let's coordinate an appropriate date and time to accomplish this.

Best regards,
Jeff

Which message is more effective? Which version communicates more clearly? Mr. Slaven was so unimpressed with the original e-mail that he cancelled a $200,000 software contract. When he shared the e-mail with me, he did so with a comment along the lines of, "This is ridiculous. It's as if a teenager wrote this." To say he was less than impressed would be an understatement. Can you imagine how the person who lost the $200,000 contract felt? I would bet he wasn't ROFLMAO[1].

Many human resource managers remarked that as the use of e-mail has increased, a corresponding decrease in grammatical skills has occurred.

In order to write effectively, you have to write *confidently*. Since the advent of electronic data networks, namely e-mail and the Internet, the importance of communicating clearly has grown. It used to be that managers would draft a letter verbally to a secretary who would convert her shorthand notes to a typed letter. Then the letter would be reviewed for grammar, spelling, and accuracy before it was mailed. Today, managers and employees are more likely to type their own letters and e-mails and often times send them off without running grammar or spell check. This opens the door to common mistakes that would have been unheard of 20 years ago. Unfortunately, the American education system hasn't armed most people with a solid foundation in business writing skills. However, there are a number of books such as William Strunk's *The Elements of Style*, Michael Muckian's *Business Letter Handbook: How to Write Effective Letters & Memos for Every Business Situation* and Harry Shaw's *Building A Better Vocabulary*, that make it possible to gain a solid foundation in effective corporate communications.

Effective communication skills extend beyond letters and e-mail. Conciseness and clarity are imperative for writing effective presentations such as those you may create in Microsoft PowerPoint. When making the presentation, clarity in speech and being able to effectively connect with your audience will lead to higher success rates than if you stand up and read what is on the screen with your back to the audience. I think of PowerPoint presentations as if each slide were a billboard. You only have a few seconds to grab your audience before they are ahead of you, so keep the bullet points and copy to a minimum and talk to each point. If you need to read the points first, turn to the screen, refresh your mind as to what the point covers, then turn to the audience and address that point. This tactic will give you a command of the presentation that is much more effective than if you simply read from a script or while facing a presentation with your back to the audience.

Communicating also relates to how you interact with employees, peers, coworkers, and clients. The biggest challenge in communicating with people today is not coping with a culturally diverse work force, the impersonal nature of e-mail or overcoming information overload. The challenge is in getting employees, your boss, and clients to trust you. If you have confidence in your subject matter you will come across as knowledgeable and on top of your game. If you think about what you want to say and then focus on conveying the message both clearly and concisely, your words will carry greater meaning. Couple your message with a positive attitude, showing that you are engaged in the topic, and your ability to articulate your point effectively is increased dramatically.

For those who want to master public speaking, join an organization like Toastmasters, enroll in a Dale Carnegie course, or take the 2-day public speaking course offered by Leader's Institute. All three offer hands-on training in becoming an effective communicator. Consider this an investment in your future and the next step in becoming successful.

What Did You Learn?

1. Make an analysis of yourself and your present situation. What are your deficiencies? What are your assets?
2. Ask coworkers for candid feedback on how your skills match up against others in your company.
3. Take steps to solve the most pressing negative traits you have. It's never too late to identify problems and start to turn your life around.
4. Fine-tune and hone your communications skills to become a more effective writer and speaker.
5. Be confident!

---

1. For those of you over age 40, ROFLMAO is Internet slang for Rolling On Floor Laughing My A** Off.

CHAPTER 6

Yes You Can: Create a Brand New You

Take charge of the most important
brand in the world: YOU.

IT IS IMPORTANT to remember that you are an entrepreneur; learn to think like one. If you are the owner of your own business you are your own brand. You are your product's brand. You must identify yourself with your product, profession or service. You must take this journey step-by-step, facing your goal, with the confidence and belief that you are going to succeed. If you paint in your mind the outcome, you immediately put yourself into the right mental condition to achieve your goal.

People tend to live up to their own expectations, so it behooves you to set expectations high. Throughout my career I have discovered that I always have choices, and sometimes it's only a choice of attitude that makes the difference between success and failure, or between exceeding my expectations or not. Henry David Thoreau, who lived from 1817 to 1862, wrote, "If one advances confidently in the direction of one's dreams, and endeavors to live the life which one has imagined, one will meet with a success unexpected in common hours." Imagining where you want to go is the perfect mental exercise to begin convincing yourself you can get there.

To succeed, you must never forget that it is your motivation and your enthusiasm that are going to put you on the path to prosperity. To get there will take guts. If you have managed to get beyond your fear of failure and have conquered that dreadful sense of loss after giving up the security of a job and steady income, then you are on the right path.

Take Risks

If, however, you aren't ready to take the leap and think you must work for a large corporation just so you can buy a big house, have some job security, and earn a weekly paycheck, then forget it. Save your sanity and do not go into business for yourself. You are not an entrepreneur. An entrepreneur understands that risk and reward go hand in hand. The old saying, "no risk, no reward" is true. The risk might include your money, your time, your effort, other people's money, or other people's time, but without that input there can be no reward. If you want to accomplish something for yourself, you must take a risk.

For Lauren Demerest, that *risk* was giving up two evenings a week to enroll in real estate courses and earn her license. Her *reward* was landing a job as a real estate agent where she earns 1-3% on every house she sells. She began by selling on weekends and as she become more confident and started earning commissions she was able to quit her day job and focus on real estate fulltime. Selling a $200,000 house puts $5,000 into Lauren's bank account. Selling three homes a month and taking home $15,000 makes the risk of giving up free time to learn the real estate business pay off.

If you are ready to devote all of your time and intensity to your new business, set your goals high. You will be a success! Take risks. You must do so to succeed! Untie any anchors that might be holding you back. A ship in port never sails the high seas.

Life is made of millions of moments, but you live only one of these moments at a time. As you begin to change this moment, you begin to change your life forever. As Oprah Winfrey puts it, "My philosophy is that not only are you responsible for your life, but doing the best at this moment puts you in the best place for the next moment." Take this moment right now and decide once and for all: are you going to take a risk and from this moment on control the outcome of your life, or are you going to continue the way you have, constantly wondering whether life could have held something better?

Strive to Be the Best You Can Be

Alcohol and drug addiction results from the act of activities undertaken simply for personal satisfaction. A one-time high makes you want another. This leads to yet more and finally you are addicted. The successful entrepreneur is addicted in the same way, but satisfies his addiction for success through achievement and self-improvement. Money plays but a small part in the equation. Achievement and self-improvement are qualities that make the difference between mediocrity and success. The true entrepreneur is the person who always strives to be better, whether it is in the professional field or their personal life. They do whatever it is they do best and do it twenty-four hours a day. This is what you will do as you start your journey. If you try your hardest, you are doing everything right. It doesn't matter what your profession is, as long as you do it well. Work for yourself and be the toughest boss you've ever had. You can do anything you want to do if you stick to it long enough and work at it hard enough. Don't worry about the money, it will follow you.

If you decide starting a business isn't for you, make the decision to live each day chasing achievement and self-improvement. Become the best employee your company has ever had. Turn your job into your career. Challenge yourself to learn more about other departments in your company and think about ways in which your special skills can improve the products or service your firm offers. Became an entrepreneur within your organization, seeking ways to improve customer relationships, product innovations, and cost-saving processes. Walk into work tomorrow and tell your boss you want to become more successful at your job and you're ready to begin right now. Ask what you can do to become a better employee. Ask how you can add more value to the company. Ask to put a career plan in place where you can lay out a plan for upward mobility. Then put every effort into becoming the best you can while becoming invaluable to the success of your company.

Developing the mental image to become a great employee is difficult. You must face the fact that no matter how superb an employee you are, there will always be outside influences that can affect your career. Someone in the finance department might embezzle millions of dollars which leads the company to bankruptcy. It's not your fault, but if the company doesn't recover, it may result in loss of your job. Perhaps the top salesperson leaves and takes the company's biggest clients with her. You may not even work in the sales department, but if a major source of revenue leaves the firm you may find yourself facing what MBAs call a RIF or reduction in force. You probably know the term by its more unsettling description, layoffs.

Regardless of these external issues, you must take pride in your job and work to become indispensable to your employer.

A Similar Recipe for Success:
Entrepreneurs and Employees

The differences between being a successful entrepreneur and a successful employee are not as vast as you might expect. Positive mental attitude drives both. Telling yourself, "Yes I can!" pushes you to excel. Focusing on goals and moving every mountain to reach those goals, leads you to success.

The characteristics that make a good entrepreneur include the following traits. A good entrepreneur expects their every need to be met. They expect the answer to every problem. They expect abundance on every level. They expect to succeed in their career, in their marriage, with their family, and every other aspect of life. Good entrepreneurs look for the opportunity in all they do. They wake every day excited about what lies ahead. They are confident and their confidence grows with each new success. They are honest and fair and understand that their high level of ethics attracts others with similar traits. They look at life not as a narrowing funnel that leads to death, but as a widening expanse that gives them the opportunity to choose any path they wish.

A great employee's traits are strikingly similar. They expect their financial needs to be met by devoting themselves to their job. They expect to find answers to every problem their position presents. They expect abundance on every level of their career. They expect to succeed in their career, in their marriage, with their family, and every other aspect of life. Good employees look for the opportunity to make their company more successful. They wake every day excited about what lies ahead. They are confident and their confidence grows with each new success. They are honest and fair and understand that their high level of ethics will be viewed positively by their boss. They look at their job not as a narrowing funnel that leads to a watch at retirement, but as a widening expanse of opportunity to become an invaluable asset to their employer.

Go ahead and tell yourself, "Yes I can!" take the first step in placing a positive mental picture of your abilities in your subconscious. Wake up, look in the mirror, and say, "Yes I can!" and start each day on the right foot. Walk into a meeting thinking, "Yes I can!" and get what you need from the meeting.   Take the steps needed to become self-confident and self-assured and you are miles ahead of everyone else.

In most companies I start, I put in place an Employee Entrepreneurship program that encourages the type of behavior outlined above. One of the core elements of this program is rewarding employees who save the company money by paying 50% of the first year's savings to the employee. By determining a way to save the firm $10,000 a year, the employee earns a $5,000 bonus. In one company an administrative assistant making $32,000 a year earned a $152,000 bonus because the field employees reporting system she designed using common software tools saved the firm over $300,000. She was able to design the system and reap its rewards because she took it upon herself to own her position as if she owned the company. After receiving such a windfall, did she slack off? Not at all. In fact, she began looking at other ways to save the company money or improve processes, each year earning bonuses that in all cases topped her base salary.

The difference between bad entrepreneurs and bad employees is also similar.

A bad entrepreneur or employee probably hit a few bumps in their first try and now constantly worries about failing. They fear they won't make ends meet. They fear they will be viewed as a failure. They immediately identify the bad elements of a situation instead of the good parts. They may have been dishonest in order to close a deal. They look to blame others for their own failings. The bad entrepreneur or employee is motivated more by greed than the desire to build a successful business. They itch for the quick buck without having the backbone to scratch for what they earn. They reach a goal and then immediately slack off, resting on their laurels, instead of focusing on the next goal to attain. And more often than not, bad entrepreneurs and bad employees focus too much on building their bank account and not enough on building success.

What Did You Learn?

1. You are your own brand. Whether as an entrepreneur or an employee, you must identify yourself with your product, service, and company. Only you can define who you want to be.
2. Motivation and enthusiasm are going to put you on the path to prosperity. Dedicate yourself to staying mentally engaged in what you do.
3. Whether you choose to start your own business or become the best employee your employer has, there are similar traits that will help you become successful. Among these traits is the willingness to strive to become better, to achieve more, and to focus on continual self-improvement.
4. If you start your own business and hire employees, don't be afraid to increase their ability to earn money: because the more they earn, the more *you* earn.
5. Shout it aloud, "Yes I can!"

CHAPTER 7

Yes You Can: Money Versus Success

Money is simply a by-product of Success.

L ET'S GET SOME things straight about money. I've found in talking with people who are starting their own company that they most often consider the accumulation of wealth as the most important decision to start a business. I hope to convince you that wealth is only one result of your success. It's a by-product. It is just as easy to be happy with a lot of money as it is with a little money. Henry Ford, the founder of Ford Motor Company, said, "If money is your hope for independence you will never have it. The only real security that a man will have in this world is a reserve of knowledge, experience, and ability." What Ford was trying to say is that if you develop your abilities, expand your experience, and continually learn, the money will follow.

There are three components of my definition of success: being successful as being able to spend time with my family; being content with the things I have instead of being frustrated because I don't have things I want; and being able to realize that what is important in my life has more to do with self-improvement than with material possessions. I'm glad I understand this. Many a successful businessman and woman continue to chase after money even after they've reached levels you and I would consider financially successful. Money has never made a person happy, nor will it ever. There is nothing about money that produces happiness. Sure, you can buy things and live more comfortably, but for most people who experience attaining any level of wealth, the more that person has, the more he wants. Instead of filling a vacuum, it creates one.

Do Your Best Work and Money Will Follow

There is no doubt that money is nice to have. Financial success is about being able to afford the things you want and being able to purchase them without taking on debt. To me, earning money is not as important or rewarding as starting a business, watching it grow, and identifying the next great business opportunity. I'll repeat it again: money usually follows success. Create a winning business and the money will be there. Develop a great new product and the money will follow. Do the best job you can for your employer and the money will flow. As you get older, and especially after you have children, you'll find your ideas of success will change. Family will take precedence over your job, especially if you hate your job. However, if you're in a career you love or running the business of your dreams, you'll find you can be successful at both, because your career success and the freedom that comes with that will give you the tools of time and money to make your family life more successful and rewarding.

Success Means Different Things to Different People

When I moved from New York City to Texas and suddenly found myself with a large yard in need of continual maintenance, I had to make a decision on how to care for it. Growing up on a farm, I had cut more than my share of grass, and as weird as it may sound, I like getting the mower out and spending the good part of a day cutting, chopping, and mulching to the smell of gasoline. On the other hand, with another startup company in the works, I knew that most Saturdays could be better spent working on my company than working in my yard. I had just decided to talk to my neighbors to find someone to cut the grass when a man by the name of Greg knocked on my front door. Greg was 37 years old and had an infectious, positive attitude, a great laugh, and a joy for life that made him instantly likable. As he stood on my porch and informed me that he would take care of my yard for $90 every two weeks, I was very impressed. His positive attitude was apparent. His neatly pressed shirt spoke of his professionalism. His pricing was reasonable. So in the great American tradition of encouraging commerce, I hired him on the spot.

Greg had one employee, a 14 year old boy named Marcus, who only worked on the weekends and during the summer months. Marcus was Greg's son. The two of them would spend three hours mowing, trimming and edging my yard, laughing and joking throughout. Greg was a hard working employer and Marcus quickly learned the values his father taught.

Greg was always enthusiastic about what was happening in his life: just the kind of person I like to hire. I never saw him angry or depressed over his choice of career. He drove over 45 miles roundtrip just to take care of my lawn, yet never once complained about the time it took or the amount of money he earned. I often asked him if he needed to raise his rates to make up for the distance, and his response was always the same: "Mr. Townsend," he'd say, "Every day I work with my son and we build a stronger and stronger relationship. I love my job and I am paid a fair wage for it. I'm happy to come out to your house to mow your grass, and my son enjoys the work, too. I like teaching him the value of earning money for a day's hard work." What is the point of this story? If a man with a high school degree, who mows grass for a living can have such a positive outlook on life, you can certainly find the silver lining in yours.

You can always defend yourself with excuses: you don't have a college degree; you don't have money; you limp; your nose is too big; you fried too many brain cells in college; and so forth. Greg had no college degree and hardly any savings at all. Yet he had dreams of success, and was meeting his goals through hard work and determination.

Develop a Positive Attitude

Greg marketed himself the hard way by knocking on doors and asking if he could mow the homeowner's yard. I suggested that there must be a more efficient means to get customers, that his approach was challenging. He replied, "The best advice I could give a person is that you've just got to start walking and stop looking back." What was he saying? Get out there and do it! Don't create obstacles for yourself. As the Nike slogan says, "Just Do It." Stop the depression and really believe that you can get anything you want out of your life. Barriers be damned! You can succeed like gangbusters if you only try, and you can't try if you let yourself be negatively influenced by your own lack of money, degrees or anything else. What impressed me most about Greg was his attitude: the willingness to succeed regardless of the obstacles.

You too have to believe with all of your heart that trying *is* doing and that you *will* succeed by trying.

You might think that I'm painting success as some rosy picture that everyone could be in if they only tried. Putting effort into trying is important, but it is often the case that a business fails regardless of the hard work that was put in it. My point in all of this is to convince you that you will need to develop a positive attitude *before* you begin your business or professional career. It is this attitude that you will have to rely on throughout your entire life. It takes more than attitude to succeed, but without the right attitude, success is impossible.

When I first met the mother of my sons she was an intern at Ketchum and was one year away from completing her Master's degree in advertising at the University of Texas. Jennifer grew up in a typical middle class household in Pittsburgh, Pennsylvania with four siblings, a stay-at-home mother, and a father who has held the same job for over 30 years. She put herself through college by taking out student loans, working, and saving every penny she could in order to finish her degree. One day I had lunch with all the interns, and while most were talking about the Pittsburgh Pirates or what concert was in town that weekend, Jennifer quizzed me about the advertising business. She quizzed me hard. I felt as if I was sitting in a job interview and I was the one being interviewed. She immediately impressed me as someone who, although not yet working in the advertising field, already had the positive mental image of where she wanted to go in her career and how she'd get there. Because she impressed me with her focus on success, I kept in touch with Jennifer after she returned to pursue her Master's degree. I liked her attitude and knew she'd be successful. And successful she was. By the time she was 28, she had worked for two major New York advertising agencies, Ammirati Purls Lintas and Grey Advertising, managing clients such as Ment-A-Dent, UPS and Dell. From there she became the youngest vice president at the world-renowned toy store FAO Schwarz and led their interactive marketing and e-commerce efforts to make their web site division the company's most profitable business unit. Jennifer's success was due in part to her incredible hard work, positive attitude, and absolute belief in her own talents. And while she worked for others, these are the same qualities you must develop to become successful as an entrepreneur.

These days, Jennifer is applying her talents to raising our children. I believe she's one of the most successful mothers I've ever witnessed and I know our sons find her to be the center of their universe. Part of what makes her a great mom is the fact that she is continuously learning how to be better by reading books and articles, talking to our kids' teachers, and gaining knowledge from her own mother.

Whether you aim to be a successful entrepreneur, lover, friend, mother or father, if you continually strive to improve yourself, then reaching your goals will become easier. Focus on becoming a better person. The best preparation for what might happen tomorrow is to prepare today. I'm not that interested in what happened yesterday because I'm focused on what might happen tomorrow. You should be too, and that focus begins with you asking how you can improve yourself today. As former Tonight Show host Johnny Carson said, "Talent alone won't make you a success. Neither will being in the right place at the right time, unless you are ready. The most important question is: 'Are you ready?'"

What Did You Learn?

1. Money is only a by-product of success. Focus on becoming successful first and the money will follow.
2. It is up to you to determine what success means. Is it family,

friends, possessions, or the ability to take a month long vacation in Italy? Or, like Greg, is it simply enjoying your work and being able to spend time with your children? This is a question only you can answer.

3. Success comes to those who are prepared to act on opportunities. Talent, attitude, knowledge, hard work, and belief in your abilities will prepare you for what lies ahead.

CHAPTER 8

Yes You Can: Make Your Job Your Career

Take control of your life in order to become successful.

Y OU HAVE ALREADY LEARNED there is no need to worry about failure and that hearing someone say "no" is not the end of the world. You know how important it is to talk with others to form an assessment of your skills, creativity, and attitude. And you know what steps you need to take to minimize any issues that need corrected. With the basics addressed, where do you start on your journey to becoming a successful person?

Take Control of Your Life

The first step is to begin to think about your life as just that. Repeat after me, "My life." This is not to say that you are going to be selfish, but rather to signify the importance of controlling your daily existence. Your life is controlled for the most part by one person: you.

If you're in a job situation you dislike, it affects more than the hours you spend slaving away on the job. If you spend 40 hours a week at a job that you hate, there are probably 30 additional hours that are directly impacted by the negative energy created while you're at work. Perhaps it's the first few hours every morning when you're getting ready for the job you hate. Or perhaps it is when you're driving to the job you hate. Or maybe you can't wait to get home and away from the job you hate. Do you see how a negative work experience parlays into additional negative hours in your day?

I challenge you to go out on your own and make your job one you love. Make it your career. Look forward to going to work every day. Are you ready? Let's get started.

First, you must have a vision of what you want to do. It helps to start by examining your background for an area of expertise. What do you know more than most people? What can you do better than most others? You can't just follow-the-leader and expect to be a success—we witnessed that during the dotcom era when every Tom, Dick and Harry (and Gertrude, Gilbert and Zoe) started an Internet company with dreams of striking it rich. Just because one person is doing something successful doesn't mean that the same idea will work for you. You have to figure out what it is that you can do that can provide you the means to generate an income, fulfill your career ambitions, and make your life enjoyable.

I was asked to look at the résumé of Manuel, a 37 year-old salesman who awoke one day to the realization that for 17 years he'd been selling insurance, and had not once made more than $65,000 a year. He asked himself, "If I haven't hit it big by now, how will I do so in the future, and how will I pay for my daughter's college education and my retirement?" Feeling that his insurance products' geographic territory was tapped, and realizing that online sales of insurance were negatively impacting his business, he wanted help identifying industries where his background in sales could be utilized. When asked what his skill set consisted of, Manuel said he was an experienced salesperson but didn't have any other skills to speak of. He never managed a sales organization, and in fact, the only management skills he had were that of a sales rep working with an administrative assistant.

Consider All Your Life Experiences and Skills

I noticed that he had been a Boy Scout leader for more than 10 years, active in his church as a deacon, and was the coordinator of four mission trips to Honduras and Columbia. As we discussed his background it turned out that he had significant project management experience through these extracurricular activities. It was also apparent that since he was bilingual in English and Spanish, he offered potential employers a better job candidate than he gave himself credit for. I suggested Manuel look for sales positions with companies that were selling to or attempting to sell to the Hispanic market both in the United States and South America. We also agreed that he should consider positions in project management as well as sales.

About a month later Manuel called to tell me about his job search. In the process of researching companies throughout Pennsylvania, West Virginia, Ohio, and Indiana, he found dozens of manufacturers that had products that could potentially sell well within the Hispanic market, but none had focused their efforts on entering this demographic. He thought he could start a manufacturer's representation business to act as the sales and product management arm for a company. For instance, his firm would help companies that made widgets market and sell those widgets to the Hispanic community, now the largest minority population in the United States and one that most companies do not know how to sell into. Manuel also believed he could do this not just for one company, but for multiple companies. "If I was selling one product to a company, why not be able to sell many if they were complimentary?" he exclaimed. He created a simple business plan that called for a $10,000 investment to purchase a computer, Internet access, a desk and phone, office supplies, a tri-fold brochure, and traveling expenses. Since he was employed at the time, he approached his bank to secure a small business loan, and with it in hand he was about to launch his company. Manuel didn't need advice from me. He had already made up his mind to become an entrepreneur and was simply using my advice to support his decision. He began working on his business in the evenings and weekends, and five months later left the insurance business to work full time at his exporting business. A year ago, Manuel sent me a copy of his yearend financial statement that showed $2.3 million in sales with $276,000 in net revenues to his company. Better yet, he was paying himself $150,000 a year. Emblazoned across the top of the page in bright red ink were these words: "I never imagined I would be here today—success is only the beginning!"

How did Manuel succeed? He took his existing skills and applied new learning in order to identify something he could do better than anyone else. In this case, he offered companies a way to increase revenues and open new markets with virtually no risk, and in doing so, created a highly profitable business by taking a 12% commission on anything he sold for his clients. He also saved money on overhead by running the business out of his home, and by hiring only one employee, a part-time assistant who took care of bookkeeping and administrative tasks, thereby freeing Manuel to focus his energies on selling and customer service. To top it off, this minimalist approach to running a business let him focus on serving and exceeding his customers' needs. All of this led to Manuel's success.

You must have comprehensive knowledge and experience with your product or service, whatever that product or service may be. Kemmons Wilson didn't have any experience in music—he was a homebuilder—and thus he didn't grasp the talent of a young Elvis Presley. But making the leap from homebuilder to hotel builder isn't that far of a jump. Add some more rooms and put a bed in each room and you have essentially built a hotel. The same is true for Manuel. The leap from insurance salesman to exporter is vast, but the jump from bilingual salesperson selling insurance to bilingual salesperson selling other products isn't. The only difference was who provided the product.

The one area of critical importance is to decide what you want to sell or offer and whether there is a market for it. It doesn't matter if you're selling manufactured products to the Hispanic market, software, vitamins, haircuts, or gifts. You must have the courage to be unique and provide a product or service that has real value. And you must believe in the product or service with all your heart, lest your customers not believe in you. How many times have you met a car salesmen who you just knew didn't like the car he was trying to sell you? You have to be convinced, and be convincing, that your product is the best.

Stand Out from the Competition

When Lycos was started in 1995, Bob Davis, the CEO, was convinced we had the best search engine on the Internet. His enthusiasm for the technology and the company funneled down to every employee who worked for us. Bob was rabid about Lycos. He wasn't just a believer; he was like a raving fan in the end zone, cheering for his team to win. What made Bob an adroit CEO was his total focus on making Lycos a success. He led Lycos from a university-sponsored research project to a multi-billion dollar acquisition. You need to have that same ambitious drive and belief that what you are selling is the best.

As part of the founding management team at Lycos, it was my job to drive revenues, so I ran advertising sales (I also ran marketing, but more on that later). I understood that our audience was tech savvy and the leaders in technology adoption. I knew that Lycos was the best ad buy on the Internet. I knew we could target messages to users based on what they were searching for, where they were based, even what company they worked for, and deliver great results for our advertising clients. I had "Lycos blood" running through my veins and would challenge anyone and everyone to be more personally involved in their company than the management team of Lycos was. We knew we had a great product; we believed in it with all our heart, and we knew we would become successful. We observed that the advertising reps of our competitors—companies like AOL, Yahoo!, InfoSeek, Magellan and Excite, were arrogant and treated ad agencies poorly, so we focused on providing superior customer service that was timely, friendly, and supportive of the agencies' clients. It made our team stand out from the competition.

When we moved Lycos from a research project at Carnegie Mellon University to a full-fledged operating company, we had a vision of creating one of the largest Internet businesses ever. The website was receiving ten million page views a month. Eight months later, with 26 employees, we took Lycos public in a widely anticipated initial stock offering that gave us a market capitalization of $300 million. By that time we were serving over 80 million page views a month. We sold $9 million in advertising space that first year and this was in an advertising medium that didn't even exist the year before Yahoo! and Lycos came along. We doubled our sales the next year. My coworker on the business development side of the house, Ben Bassi, devised content deals with major US and International companies that brought in millions of dollars of revenue to what was then a 2 year-old company.

Lycos became one of the most popular destinations on the web, with millions of customers from around the world. What helped it grow so quickly? We had super salespeople. Bob Davis wasn't just the CEO of Lycos; he was the Company's #1 salesman. Ben Bassi wasn't just VP of Business Development; he was a super salesman. The advertising sales department didn't succeed because I was a super salesman; it succeeded because I hired super salesmen (and women).

Newegg.com is the 2nd largest pure-play online retailer in America. The company sells information technology and consumer electronics products and operates e-commerce websites in the United States, Canada and China. Newegg is wildly popular with the geek crowd because not only can you buy PCs and laptops but you can also buy motherboards, memory, CPUs, graphics cards and all the other parts that enable one to build their own computer. Newegg backs the thousands of products it sells with what many consider to be the industry's best customer service. If there is a problem, Newegg will go to great lengths to resolve it.

Newegg's customers are incredibly loyal and much of that loyalty stems from the fact that Newegg's employees are clearly focused on making the customer's experience ideal. They are dedicated to offering the best products at the best price, backed by the best service. In fact, you could say that Newegg's employees are loyal to the customer and the customers know it.

You must be able to convince your customer, whether he is the end user or represents a commercial or industrial account, that you can provide the very best product and service in all areas. Lycos and Newegg do this over and over, again and again. The passion and dedication of every employee, from the CEO down, is apparent through service that customers are passionate about, and that is what makes a company grow.

As you begin to think about what it is you want to do with your life, you'll need to focus on what you're going to sell and how you'll do it. You have to have confidence that you can sell yourself and your product or service. You must believe in your inner strengths to be successful. You must wake each day and say, "Today is going to be a great day. If I think you can do it, I can. If I believe I can do it, I will. If I trust I can do it, nothing can stop me."

What Did You Learn?

1. If you want to become successful you must take control of your life. Only you can do it and it must be done. Start today.
2. Understand what it is you do that has value. Assess your skills and abilities and focus on creating your career around those attributes.
3. Become dedicated to yourself and your company. You must be the #1 salesperson in your life. You must be enthused, ambitious, and willing to start every day by saying, "Yes I can!"

CHAPTER 9

Yes You Can: Earn Your MBA In A Few Minutes

Understanding how a business operates isn't difficult.

HERE IS THE basis of a $50,000 MBA education boiled down into one sentence: there are a handful of areas that are very important to any business: *product, cost, pricing, sales, profit,* and *people.*

Let's apply this to your situation. Once you have established the idea about your product or service and you feel you have a good concept, you have to begin testing your concept by thoroughly researching the market. You need to talk to potential customers, learn as much about the competition as you can, read as much as you can about the industry you'll operate in, and be ever vigilant to new competitors. Call similar companies outside of your territory to learn what challenges the owners faced when they launched their businesses. Visit their stores and see how they present themselves to the public. Try to learn as much about their operations as possible.

Before launching his company, Manuel called a dozen firms and talked to the CEO, COO, and/or Vice President of Sales to gauge their interest in selling to the Hispanic market. He identified a desire on the part of manufacturers. Then he called potential buyers of these products to understand their needs. When he saw a match between the two he decided to start the company. It wasn't a costly process and it didn't take a long time. It was Manuel sitting at his kitchen table, calling prospects over the course of a couple of weeks. He estimated it cost him $50.

You may find that the market is currently saturated with your product or that there is no demand for it. For example, perhaps you have worked for a certain company in a sales capacity for five or ten years. You think you could do as well on your own with the same product, but after conducting your market research, you find that there isn't any room for competition. The only way you can be successful in the same field is to build a better product, sell the product at a better price and/or offer better service. (Think back to Joe Hardy and his cash and carry plan at 84 Lumber Company. Wood is wood, but because he could sell it cheaper than his competitors, his business blossomed.) This is where you must rethink your business plan to outsmart the competition. By researching the market early you avoid costly (in terms of both money and time) mistakes that could have derailed your ability to reach your goal.

In 1998 I was hired to help turn around a financial services company. As it turned out, this company was attempting to do too many things at one time. They had 2,916 customers and offered 200+ sources of data. The first thing I looked at was where their margin was; that is, what was making money and what wasn't. Their most popular service cost $195 a month and was sold to about 800 customers, resulting in $156,000 a month in revenue. This service cost the company $105 a month per subscriber resulting in a profit of $90 per subscriber or $72,000 a month. Or so they thought. What the management team failed to understand was that of the 1,200 customer service calls each month, 87% were for this one service. Each call lasted an average of 17 minutes and typically came from clients who subscribed to only one or two of the company's services. The company employed six customer service reps, which cost the company $33,000 a month in salaries and overhead. They never bothered comparing revenues with the costs of servicing the accounts. Once analyzed, it became clear that their most popular service wasn't generating $72,000 a month in profit as thought, it was making $39,000.

After spending a few days talking to customers and running financial projections on my PC, I presented the owners with my recommendations. We would raise the monthly subscription fee to $595 with the effect of eliminating about 70% of the subscribers, reducing gross monthly revenues to $119,000. As you might imagine, the thought of eliminating 1,500 subscribers scared the management team.

I then demonstrated how eliminating customers this way was actually good for their business. I explained that we would eliminate four customer service positions and supplement the remaining rep with a robust online help section. This reduced the monthly burn rate from $33,000 a month to $5,400 a month. Subtracted from the $119,000 in revenues, this meant that net revenues from the remaining subscribers would total $113,600, which was vastly more profitable than the existing model.

The Customer Connection Solution

How could we raise prices like this? I understood the customer. I utilized something I call the "Customer Connection," which is a tactic that focuses on understanding why customers like or dislike a product. The Customer Connection is centered around understanding what is inside customer's heads to try to determine what a company can deliver to them, and to fulfill their wants and desires, sometimes before they realize they need what the company is offering. I want to know more about their business than they know and I want to understand what drives them to support my product. I knew that at least 150 clients absolutely had to have access to this data and wouldn't cancel unless a 500-mile wide meteor hit the earth destroying everything in its path. I also knew that another 60 to 90 companies relied heavily on the data and probably wouldn't cancel if we raised prices slowly and explained why we were doing so.

We sent a personal letter to each subscriber detailing the need to raise prices and featuring all the normal marketing speak of better quality, redundancy, and shorter time on hold for customer service. There was one other note: We told subscribers that we were in business to make a profit, and that under the existing rate structure this was not possible. We stated that we had two options: continue delivering at today's prices and go out of business, thereby leaving our clients high and dry; or raise rates slowly over the next six months in order to insure we'd be here for our clients in the future. If your business relied on this data, which would you rather support: a company that was honest with you and described the problem and solution, or a company that didn't say a word and just jacked up prices unexpectedly? In this case, the former approach, the honest approach, worked well. The management team and I altered the business model on an additional 37 subscription services, eliminated 18 altogether, and combined all the firm's services into easy to understand packages. When it was all said and done, the company increased their net profit margin by 71%, cut expenses by 18% and positioned themselves for an acquisition the following year.

It is nearly impossible to create a successful business if you don't understand why your customers value your products or service. You have to understand what it costs you to provide a product (the cost) and what your customer is willing to pay (the price). The difference is your profit. This understanding will not only help you fine tune your product offering, but will also enable you to create a more profitable business.

Manuel understood that the average cost of sales for manufacturers was 17%; therefore he felt a 12% commission was a fair way to provide service to his clients while reducing their sales costs. He approached each manufacturer by stating that could drop their cost of sales 5% by representing their products.

He estimated the cost of running his business to be between $5,000 and $6,000 a month which meant he had to sell $50,000 of goods each month to break even. He felt that would be easily attainable in the first year, and as you saw earlier, he was selling $191,000 a month in no time at all.

Keep Expenses to a Minimum

Once you have researched your product or service and have a good understanding of what you can charge, the next thing is to organize your business. Always remember, keep it simple. If you can start the company by working out of your home as Manuel did, then by all means, do so. Or consider an executive office space where you share the receptionist and office equipment with others, thereby keeping your costs down. Plus, by running a business from your home you can deduct certain expenses such as electricity and Internet access from your taxes. And with rising gas prices, you can't beat the commute!

Keep your employees to a minimum. Unless you are venture capital backed or have deep pockets, every dollar you pay an employee is a dollar you could pay yourself, or better yet, put back into growing your business.

Most businesses today can be started with a computer, Internet access, printer, and telephone line. You won't need fancy signage, company cars, and other non-necessities. What you do need is a good idea, a good product or service, and the dedication to make it successful. You'll probably want to incorporate in order to protect your assets and limit your liability. This can be completed inexpensively through one of many online services.

Be flexible in your business plans and operational activities and keep an open eye to remaining adaptable to changing customer demands. Jack Welch, the legendary ex-CEO of General Electric, once said, "It you're not fast and adaptable, you're vulnerable." By remaining adaptable, you can change course on your way to your goal. Much like laser guided and satellite-guided missiles fly this way and that on their way to their target, you will be able to slightly or dramatically alter your business to continually provide the best products for your customers.

Be a Great Salesperson

So now you have done your research and determined what product you will offer that will be priced competitively and provide enough profit to make running the business worthwhile. You've formed your company, purchased a computer and telephone, and are ready to start tackling the marketplace. Now it is time to sell. The best of the best have one thing in common and there is one way to describe them – you guessed it – they are outstanding salesmen. You can have the best product, but it has to be sold. You can have the best service, but it has to be sold. You say you're not a salesperson? How can you expect to succeed if you don't believe in what you are doing and your capabilities to deliver what you can't sell yourself? You can have the best product, the right availability, the best price and the demand, but it still has to be sold.

Of course, once it is sold, it has to be worthwhile to the customer; otherwise, he won't keep coming back. Part of maintaining a healthy customer relationship is in the level of service you will provide your customer. Every time I close an order or sign a contract, I send a handwritten thank you note expressing my gratitude for their business. Especially today, in an era of electronic mail, a handwritten thank you goes a long way to reminding your customer of how important his or her business is to you. This little act of gratitude helps build solid customer rapport that may come in handy should a disagreement or error in product or service delivery increase tension between you and your customer. Customer service is becoming an area where the underdog can shine. As businesses become more pressed for profits and timeframes are compressed, companies look for suppliers who can provide quality goods coupled with exceptional customer service.

Product, cost, price, sales, and profit all work in tandem. If one is out of step with the others, the circle is broken and it must be fixed.

Be Adaptable and Open to Change

Another company I helped troubleshoot had a centrally located sales force in a city that wasn't well-served by the major airlines. Every single flight seemed to have to connect through Atlanta, Houston, or Tampa. I suggested the company determine their top markets and place a sales representative in each of 5 key markets, with the vice president of sales based in the home office. We hired a young woman who was a paralegal by training and gave her the role of Team Coordinator, which meant she was a centralized administrative assistant to all six employees. We hired three regional sales reps and moved two home office reps into the field. We then fired four internal reps who weren't hitting their sales quotas so they could go about their life's work. What happened? The money that was saved by having a rep in the field instead of flying to meet clients reduced travel costs by 82%. Customer orders increased because the reps simply drove to serve their customers and this led to better customer relationships and more orders. And finally, the field reps began giving feedback to the product development team that helped them continually fine tune and alter the products to suit customer needs. The president, who spent 20 years working for a big company in a centrally located, monolith office building, still can't believe that putting reps in your customer's backyards was more effective than having them sit in their cushy corporate office building or spend countless hours each week waiting in airport check-in lines. But his business is more profitable than ever because he was willing to be adaptable to a changing marketplace.

As you begin to think about how to make your new company or your existing employer's company more adaptable and profitable, try to view your business through the eyes of your customers. Ask your customers what you do well and where you need help. Ask them where their business is heading and what you can do to be ready to serve them in the future. If your widgets are being used by a shop technician, talk to that person, not the purchasing director. Corporate restructuring and merger integration expert Frank Federer likes to say that if he really wants to find out what is happening in a company, he need only talk to the guys on the loading dock. Get to the person using your product or service and ask them to be brutally honest with you to help you provide them with better service. In almost every case I've ever encountered, your customer will be happy to give you the feedback you need to succeed.

What Did You Learn?

1. Identify what you can do that others can't, and build upon that knowledge to build a company with a dedicated focus on product, cost, pricing, sales, and profit and the elements that go into making each one successful.
2. Research your product or service and quickly determine whether you have a shot at building a successful business.
3. Keep your expenses to a minimum. You don't need fancy conference rooms, thousand dollar fish tanks, or fifty employees to start your business.
4. Create a flexible business that can adapt to changing customer needs. Continually work at providing the best products and service and be willing to reexamine your business from all angles, eliminating unprofitable lines.

CHAPTER 10

Yes You Can: Commit To Being The Best

Lining up your ducks.

NINETY PERCENT OF new businesses fail during the first year. The reasons are often that the new entrepreneur failed to properly research the market, offered a "me-too" product or service that several competitors also offered, or simply didn't work hard at making his business a success. This lack of preparation and action, combined with limited funding, spells disaster for a new business. Successful entrepreneurs utilize the tools of good market research before sticking their necks out.

As mentioned earlier, the first obstacle to overcome in starting any business is to determine whether or not there is a market for your product, hence, the overwhelming importance of market research. For the most part, you will discover that there are lots of other people in your same field. Therefore, you must develop an advantage over your competitors. The three most valuable advantages you can offer are price, availability and service.

Recently, a new business opened in a town near me. To date, the business is growing in both revenues and customers, and a major factor in this early success was proper market analysis. The owners began with the idea of creating a small business within the service industry to target a niche market they saw developing. Their field is relatively new, but nonetheless, quite competitive. Rather than investing a lot of capital purchasing equipment, these entrepreneurs decided first to analyze other similar businesses in their area to determine the going rates and how their young company could better shape itself to serve their own business community. Consequently, the new business was prepared to service their customers before they even had a product for sale, much less a customer to deliver it to. Their research paid off as they had already established a solid list of potential customers to call when they began. After opening their doors, they quickly signed contracts with more than 20 companies they had profiled. Had this young company chosen to ignore market analysis, they may well have ended up wasting both time and money. Worse, they may have failed.

Research, Research, Research.

It often happens that a new company begins with what they think is a tremendous product—so tremendous, in fact, that they rush to invest all of their capital producing this wonderful thing and never bother to take the time to determine the existence of a market for the product. Nine times out of ten, the company that rushes to produce before evaluating the potential market for customers will find itself bankrupt before the first year is over.

I mentioned earlier that I've had my share of business failures. Several years ago a friend of mine invented a golf umbrella that was exceptionally well suited to keeping golf clubs dry when in the rain, a problem most golfers will face at one time or another. This high-quality, low-cost product had all the indications of becoming a successful product. It could be produced inexpensively; it could be personalized with sponsor logos; and it kept club grips dry if you're caught in the rain. My friend raised money from me and several other people. The company had several dozen prototypes made. They spent thousands of dollars to attend the annual PGA show in order to show off the product and secure a licensing deal or direct sales. Everything looked rosy, except that there were three weak areas that would have been uncovered through market research, had it been properly undertaken prior to launching the company. First, the company was based in a small town outside of Pittsburgh, far from the heavily populated golfing centers in the United States. Second, the product required a national sales force for which the company never budgeted. Finally, had more research been done on the demographics of golfers, the company would have found that per capita golf merchandise spending was decreasing, meaning people were spending less on the very type of product it wanted to sell. The company no longer exists, and the shareholders lost everything we invested in the firm. Properly researching the market could have exposed these danger signs and saved the investors a lot of money and the inventors a lot of heartache.

Another business that I started had projections to grow into a $200 million firm within a few short years. The technology we developed would have revolutionized video across the Internet, providing users with the ability to view their cable TV programming from anywhere around the world and post their own videos, creating their own broadcast channel (this was before YouTube). We developed the technology, built a working prototype, and were ready to build out the business when we found that our technology—that we built on our own—infringed on a much larger company's patent. Without the millions of dollars needed to defend ourselves from a likely lawsuit we decided to abandon the company and close the doors. Since that day, any time I am involved in a technology startup or other new firm that has a patentable product, I make sure a patent attorney is reviewing existing patents and monitoring new patent applications so ensure we don't get into the same predicament.

If You Want to Win, Prepare for Failure

An important thing to remember in your research is that it pays to look at failed businesses or those that are operating in the red months or even years after their initial creation. Think about successful merchandising, marketing and production, and use your head to determine why these didn't work for some people. It is better to plan to avoid pitfalls before you find yourself falling into them. An effective tactic is to look at a business concept and come up with a list of things that could go wrong. Then try to design a plan around each challenge to see if you could survive it. If you can, you're on to something. Recognizing that failure is a possibility, you must devise a strategy to prepare for it. Identifying the worst-case scenarios and devising methods to deal with them puts you in a much better situation than the swimmer who ignores the alligators lurking in the river.

Contact stores in other states and ask the owners for the five best and five worst things they did starting out. If you see a pattern develop, be sure to plan for that expected contingency. I evaluated a Jacadi franchise a few years ago. Everything the company presented to us looked rosy and our initial financial calculations made the franchise appear to be a sound investment. But having learned from the golf umbrella failure, I called and visited other franchisees around the country. I soon learned that there were inventory problems, ordering system problems, and a host of other issues we would have not learned about until it was too late. We politely declined the offer to buy a franchise. Even though we spent three months evaluating the opportunity, we saved hundreds of thousands of dollars by uncovering what appeared to be significant obstacles to success.

Sometimes getting access to research is as simple as making a few phone calls. When I launched my advertising agency in 1989, I contacted a local college and found they had an entrepreneurship program. I asked if a group of students would be interested in evaluating my business plan and giving me feedback and suggestions on how to better structure the business. To my delight, a team of five students was assigned to Townsend Advertising Corporation to write a comprehensive business plan to maximize revenues and profits. They identified four types of clients that, whether because of decreased spending or cyclical spending, could cause money flow problems in my business. I soon avoided clients from these areas. Their plan helped me see an opportunity in representing law firms, which became the most profitable segment of my business. This plan cost me nothing except the time I spent with the students, yet it highlighted an opportunity in legal advertising which accounted for substantial profits. Of equal benefit, in the spirit of doing good while doing well, the exercise helped five college students learn the real world ins and outs of launching a small business.

Even when you have good contacts from either your last employer or personal friends within a given field, a great product, and the knowledge to run a successful company, it isn't easy to start a new business. I am a successful entrepreneur and might be willing to fund and support a new business, but *only* if I am convinced that the future entrepreneur has come to my door armed with enthusiasm and concrete evidence that they have properly researched the potential market for their product. Without these two important elements, I could throw my whole fortune behind their idea and end up a penniless man. It takes far more than money and connections to make a go of it in the world of free enterprise. There were plenty of companies in the Dotcom era of the late 1990s that raised $20 million, $50 million, even $100 million dollars and are no longer in existence because they simply did not have a sustainable business model. WebVan, Pets.com, iHarvest.com, Furniture.com, BitLocker.com, BeautyJungle.com, Boo.com, and Z.com burned through an estimated $200 million dollars before disintegrating into what have become known as "DotBombs." It is as if the founders of these companies and the people who invested in them never planned for what could go wrong. I'd rather invest in an entrepreneur who has thoroughly probed his product and its placement in the marketplace, understands his differentiation from his competition, has contingency plans for worst-case outcomes, and expects an 8% investor return than some hotshot who, based on his unsubstantiated personal beliefs, thinks his product will gain 50% market share, make hundreds of millions of dollars, and return 40 times my investment.

The rules of the game are not all that complicated, but they do require time, research and sound common sense. There is nothing that can substitute for good market research: not connections, money, experience nor college degrees.

What Did You Learn?

1. Thoroughly researching your market is critical to identifying obstacles you may face in launching your business.
2. Talk to prospective customers to identify what they need, what they're willing to pay, and whether or not you can fulfill their

needs.

3. Conduct research before starting your business and you'll save thousands of dollars and hundreds of hours of your time, should you find that your product doesn't fulfill customer needs.

CHAPTER 11

Yes You Can: Three Questions You Should Answer

Work, Win, Worth

THIS IS THE shortest chapter in the book, but when it comes to organizing your business, it is one of the most important.

Frank Federer, President of Federer Resources, is one of the most talented corporate turnaround and post-merger integration specialists in the country. Investment banks hire him to act as interim CEO to straighten out a faltering company in which they are invested. He's worked in fields ranging from medical devices and beverages to printing and snowshoes, and in each case he's usually brought into a company when the banks are about to foreclose and it appears all hope of continuing in business is lost. Frank is fairly unique in the turnaround industry because unlike famous turnaround artists like "Chainsaw" Al Dunlop, who tends to break apart firms for salvage value, Frank prefers to build firms so they can operate profitably into the future.

Frank has a unique and effective approach to evaluating a company and its product that can be applied to companies of all shapes and sizes, including yours. He calls it "WWW" or "Work, Win, Worth," and it goes like this: The first thing to ask yourself about a product of service is, "Will it Work?" meaning, does what you want to offer to the marketplace work? If it's a technology, does it work? If it's a new water bucket design, does it work? If it's a new skin care treatment, does it work?

Once you've answered that in the affirmative, you move to question two: "Can we Win?" You have a good product, but can you win in the marketplace? Can you gain enough market share to build a profitable business? If so, you may be on to something. If not, then the product doesn't differentiate itself enough or the market simply doesn't need it and you'll end up wasting valuable time and money trying to win. You probably wouldn't open a copy shop next door to a FedEx Kinko's even if you had better printers and copiers. Even with a product that works, taking on a competitor such as FedEx Kinko's isn't a very smart move.

The third part of "WWW" is "Is it Worth it?" meaning, can we make this product and sell it to win and then when it's all said and done, have a sufficient amount of money left over to constitute a profitable venture? If you sell 10,000 widgets at a profit of $1 a piece, you make $10,000. But if you sell 500 widgets at $20 apiece, you make the same $10,000. Which requires more effort? Which is likely to be more appealing to you: selling 10,000 widgets or selling only 500? Or perhaps you have a great product, feel you can capture significant market share, but the startup costs mean it could take 10 years to recoup your investment. That's too long for professional investors, who typically look for a return on investment in 18-36 months, and that should tell you that it is probably too long for you, too.

Frank and I were assisting with the launch of two companies. Dorio, Inc. is an online media distribution company that uses technology to provide multi-channel live and prerecorded content via the Internet to broadband enabled PCs and televisions. It's an offshoot of my company that failed, although this time the patent issue has been solved and the technology is even better than before. The company intends to utilize its technology to operate multiple content-specific broadcasting channels such as theaters, symphonies, and other unique performance venues. By themselves these content providers attract small numbers of people, but when combined, have the ability to produce large audiences from around the globe. The first market we're pursuing is repertory theaters. We identified 100 theaters across America that stage live productions throughout the year. Our research indicated high interest from the theater companies and actors. The technology is proven and capable of streaming broadcast quality images across the Internet and via satellite TV (it *works*). Management believes they can own the market because of their technical know-how, focus on a niche market others haven't shown an interest in, and unique subscription model. The board of directors, which includes industry veterans like director Michael Kahn (*Cat on a Hot Tin Roof, Henry V, Showboat*) and Golden Globe winner and Emmy nominee Stacy Keach, has deep influence in the live theater industry (we can *win*). The financial models suggest a 34% operating profit after 3 years and a required investment of under $8 million (it is *worth* it).

Even with positive answers to *Work, Win, Worth,* not every situation will unfold as expected. The company ran into a roadblock that so far has proven difficult to solve. It turns out that even though the theater companies and actors want to offer live productions online, the actor's union is unwilling to negotiate with the company to develop a win/win financial solution. Their inability and unwillingness to look at online streaming and its smaller audiences as different from broadcast television means their members will not benefit from Dorio's activities. Management believes it can increase revenues to theaters and actors—even if it is small at first—a win/win situation for them and us. However, the union, demanding broadcast television level payments would rather see its members not receive a cent than have to capitulate and lower royalty fees to explore a new product. At the end of the day, with the union blockade preventing the company from moving forward, management finds themselves in a situation that does *not work*. This unanticipated obstacle isn't stopping Dorio's founders. After all, it's just an obstacle to be overcome and since they planned for failure from the beginning they have an alternative route available to us. Our market research indicated there were hundreds of non-union theaters across America and Doris is now soliciting those theater companies to participate.

The second venture was for the development of a state-of-the-art, four-place, single engine aircraft company. The airplane will outperform and fly farther than any of its competitors. It is a proven design, with FAA clearance to begin manufacturing. The avionics are top of the line, and the composite body structure is so slippery, that the plane will fly at over 200 miles per hour from Austin, Texas to Seattle, Washington on one tank of gas. The plane *works*. Our research and hypothesis testing suggested we could *win* in the marketplace by reaching just 15% market share within our segment. But the venture was expensive to launch and would require securing over $70 million dollars. In addition, the first plane wouldn't roll off the assembly line until six months after a manufacturing plant was built, which would take at least 18 months to complete. As we met with venture capitalists, private equity firms, and investment banks, we found that the returns we projected, coupled with the long timeline from breaking ground to delivering a finished product, made the investment unattractive to the very people we needed to solicit funds from. We had a great product, exciting market, wide open opportunity, and we believed we could *win*. But the investment wasn't *worth* the risk and we shuttered the company while we were still in the business planning stage, saving our management team and investors millions of dollars and hundreds of thousands of man hours.

By looking at your business through the *Work, Win, Worth* lens, you can quickly determine whether the idea you have is a good one and more importantly, whether you have a reasonable shot at turning it into a success.

What Did You Learn?

1. Will it work? Will the business I want to start work in this market?
2. Can I win? Will I be able to find a niche market to service or will I compete head-to-head with competitors? Can I beat these competitors?
3. Is it worth it? Can I launch this company and make it pay off financially? How long will it take to recoup my investment?

CHAPTER 12

Yes You Can: Take Control

What kind of hat will you wear today?

DURING ONE OF my many meetings with Ed Smalis I told him about the flier I sent to the Cleveland company's president with my picture next to all the job titles. He dug into his file cabinet and handed me a copy of a letter he had sent to a customer many years ago. It read,

"Your sales department is in dire need of a complete overhaul!!! The Smalis Corporation has no sales department and no purchasing department, yet it performs every function, national in scope, the equivalent of U.S. Steel, carrying a total payroll of three people!!! Computers be damned!!! Receptionists be damned!!! Vice presidents be damned!!! Stockholders be damned!!! Purchasing agents and salesmen be damned!!! Watchmen be damned!!! Company cars be damned!!! Parts departments be damned!!! Service departments and personnel departments be damned!!! Legal and accounting departments be damned!!!"

Wear as Many Hats as Possible

What was he trying to say? As you get started in your business, all of these functions will be performed by the most important person in the company – YOU. Otherwise, you will be paying out money unnecessarily. This will probably lead to an immediate and constant cash flow problem and, if you're like 9 out of 10 small companies, can give you a speedy head-start to declaring bankruptcy and closing your doors. You are the one who will have to wear twenty hats. You have to be shipping, receiving, sales, bookkeeping, purchasing, sales, customer service, etc.

I especially enjoy the rush of adrenaline in starting companies and getting them through their first two years of infancy. It is during this time that every decision you make and every action you take directly impacts whether the company will thrive. It is also the time when you will know the most about the inner workings of your company. As it grows you will invariably become more and more isolated to various divisions of the firm. For instance, after a company I co-founded with Ben Bassi, CommonPlaces, merged with another company to become the largest publicly-held young adult marketing firm in America, we suddenly found ourselves with 1,100 full- and part-time employees and a human resources department of several people. Previously, if Ben or I wanted to hire someone, we just did it. Now we had processes and diagrams and booklets and headaches...oh, the headaches. That's why you hire people to handle those tasks, but you do so only after your company has reached the size where it *must* make those hires. To do so before that point is to waste money that could be going into your pockets or back into building your business.

Make no mistake: if you are like the majority of small businesses, it will be you and perhaps two or five other employees who will grow and support your business throughout the years. The local Subway sandwich shop franchisee has four employees, but it is the owner who opens the shop in the morning and closes it at night; the owner who deals with vendors, accountants, and sales tax collection agencies. Get used to wearing many hats and staying involved in all elements of your business. Know what is going on within your company as much as you need to know what is happening outside your company. J. Paul Getty summed it up best when he said, "To succeed in business, to reach the top, an individual must know all it is possible to know about that business."

If you are intent on adding employees, make sure that you get into a service or product line that will allow you to charge a decent profit to cover the additional costs associated with employees. Keep in mind that it isn't just an hourly wage you'll be paying; you'll add Social Security taxes, benefits, unemployment insurance, and a host of other costs that will typically add 20% to outright labor costs.

Employees Should Add to the Bottom Line

Remember the question, "Is it worth it?" You have to sell a lot of inventory if your profit is based on one percent to ten percent. For example: based on a ten percent profit, one hundred thousand dollars in sales will only generate ten thousand dollars in gross profit. Out of this profit you must pay overhead such as taxes, rent, computers, marketing costs, payroll and other expenses. At my ad agency I believed in charging hourly fees that covered overhead, salary, and profit. If I added an employee, I simply adjusted the hourly rate to coincide with their costs and maintained the percentage profit I wanted from each employee. This hourly rate gave me the flexibility to pay my expenses and plan for future growth. And I never took on employees who subtracted from the bottom line. If they couldn't bill their time, I didn't need them. Hourly fees work great in consultancies and service oriented businesses, but aren't applicable to product sales. In product sales you must determine whether the addition of an employee will enable you to sell enough additional product to justify that employee's working for you. A $25,000 a year employee will cost you $30,000 with overhead, plus a computer, additional telephone, and other expenses you might not realize, easily increasing the cost to $35,000 or more. If you're selling those widgets at a 10% profit, you now must sell a minimum $350,000 more in products just to break even on the additional hire. And if you're hiring someone, you probably don't want to break even; you want them to increase revenues enough so you can earn more, too. That means your hire should bring in $500,000 or more in new business.

Keeping a good cash flow is a necessity to a successful business, and having too many employees early on can severely hamper your ability to maintain cash flow. Cash flow is simply the amount of money you have available to work with. Or as an MBA would say, "the cash receipts or net income from one or more assets for a given period, reckoned after taxes and other disbursements, and often used as a measure of corporate wealth." Let's stick with the easier definition. How much cash do you have that you can use to run your business? That's cash flow. If you have $3,000 a month coming in and you are paying $2,000 of that to an employee, then you don't have much left over to buy your product and pay yourself. You will need to put on one of your many hats and do the job yourself in order to keep that $2,000.

Have a Cash-on-Delivery or Cash-in-Advance Payment System

The only things of monetary value in a company are inventory, which you can sell, and cash. One can only borrow against cash and collateral (inventory or accounts receivable). With an eye on cash and collateral, forget about thirty-, sixty-, or ninety-day accounts. These won't generate money for you; they only keep your money tied up. If you think it's difficult to ask for money up front or on delivery of product, just try getting money out of an overdue account. You can go to all the bill collectors you want, but if the person doesn't want to pay, he won't. You will be spending additional money for lawyers trying to get only a percentage of your original money due you. By this time your cash flow is dwindling because you're spending all your time collecting and meeting with your attorneys instead of being the great salesman you are.

At Townsend Advertising I used to bill customers their monthly retainer 30 days in advance. This meant I received the money in the first two weeks of the month in which I was representing them, not six weeks later like a traditional agency would. This gave me more on-hand cash than most of my competitors. Was it difficult to explain to clients why I did this? At first it was. But once they understood that I could better serve them if I knew they were paid for the month, they understood I was actually putting their best interests first. There are always liabilities to be taken into consideration, and it's better to err on the safe side and bring in more cash than you need.

Create Win-Win Relationships with Your Clients

Most of your clients will understand your need to generate a profit. If they don't, you have to ask yourself if they're worth having as clients.

Each time you do business, it should be a win-win situation. Win-win means your relationship is based on a 50-50 deal. You win; the customer wins. You make a profit; the client gets what she wants. You keep your doors open; the client has a source for future products. You sell more products and thus lower your cost of doing so; the client saves money by becoming a faithful return customer. If you try to move the scale up to 60-40 it is no longer win-win because one party is losing. Keep it simple, treat your customers fairly, charge accordingly, and you both win.

What Did You Learn?

1. As the CEO of your business, you will wear many hats and you must be prepared to excel at all of them.
2. The only thing of immediate value in your company is inventory and cash, both of which can be used to fund the company.
3. Cash is king. If you have customers who are delinquent payers, they are no friends of yours.
4. Keep your client relationships a 50/50, win-win situation.

CHAPTER 13

Yes You Can: Be Your Own Boss

*Going out on your own is a challenge
you will never forget.*

I'T IS TIME to put your foot forward and take the next step on your journey toward success: Going out on your own.

The fear of going it alone implies a fear of failure. But remember, we don't have to fear failure because we can learn from it. Going it alone takes more than ability, motivation, skill, luck, guts or enthusiasm. It is believing in yourself and having the necessary independence that goes along with that belief. Having a strong belief in yourself can make all the difference between mediocrity, failure and success. For example, in 1956 when Joe Hardy started 84 Lumber Company, he believed he could deliver a better-priced product than the competition through his "cash and carry" business model. He did this alone. Today, 84 Lumber is the largest privately owned lumber company in the United States, with over 400 stores and sales in the $2 billion range. Needless to say, Joe has prospered throughout the years.

A few years ago, he turned the company over to his daughter, Maggie Hardy Magerko. She is now CEO of 84 Lumber, and Forbes magazine ranked her among the 400 wealthiest Americans, with a fortune over $2 billion. Maggie may have inherited a good head start, but I can tell you she works as hard, if not harder, than anyone in the company, and may in fact be one of the hardest working executives I know. While you and I may not inherit an opportunity like Maggie did, we still have a responsibility to work at our business as hard as she works at continuing the success of 84 Lumber Company.

After his historic flight, people called Charles Lindbergh "Lucky Lindy." Luck had no part in Lindbergh's perseverance and the courage of his decision to go it alone. It was Lindbergh's skill, determination, and risk taking that made him successful. J.C. Penney, Walter Chrysler, Henry Ford, F.W. Woolworth, and Robert Wood Johnson (Johnson & Johnson) all started their businesses on their own. They didn't have a security umbrella or a parachute for safety.

For the vast majority of small businesses, a partner, an associate, your brother-in-law or even your wife makes no real contribution to your business and is used as a convenience, or more often, as a crutch. Such an arrangement only dilutes the strategic thinking, the risks, and also the rewards. In the case of Charles Lindbergh, what real purpose could a co-pilot have served in the mid-Atlantic except taking up space and burning more fuel? What benefit would a partner serve J.C. Penney, starting out with a horse and wagon, other than adding extra weight and having less room for his merchandise? If Henry Ford had taken on three partners, would we be driving FordMayerGersonLindenbaums? Most small businesses don't require partners if you have the determination to walk alone.

The true spirit of an entrepreneur centers in developing one's own ideas. It is not using someone else's ideas, nor taking your ideas and sharing them with others. One word describes the entrepreneur best: *original.* She is not only an original but she is creative in her field, be it business, religion or politics. Her greatest asset for herself is being the best of the very best because she focuses on reaching her goals. An entrepreneur will never be content with falling into the daily grind. Instead, she'll continually seek ways to improve her business and her professional and social skills. She views her life as if she were the captain of a majestic ship. Regardless of her wealth and fame, she is in full command. She explores the horizon in fair or stormy weather: seeking, searching and probing. She isn't content to keep the boat docked, but instead wants to travel the world, continually seeking new adventures.

Immediately looking for a partner or an associate shows a lack of confidence in yourself and indicates that you are seeking someone to fall back on. Going it alone means that you don't have to rely on anyone else. It also means that you don't have anyone but yourself to blame if and when things go wrong. Along that same vein, you alone take the risks and you alone reap the rewards.

Virtually every entrepreneur starts out small (if he or she is smart), but with hard work, perseverance, total dedication and devotion to the task, he or she will be a success. Steve Jobs started Apple Computer in a garage. Lycos' first office consisted of a few cubicles that Bob Davis, Bev Wilson, and I shared in Andover, Massachusetts. 84 Lumber Company started with one lumberyard. Ryan Homes started with one house. Kemmons Wilson started with one motel. Yahoo! started from the campus of Stanford University. Same with Google. Kinko's was founded in a little shack near a University of California campus. A great idea, backed by hard work and enthusiasm, doesn't care where it starts geographically. It just cares that it starts.

Lone Entrepreneurs Who Beat the Odds

John Rogers started Pay By Touch, at the time the world's leading biometric technology services company with an idea. Faced with increasing rates of credit card fraud and identity theft, John premise was the belief that tying your financial accounts to something that is uniquely you, in this case a finger scan, would be an efficient way to eliminate fraud at retail establishments and increase consumer privacy and security. A person simply enters an access code and scans their finger to gain access to their checking accounts, credit card accounts, loyalty programs and more, all without ever having to carry a plastic card or check around. Pay By Touch not only solves the fraud issue associated with transactions, but it gives consumers the freedom to access their cash no matter where they are. You could be out jogging or biking and simply by scanning your finger, purchase a bottle of water. You might visit the grocery store and without ever removing a credit card, pay for your groceries and earn valuable rewards points simply by scanning your finger. John's great idea, backed by his tireless dedication, has led to the creation of a global company with several hundred employees, over 70 issued or applied patents, and a multi-billion valuation.

Mary Crowley's mother died when she was eighteen months old, and at that age Mary was sent to live with her grandparents on a farm in Missouri for five years. She then lived with her father and stepmother for several years until her stepmother was declared unfit, and she was sent to live with her grandparents again. Years later, divorced and with two children to support, Crowley got a job in Dallas, Texas and attended Southern Methodist University at night. She worked in sales at Stanley Home Products and for a home accessories importer's firm before starting Home Interiors and Gifts. She started her business with virtually nothing and turned it into a multi-million dollar corporation.

J. M. Haggar, Sr., was born in Lebanon, and after visiting an uncle in Mexico City, he decided to stop in New Orleans on his way home. It was there that he decided to stay in the United States. After marrying and having a child, the Haggar family settled in Dallas, Texas, where he worked for the Oberman Pant Company. In 1927, Haggar started his own company, mass-producing fine pants at popular prices, using assembly-line methods patterned after those developed by Henry Ford. Instead of using denim or other work fabrics, Haggar bought the ends of suit materials and made a new kind of dress pants he called "slacks." J. M. Haggar, Sr. never had a formal education and he never let anything stop him from starting his own company.

Norman H. Stone was born into a poor Chicago family shortly after the turn of the century. In his youth, he delivered papers, turning most of his weekly 50 cent salary over to his mother to help support the family. At age 13, he dropped out of school and worked as a messenger for Western Union at $4 a week. At age 15, he became a messenger at Sears Roebuck for $6 a week. By age 17 he had worked his way up to head office boy, eventually earning $8 a week. In 1926, he founded the Stone Container Corporation. Established with only $750 in capital, the new company had sales of $68,000 the first year. The Stone Container Corporation has since grown to be one of the largest packaging firms in the world, with 2004 sales of more than $8 billion.

Having a partner or partners in itself poses many problems, not the least of which is the problem of identity. In a business, whether you supply a service or product, there is one and only one key person – *you*. It doesn't matter whether you are a lawyer, engineer, doctor, accountant, janitor or storekeeper. You reflect your enterprise. You convey your identity to the customer. When you are the sole owner, you put yourself on a one-to-one basis of responsibility. In effect, you become your brand.

Brand Yourself and Be Responsible for Your Brand

Thinking of yourself as a brand is a unique means to help identify how you want to present yourself to customers. Are you an IBM that is smart, sophisticated, and helps businesses through the long lineage it has, or are you an Apple Computer that is young, aggressive and looks to accomplish goals by being different? Are you Nike or Reebok? Pepsi or Coke? American Airlines or Southwest? Wal-Mart or Saks Fifth Avenue? Figure this out and you'll know how to present yourself and your product on a continual basis. Deviate from your brand identity and you'll only muddy the perception you have in your customers' and prospects' eyes.

When I ran my own advertising agency, I sent new clients the following note:

"I am the owner, founder and President of Townsend Advertising Corporation. We are an established, marketing company that has a reputation of providing our clients with exceptional service and meeting our responsibilities head-on. Only the owner of a successful company has the authority to do this and I take it upon myself to personally see that you are pleased with the work we provide."

Think about the effect this had on people. Here was the president of a company stating that he was personally responsible for their success and happiness. When is the last time the president of any company told you that if you were unhappy you should contact him?

Titles command attention and respect. Well, I should say, some titles. The titles of director, manager, and vice president are all overused. During the dotcom era, one firm made every single salesperson a director or vice president in order to give them the appearance of power, yet when it came down to it, the sales team couldn't even sign contracts because they had to be signed by the *real* vice president, or in this case, the senior vice president. In the corporate world every company has a president, and unless the president of the company is also the majority or sole owner, his ultimate responsibility doesn't lend much weight. Just look at the public companies in the past few years whose presidents and CEOs raped the public trust, and the assets of the companies, and got off with a slap on the wrist. The one title that commands the most attention (and has the most responsibility) is "owner." Which of the following conveys a meaningful purpose: a letter signed "president" or a letter signed "Owner"? The latter shows that responsibility is on a one-to-one basis and won't be diluted by excuses of "that's not my department," "it was a vendor error," or "it was held up in shipping." As I always say to my customers, "The responsibility is mine and mine alone." It is with this type of relationship that the customer will begin to feel comfortable and trust will be built. He doesn't feel that he is dealing with subordinates, partners or associates. These people only dilute the responsibility and with the dilution, there are added risks to the customer.

Now before you read further, you may be saying to yourself, "Well, if I were President of General Electric I'd be able to ensure a customer that I'll fulfill an order." This may be true as the president of such a large concern can put into motion the actions needed to solve a customer issue. However, the president of GE is not going to go down to the aircraft engine plant and make sure the bolts are secure for the customer. He'll delegate it to an underling who will delegate it to another. And so on and so on. Then when the bolt is tight, the mechanic will let his superior know it's tight and he'll then tell his superior and so on and so on, back up to the CEO who will tell the customer that the bolt is tight. Keep in mind that the majority of companies around the globe are small businesses, employing fewer than twenty-five people. You, as president and owner of your company, will be able to guarantee to your customer that an issue will be resolved, because you will be the one resolving it.

Terry Hernandez is a homebuilder in Austin, Texas. While he didn't build my home, he built the home behind mine and the one across the street from mine. I admire Terry because he loves his work and stands behind it. He is ultimately responsible for his product and it shows in every job he undertakes. A few years ago when I wanted to build an eight-foot wall around my property, Terry was the only person I called. I didn't need to get competing quotes because I knew Terry would be fair in his pricing (remember "win-win?"). I was spending the majority of my time in New York City and, because I knew Terry would guarantee the job would be done right, I had no qualms about having him begin construction while I was halfway across the continent. He told me what it would cost, I mailed him a check, he completed the job, and the wall is everything, if not more, than what I expected. As an added bonus, Terry integrated electrical wiring throughout the wall in case I ever want to add lights to the pillars, a good idea I hadn't considered. Terry lives up to the axiom of "The responsibility is mine and mine alone." If you do too, customers will trust you, reward you, and help make you a success.

Another homebuilder, Gary Rostic of Tara Homes, has quickly built a highly respected business in Springfield, Missouri because he constructs quality homes and, as the owner, stands behind his product. He uses higher grade materials than his competitors because, as Gary says, "When someone buys a home from me they are making a significant investment, and deserve to have the best quality they can afford. I wouldn't want cheap materials in my house and I don't treat my customers any differently." This dedication to quality and responsibility illustrates daily how Gary lives up to the title of owner.

A Little Bit More

Many years ago I was visiting a client, Jim Springer, when he received an urgent phone call. Jim, was the owner of a manufacturing company in the steel industry. The call was from a client in Indiana who was dealing with electrical glitches in a smelting furnace Jim's company had designed, and his client was screaming that he was losing thousands of dollars each time the line went down. Jim hung up the phone, turned to me and said, "Let's go for a ride." We walked down the hall; he pulled his head engineer out of a meeting, and the three of us climbed into Jim's car. Twenty minutes later we were chartering a plane to Indiana to solve the problem. Now I didn't wake up that morning planning to fly to Indiana and I certainly wouldn't have worn a suit into a steel mill had I known I was going to be mucking through a smelting plant, but Jim asked me to come along so that I could see a physical installation. Since Jim was my client, I felt a responsibility to take him up on his offer and see his company's products in action. I didn't realize it until a few hours after landing that what I was experiencing that day was the president and owner of his company dropping everything in order to solve a customer's problem. Where many would view taking an unscheduled trip as a hassle, Jim saw it as an opportunity to please his customer and put him one step closer to his goals. He knew that his competitors would have scheduled a flight the next morning. He was there within four hours of the client's phone call. Jim understood that the customer comes first and without customers, he wouldn't have a business. Four short words sum up what places Jim Springer and other successful individuals above the crowd: a little bit more. They do all that is expected of them and a little bit more.

Laura Schlessinger once said, "People with integrity do what they say they are going to do. Others have excuses." As owner of your company, you have the final say in the culture of your business. Will it be one of honor and professionalism, or one of blame and excuses? Which would you rather work for?

The decision to become an entrepreneur is the most important decision you will ever make, and it is also the most difficult. Your reputation is on the line day in and day out. Forty-hour workweeks will become a thing of the past. You will be responsible for your success or failure. But you won't mind if you love what you're doing. Challenges are what make life interesting, and overcoming them makes life meaningful.

What Did You Learn?

1. As owner of your company, ultimate responsibility rests on your shoulders. Don't carry this responsibility as a burden; carry it with honor.
2. Great business owners earn their clients' trust and maintain that trust by continually being involved in their business.
3. Starting your own business will be the most important decision and challenging project you will ever make. If you do it correctly, it will be the most rewarding and meaningful endeavor you will ever undertake.

CHAPTER 14

Yes You Can: The Benefits of Partners

Sometimes it pays to be in business for yourself,
but not necessarily by yourself.

WHEN MY CAREER took me to Ketchum Advertising, I was
responsible for new business activities for a $1.3 billion
advertising agency, ranked in the top 20 of all global firms by billings.
Ketchum had always been highly regarded in the public relations
industry and for the level of talent the firm's managers cultivated. Their
advertising business produced solid work that sold products for clients
like Heinz, Acura, Nationwide Insurance, Digital Equipment
Corporation, the Pittsburgh Pirates, the California Raisin Board, and
others. Ketchum prided itself on customer service, which was reflected
through the numerous clients who had been with the agency for years,
including PNC Bank, a client for over 70 years. Taking my career from
my own firm to Ketchum was a logical move in my career track because
I essentially ran my own business within the Ketchum organization, yet
also had the opportunity to learn from some of the best people in the

business. I gave up running my own ad agency because I wanted to gain experience in the big leagues and I knew that I could always start another ad agency if Ketchum wasn't a good fit for me. I reported directly to the president and he gave me wide leeway in how I approached our new business goals.

Ketchum had a mission statement much like many other firms in that it was a lengthy, elegantly-worded overview of what the company hoped to do. It began, "At Ketchum we believe in…blah, blah, blah" and continued on for far too many words. As part of our new business efforts we changed the mission statement to this simple statement: "Ketchum: Have fun. Get it great. Make money." This summed up what the agency was all about. Have fun: because if you're not, you're in the wrong place. Get it great: because if the work isn't great, we don't deserve to keep our clients. And make money: because if we don't make money, we don't eat. The Ketchum brand combined a little cockiness with attitude. Our entire new business efforts reflected this attitude. We devised processes for bringing clients through the agency that focused on what was of interest to the client. Someone who was interested in awards and great creative work took a tour past the award showcase, the art director's studios, the pool table in the lower conference room. We might even stop in on an art director evaluating slides and let the new business prospect give their opinion, making them feel important and a part of the Ketchum family. Someone interested in process-oriented tasks like media planning and analysis took a different tour; this one past the process wall where the Ketchum philosophy was spelled out in charts and words, then past our media director's office, then into a conference room where more "we do this, thus this happens, resulting in this" conversations took place. CEOs, often focused on bottom-line conversations, were usually taken directly to the president's office where one-on-one conversations about business could occur.

I ran our new business efforts as if I were the owner of Ketchum. Prospects knew I was ultimately responsible for the client/agency relationship and that I had a direct line to the president's office. Did it work? We went from pitching $11 million in new business the year before I became Vice President, Director of Marketing, to pitching over $120 million in new business in eight short months. I took what I already knew about selling and expanded it greatly by virtue of the types of clients I was calling on at Ketchum. Whereas Townsend Advertising could easily manage a $250,000 piece of business, Ketchum was used to handling $20,000,000 pieces of business. For an advertising guy, working at Ketchum was a dream job. It involved exciting clients, travel, the thrill of pitching new business via elaborate presentations, and high levels of creativity. I managed some of Digital Equipment Corporation's business and was exposed to the PC and microprocessor industry: areas I would have never seen within my own agency. As a learning experience, my stay at Ketchum was invaluable. The exposure to Fortune 500 clients and global marketing challenges presented hundreds of learning opportunities for me. Plus, we had fun, got it great, and made money.

I probably would have stayed on for an indefinite time had it not been for a call from a close friend, Mark Coticchia. Mark worked in the Office of Technology Transfer at Carnegie Mellon University (CMU) in Pittsburgh. A research scientist at CMU had created a piece of technology called a search robot that was capable of searching through large amounts of online data in order to create a type of searchable database of the contents of the Internet. It just so happened that I had been using the technology, called Lycos, for the past several months. Mark knew that in 1992 I had started running advertising for my clients on the Internet, primarily in a section of the Net called

USENET, which were text based discussions on multitudes of topics. He thought I'd be interested in the Lycos technology so we discussed Ketchum's licensing the technology. I took Jim Ficco, Ketchum's President, to CMU and as we met with Mark it became clear to me that this technology would have great implications for the millions of Internet users who had trouble finding information. At the time, Ketchum had the third largest directory advertising business in the country. They placed yellow page ads for hundreds of clients in cities all over the U.S. I believed CMU's technology was a natural extension of Ketchum's yellow page business. For the $2,000,000 it would take to license the technology and launch a company, it seemed like a promising opportunity for a major advertising and public relations firm to get involved in a new means of communicating.

Jim didn't quite see it that way. He wasn't a big believer in this new technology called the Web (remember, this was 1994 and the Web was still mostly text-based and not widely used.). He couldn't believe that people would choose to gather information via computer when magazines, television, radio and other traditional forms of media were so ingrained in our culture. And rightly so, he pointed out that Ketchum was a communications firm, not a technology development company. Ketchum politely turned down the opportunity to license the Lycos technology. As you may have experienced, when your manager doesn't agree with your assessment, it hurts. I felt Ketchum was missing a large opportunity. In a way I felt that the company wasn't paying enough attention to what was happening with the Internet and they just didn't understand how it could change the advertising industry. But like any good employee, I quickly put the notion of owning Lycos behind me and returned to my glass office to use Lycos to find the information I wanted in my pursuit of new clients for Ketchum. I still loved working for Ketchum and the advertising industry, so I resumed my goal of being the best ad man I could be…at least for several more weeks.

I left the agency I so loved when Mark called back with another offer. There was a venture capital firm in Massachusetts that was interested in licensing Lycos and he thought I'd be ideal to be part of the founding management team. It would be five core team members who would take the company out of CMU and launch it into a commercial enterprise. It was a ground floor opportunity with no guarantee of success, only the guarantee that if we worked hard at it, it could become a success and we all might make a little money for our efforts.

I had been at Ketchum long enough to know that there was a limit to how far I could go with the company. Jim Ficco was in his late 30s and Dave Egan, a talented and bright executive who was most likely next in line for the president position was about the same age. The money I was being paid was good and I knew that the money and security could continue. However, in all corporations there is a matter of office politics – if you graduated from college, what school you attended, where you got your MBA, what your family background is, where you live, etc. All of these things determine whether you advance in a company. I decided I was better off taking a chance with Lycos. Giving up my so-called security and income was one of the scariest decisions I had ever made, especially since I had all the usual commitments: rent, car payment, insurance, not to mention groceries and other necessities.

At Lycos, Bob Davis was the President, I was Vice President of Advertising, Mike Olfe ran marketing, Michael "Fuzzy" Mauldin was the inventor, John Leavitt and Brian Milne ran the technology. Bob had a long career in sales at companies like Wang. Fuzzy, John, and Brian were all technologists, working and studying within the halls of

Carnegie Mellon University. Then we hired Beverly Wilson, who worked for Bob when he was at Wang. Ben Bassi, an Oracle executive, joined the team as Vice President Business Development. Mike left and I soon added the role of VP of Marketing and we began our quest toward an Initial Public Offering.

While in the last chapter I preached about not taking on partners, in the case of Lycos, and most technology companies started in the mid-1990s, having partners with diverse backgrounds was what the venture capital and Wall Street's investment banking community wanted. Could Fuzzy have gone off and launched Lycos by himself? Sure. But in this instance, the hiring of Bob, Ben and me rounded out a management team that brought many years of experience in operations, sales, and marketing to a company that didn't have the luxury of growing slowly over many years. We had to make our mark and make it quick. We had to devise a means to generate revenue, hire a staff, brand the company and website, and ultimately, shoot for an IPO of our company's stock while the market was hot. Netscape had gone public that summer and we knew the interest in Internet companies would only grow and that search was the next great online opportunity. But at the same time, we knew we had to build a business that would last past an IPO. The foundation that was built from 1995 to 1997 is what has helped Lycos outlast thousands of other dotcom companies.

There are many success stories where two or more people join together to launch companies. Many times the working relationship lasts for years. Many times it doesn't. That is one of the biggest risks in taking on partners, and why I don't recommend it for most people who want to seek their own independent small businesses. But it is not for me to tell you not to have partners. If you have a good business partner who balances your skills and with whom you believe you can work effectively, then by all means do it. However, make sure you have a clear – and written – agreement between you that will define how the business is run, the roles of partners, and address circumstances such as dissolution of the company or death of the partner. Pre-planning can help avoid disastrous consequences that might lurk down the road.

Successful Partnership Stories

Partnerships can prove to be very successful. John Paul DeJoria lived in Austin in the early '70s and sold beauty products. He teamed up with his friend Paul Mitchell and with $700, most of it borrowed, started their business, John Paul Mitchell Systems. DeJoria lived miserly and spent only $2.50 a day on food. He had no money for advertising, and had to rely on himself to promote his products. Resources were so tight that the John Paul Mitchell brand's now famous black-and-white packaging was a result of not being able to afford color ink. John Paul provided the business and marketing brains and Paul Mitchell was the expert hair stylist. Today, John Paul Mitchell Systems has become a $600 million-a-year beauty empire. According to John Paul, "We should have gone bankrupt perhaps 50 times during the first year," but the skills each partner brought to the table enabled them to become successful.

In 1958, Dan and Frank Carney started a pizza restaurant in Wichita, Kansas. After learning about pizza's newfound popularity in New York City, the brothers borrowed $600 from their mother and opened a shop inside a small tavern. By 1967, the brother's owned 43 restaurants. In 1977, after the brothers had expanded to over 1,800 restaurants, mostly run by franchisees, they sold Pizza Hut to PepsiCo for $320 million. That's a lot of dough.

Davre J. Davidson was born in Portland, Oregon, in 1911. He only attended college for one year. In 1936, he founded a small business on $500 of borrowed money. Three years later the business had grown to the point where his brother could join him, and the firm was renamed Davidson Brothers, which they built up to generate annual revenues exceeding $65 million. Eventually the firm became known as ARA Services, Inc. which later began operating under the name ARAMARK, a leader in dining, catering, uniforms, and other service related industries.

While I've launched a lot of ventures on my own, there have been times when I've teamed with others. My view is that it is preferable to be the sole owner, but when another person can add talent that is required to make a venture successful, then taking on a partner makes sense. The aircraft company Frank Federer and I were trying to launch was of such vast scope that a well-rounded founding management team was critical just to develop the business plan.

There will be some of you that will want the security or balance of a partner. If that is what it takes to get you to charge down your road to meeting your goals, then so be it. I only warn against it because, as I've seen so many times, it is nearly impossible for two people with different backgrounds and interests to maintain the same level of enthusiasm and commitment to a company year after year. For some, like John Paul Mitchell Systems and Pizza Hut, it works. For others, it is a disaster and often results in the business being sold or worse, closed.

Funding Your Business

The most difficult part of becoming a business owner is finding financing. At Lycos, we were fortunate that the venture capital firm CMGI provided adequate funding for the company to become operational. Our product, a technology that made searching remote computer systems accessible, hit the market at the right time, just as the Internet began to move from science- and education-based computing to mainstream consumer adoption. John Roger's Pay By Touch hit the market at the right time, when people were growing increasingly concerned about fraud and identity theft, and based on the company's unique patent portfolio that covers biometric authentication, transactions, and loyalty, the firm was able to raise of a quarter billion dollars in funding from individuals, venture capital firms, private equity firms, and hedge funds. In reality, very few people have venture capital or angel (wealthy individual investors) backing. And even fewer people have any savings to count on these days. Few have the foresight to start scrimping and saving while they're young so that if they do end up in a dead-end job, they have savings to fall back on if they choose to start their own business.

Manuel started his export business by working nights and weekends while maintaining his day job. This allowed him to secure a bank loan and to drastically limit the negative effects should the company have gone bankrupt.

When I was 24 and decided to start my own advertising agency, I certainly didn't have any savings to speak of. I had a snazzy sports car, bought all kinds of nice suits, lived in a 2 bedroom townhouse, and it took all my savings power just to fund my IRA with $500 once a year. All of a sudden I was moving 300 miles away and had no idea how I was going to fund my new business. I went to three banks to no avail. I sought funding from several individuals and ended up borrowing $25,000 from an attorney in Pittsburgh to start my company.

If you are a young person starting out and thinking about starting your own company in a year or two, take my advice and seriously attempt to save a minimum of 5% of your take-home pay each month. 10% is even better. Call it a rainy day fund and only use it for emergencies or for opening your own business. Put half into your IRA and the other half into a certificate of deposit or other investment vehicle where you can begin to build your "business startup fund." Successful entrepreneurs are willing to face the pain of being an entrepreneur. Smart entrepreneurs have set aside money over the years to enable them to alleviate the financial pain to some degree.

An entrepreneur is the commander-in-chief. There would be sacrifices made not only by him but his family as well. He will be working ten to fourteen hours a day, six or seven days a week. No excuses! No exceptions! Now one does not need to neglect his family, and you must work at creating good family time since you won't be spending a great deal of time at home, especially in the beginning, but both you and your family must be willing to make sacrifices in order to reap the benefits of success.

If you're ready to take the first step in becoming a successful entrepreneur, then lace up your shoes and get moving. If someone else presently employs you, you can begin by working on your business plan while retaining your current position. Just make sure you don't develop your plan on company time or you may find that legally, they own it. Many companies require their employees to turn over ownership of any and all inventions and concepts that are developed on company time. Because of this, be extra cautious about not working on your new company while on your employer's time clock.

Cutting Expenses to Invest in Your Business

The first thing you must look at is how to cut your living expenses. If you are earning $40,000 a year, find a way to live on $24,000 a year. You will need every nickel you can beg or borrow to support your business. There is no reason why you can't live on $2,000 a month.

$2,000 a month should cover your mortgage or rent, utilities, food and other basic *necessary* expenses. Now, no screaming! If you're read this far you must have a keen interest in becoming successful. You already know that becoming an entrepreneur means you have to face the pain and uncertainty of running your own business, and this is the start of the pain. If you have large payments to make as a result of credit card debt or to banks then you probably don't know how to budget your money. And if you can't budget, you won't be able to have money for the business and you probably won't make a successful entrepreneur. If you're driving around with a $500 a month car payment on a fancy BMW, get rid of the car, buy a used vehicle and avoid a monthly car payment altogether. If you can't afford a used vehicle, lease or buy an economy car. Let's be honest fellas, your girlfriend doesn't go out with you because of the kind of car you drive. If she does, then you need to trade her in on a more reliable model. Heck, I used to drive a $90,000 Acura NSX sports car and Jennifer's opinion of it was a somber, "Oh, it's nice." And ladies, would you rather spend $300 on a pair of shoes or a Coach™ handbag or have that money available to incorporate your new business? It all comes down to priorities, and you need to start prioritizing today.

I recently met a 26 year-old woman, single mother of one, who is starting her own hair salon. She asked for my advice on how to make it as profitable as possible. We met four times, each time at Starbucks. I noticed she spent $7 on her café mocha caramel whateveritzcalled and accompanying biscuit each time we met. During the fourth meeting I asked her how often she came to Starbucks. She said, "Every day except Sunday, why?" I pulled out my phone and accessed the calculator function to show her something. I told her the first thing she could do to make her business more profitable was to quit the $2,000 a year café mocha habit and sink that money into marketing her salon. Up until that point, she had never thought about how $7 a day can add up. It does and it does so quickly. $7 a day for six days is $42. In one month that equals $168. Multiply that by 2 months and you have $256 which is about what a good laser printer costs these days. Six months savings buys her a computer with a built in point-of-sale system.

The same is true for eating lunch. I recently determined that the people who have offices down the hall from me are spending an average of $12.37 each day for lunch – almost $250 a month! And that doesn't include the cost of gas to drive to and from the restaurant. In many cities, $250 is enough to rent a one-room office for your business. The point of this is that if you really want to free capital for your business, start by evaluating your current spending practices and determine where you can save money. If you visit a coffee shop each business morning and eat out at lunch five days a week, you're probably spending $5,000 a year needlessly. Add in two dinners out per week at $35 a pop and that number increases to over $8,600! I'm not saying don't have fun, but for $8,600 you could completely outfit your office, incorporate your business, and buy business cards, letterhead, marketing materials and, well, everything you need to get started.

A Small Price to Pay for a Lifetime of Financial Freedom

You will know within the first three to six months whether or not the business you are after is enough to support you. So count on needing at least $10,000-$15,000 to support yourself for six months. If in this time you establish that the business is not there, then it is time to get out and find yourself a regular job. If you've been able to work on your business while retaining your existing job, then you haven't lost anything except time and some money. Return to your job and become successful at it.

Now think about that last paragraph. Would you invest $10,000 to $15,000 if it meant you were on your way to financial independence? Would you commit six months of your life to determine if your idea can produce a comfortable living for you and your family for years to come? I would. I have. You can, too.

Kelie Plank is the founder of Austin Women & Wine, a networking organization for women that empowers women by leveraging their assets amongst themselves. In the development of a local organization, Kelie developed a business model for other young women who want to take control of their financial lives. For about $15,000 in startup costs, a person can license the AWW business model, purchase all the required equipment, and create a business in their city that has the potential to provide $140,000 a year in income or more, while offering numerous networking opportunities to expand their sphere of influence among the business community. What a deal!

Product Partners has a program whereby a person can become a "coach" for just a few dollars a month and sell the Beachbody.com line of products while supporting others who are interested in fitness and healthy living. Most people are making thousands of dollars a year, and many are making hundreds of thousands, all doing something they love…expounding the benefits of being in good physical shape, eating well, and taking the right vitamins to stay healthy.

There is really nothing stopping you from starting your own business. The opportunities are out there. Thousands of people start new companies every single day. Many start out with their own product ideas. Others, like Manuel, become manufacturer's representatives. Still others purchase a franchise. Individuals have opened General Nutrition Centers (GNC) stores in more than 30 countries. 7-Eleven franchisees added 2,000 stores in a recent year.

There are hundreds of franchise opportunities where $15,000 or less would give you the framework to begin your march to success. A recent Internet search at the International Franchise Association website (www.franchise.org) revealed more than 100 such opportunities, ranging from concrete coatings and tutoring firms to cleaning systems and cruise consultants.

If you are without a great idea, purchasing a franchise may be a viable alternative as you start down the path to success. With a franchise, you don't need an original idea as it is provided for you. A proven business model already exists and all the supporting materials such as brochures, product, training, signage, and operating manuals are provided as part of your franchise fee. Franchising is a relatively easy way to get started in owning and operating your own company.

I recently met a young woman who told me she became a dealer for a fire suppression product called No Burn®. It cost her $175. She incorporated as an S-Corporation for $400. She invested $80 in a cell phone, $900 in a computer, $200 in letterhead and business cards, $60 in office supplies, bought a desk, chair, and filing cabinet for $270 at a used furniture outlet, and set up shop in her house as an independent representative for the company. For under $2,500 she launched a new career where she spends the majority of her time outdoors, calling on commercial and residential contractors, selling her fire suppression system.

But you may ask, "What if my business fails?" Great! You'll learn more in running a failing business than you would working for a big corporation for ten years. You'll become more appealing as a job candidate because you'll have been exposed to all facets of an operating business. You'll learn what works and what doesn't work, and you'll bring that knowledge with you to any position or future business endeavor you undertake. Have I had businesses that failed? You bet. Does it worry me that my next business may fail? Not at all. Each time

I start a company I know what to do to avoid the pitfalls of past mistakes. Does that guarantee me success? No, but it helps me to better understand what it takes to succeed. It really is true that there is no better teacher than experience.

What Did You Learn?

1. Finding a partner who rounds out your skills is an option for those who feel that sole proprietorship of a business is not up their alley. Just be sure you choose a partner with common interests and goals, and write an agreement that you both can live with for years to come.
2. Launching a company doesn't have to cost an arm and a leg. Thousands of firms are started each year for under $10,000; many for as little as $1,000.
3. Even if your business fails, you'll have learned more and become a more attractive job candidate than if you had not started the business in the first place.

CHAPTER 15

Yes You Can: Fund Your Company

Brother, can you spare a dime?

EVEN THOUGH SOME very successful people have started businesses with as little as a few hundred dollars, it is nearly impossible to start a business unless you have a source of at least a little money. Let us suppose that you have already resigned from your former company and you have no money, not even the $2,000 a month you need to live on. How do you get money? You won't get money from a bank to start a business so put that idea out of your head. The ideal situation would be if you had a wealthy relative who would be more than happy to give or lend you the financing you need. Unfortunately, not many of us have a wealthy relative. So now what do you do? First, swallow your pride. You are starting your own business and you must focus on the tasks at hand, which include developing your idea, projecting your revenues and expenses, determining your growth plan, and figuring out how to ask for money.

The Small Business Administration offers programs to help you write a business plan, apply for a loan and even guarantee the loan if you don't meet a bank's loan criteria, as it did for over 50,000 people last year. Computer programs can help you create a professional business plan, and some good ones can be had for under $100. Local colleges, especially community colleges, often offer business startup courses. Accessing these resources and absorbing as much information as you can will help guide you in financing your endeavor. Obstacles can't stop you. Problems can't stop you. Most of all other people can't stop you. Only you can stop you.

Let's be honest, it is difficult to ask someone for money. Practice by asking your closest friends to loan you $500 and listen to their reactions. You'll hear everything from, "Are you crazy?" to "Yeah, me and what bank?" to "What for?" It's that last response that you want to hear because that person has opened the door for you to make your pitch. Tell them your idea and then give them a few minutes to ponder the concept. The worst that can happen is they will say "no," and we already know that that's no big deal. Just get over your fear and ask.

Begin making a list of all friends and family who could help finance your operation. Since perhaps not many of your friends have a spare $15,000, tell your friend that you don't want the entire amount at one time but that you will ask him for the money, as you need it. Or ask 15 people to loan you $165 a month for each of six months. If you keep your investors aware of what is happening with your company, they will likely continue to support you and may also offer free advice that can be of benefit in times of trouble.

To be honest, you may have to beg, borrow, and sell equity in your business to raise the funds you require. The poet Charles Baudelaire summed up this approach when he wrote, "Nothing can be done except by little." Take baby steps. Figure out what you need to raise and start asking people to help guide you to those who could lend

financial assistance. They may be your parent's attorney or accountant, your childhood dentist, the neighbor down the street who always seems to drive a new car, the local business owner that may buy your products or services, or people you meet in what are called Angel Networks (groups of wealthy individual investors who often lend $20,000 to $200,000 to entrepreneurs). Regardless of where you find the people, find them, and do so by asking for advice from everyone you can think to ask.

In 1978, at age 25, John Mackey had just dropped out of the third college he had attended when he decided to go to work for himself. He borrowed $45,000 from friends and family to open a health-food store/restaurant in Austin, Texas. He started with a unique concept that wasn't easily replicated by the large chain grocery stores, focusing on healthy, organic foods coupled with impeccable service. Since then, Whole Foods has grown to more than 150 stores and $4 billion in revenues.

Use Credit Card Cash Advances…Wisely

If you don't have anyone to ask for money, and you truly believe in your idea, borrow from your credit cards. Robert Townsend, the comedian and filmmaker, financed his entire first film on credit cards. Without having faith in his abilities, and taking that chance, he never would have won his first studio deal.

Unless you have a really bad credit rating, most everyone has credit cards. Granted, the interest rate may be high (from nine to twenty-one percent) but you only need to pay back the minimum balance each month plus a little bit more. Of course, that minimum balance will increase substantially each month when you are borrowing at least $2,000 a month. Be warned: borrowing on credit cards is extremely risky, and if you pay back the minimum each month you'll be in debt for a long time. Let's suppose you borrowed $6,000 over three months at 18% interest. Your minimum monthly payment would be around $150.00. If you pay back the minimum due it will take you 331 months – 27 years – to pay off your debt. In that time, you will pay $8,615.25 in interest. Here's the trick to borrowing from credit cards: pay off more than the minimum. If you paid back $200.00 every month, just $50 more than the minimum due, it would be paid off in 41 months, and would cost you $2,030.99 in interest. If you increase the payback amount to $250.00 a month, it will be paid off in just under three years. Whether you start a business or not, if you have credit card debt, do yourself an enormous favor and pay back more than the minimum each month. This tip alone is worth the price of this book.

You can consider selling stock in your company, perhaps setting aside 25% - 60% of your corporation for investors. An organization such as SCORE (Service Corps of Retired Executives, reachable at 800-634-0245) may be able to provide you with mentors who can help assemble the documents and terms for a private equity offering. Keep in mind that when you raise money through a stock sale you now have shareholders. If you don't feel 100% confident you can repay their investment and provide them an adequate return on their money, you should probably avoid this route. This is especially true if you intend to raise money from family members and friends. Many a relationship has been destroyed because Aunt Vera invested in Charlie's get rich quick scheme.

Use Your Current Job as Collateral

Another avenue is to borrow the money before you resign from your current job. This is the only way you will be able to borrow from a bank or lending institution without a track record. If you were to borrow $15,000 and use your current job as proof you can make payments, you might obtain a loan and continue with your current job as you put the foundation of your new business together. To do this, it helps to be well established with a bank or finance company, so get to know the manager of your bank's local branch office and be friendly with all the tellers. Don't use the need for a loan to be the basis of meeting the manager. Just pop in to say hello and mention how long you've been a customer of the bank and how you've always wanted to meet him or her. Then, when you return in a few months to seek a loan, there will be an element of recognition there, which can only help.

One of the more clever forms of fundraising I've seen was undertaken by a young woman who hosted what she called "a fundraising presentation." Jill sought to raise $8,000 to fund what began as a part-time business to assist high school students with financial aid applications. She invited eighty people to her parent's house, including family, friends, old employers, high school teachers, and even people she babysat for back in high school. The invitation explained that those invited had touched her life in some form and would now have a chance to do so again. Jill asked for each person to come with a $100 bill in their pocket and to hear a pitch for her new business.

To a curious crowd gathered at her apartment, Jill explained that if those in attendance liked what they heard, she'd ask them to write their name on the bottom of the bill and leave the $100 behind as an investment in her venture. If successful, she would repay the money, plus 15% annual interest within 3 years. Think about how clever this tactic was: instead of asking someone for $8,000, she was simply asking for $100. By itself, it is not a lot of money to invest in a company, but combined with other people's $100, it adds up. Of the eighty invitees, fifty-seven people attended the presentation and forty-six pieces of currency with Benjamin Franklin's smirking mug were left in the fundraising basket. To her surprise, on top of the $4,600 in cash were six checks: three for $250, one for $300, another for $500 and one for $1,000. In one evening, she raised $7,150, an amount just shy of her goal. As it turned out, Jill didn't need the rest of the money; her business was so successful she quit her job and became a full-time entrepreneur. She repaid her investors within twenty-six months. I never cashed my check for $132.25, choosing instead to keep it as a reminder of Jill's clever fundraising technique.

Finally, you might seek funding from a customer. Let's suppose your product can save XYZ Corp. $50,000 a year. If management believes these savings to be realistic, they may be willing to prepay you that amount or more in exchange for equity in your company. If you can show that an investment in your company not only helps them with an internal issue, but also offers the ability to realize revenue gains from sales to their competitors and other companies, bringing XYZ Corp. in as an equity partner may be a solution worth pursuing.

Setting Up Shop on a Budget: Money-Saving Tips

While you're pursuing funding, keep in mind that in today's economy, it may be less risky to start a business than in the past. Major costs such as labor, office rent, and equipment are down from previous years. Part-time and freelance help is available at a discounted cost compared to just five years ago. Used office furniture can be purchased at auction for pennies on the dollar. Broadband Internet access can be put into your home office for under $50 a month. Corporations can be formed online for a fraction of the fee most law firms charge. Cell phones can double as office phones and wireless service can be had for $30 - $50 a month. A decent computer system with a color printer that will enable you to keep your financial records, generate invoices, write sales letters, and produce basic sales materials now costs under $1,500.

Here's another tip: when purchasing a computer, buy one with at least a 1.5 gigahertz processor, 1 gigabyte of random access memory (RAM), an 80 gigabyte hard drive and a CD R/W or CD/DVD R/W drive so you can backup your files each month to inexpensive storage such as CDs. Or purchase an external hard drive of 500mb or larger from Newegg.com. That will give you enough computing power for most programs and provide a workhorse PC good for several years use. You can save money if you purchase the minimum amount of RAM, usually 256K, and buy an upgrade memory module from a company like Crucial Technology (www.crucial.com). The notebook computer which I use was purchased with 512K RAM. Instead of paying the manufacturer $329 for an additional 1G of RAM, I bought it from Crucial for $130 and installed it myself in about 10 minutes, saving nearly $200.

So there you have it, the written word on how to raise money and save money in order to get your business off the ground. That's the easy part. The hard part is in running your company professionally and honoring your word. Tens of thousands of companies are begging for suppliers who will provide them with exceptional customer service. Investors are seeking opportunities to invest and increase the value of their portfolio. Banks, the Small Business Administration, and other funding sources are in the business of supporting people with good ideas. Don't let the naysayers fool you; *right now is a great time to start your company.*

What Did You Learn?

1. You will have to be resourceful to raise the funds needed to launch your business. You'll ask friends and family, seek help from the Small Business Administration, and pursue every avenue to reach your goals.
2. If you use credit cards to borrow money for your business, or carry credit card debt in general, always, always, always, pay more than your minimum monthly payment. Otherwise you will be throwing money away for a long, long time.
3. If you hope to borrow money from a bank, do so while in your current job to prove you are able to pay back the loan.
4. From the standpoint of buying the tools you need to launch a company, items like computers and broadband have never been cheaper. It's a great time to start a company!

CHAPTER 16

Yes You Can: Calling All Who Want To Succeed

Success begins right here, right now. Let's get started.

ONE THING THAT has always bugged me, and I'm sure it does most of you, is to sit down at the dinner table only to be interrupted by a phone call from a telemarketer. I decided, on one such occasion, to try to be as irritating to them as they were to me. This particular call happened to be from AT&T and it went something like this:

Me: Hello

AT&T: Hello, this is AT&T...

Me: Is this AT&T?

AT&T: Yes, this is AT&T...

Me: This is AT&T?

153

AT&T: Yes, this is AT&T... *(I can tell he's getting a little irate now)*

Me: Is this AT&T?

AT&T: YES! This is AT&T, may I speak to Mr. Townsend please?

Me: May I ask who is calling? *(I couldn't resist)*

AT&T: This is AT&T.

Me: OK, hold on.

At this point I put the phone down for a solid 5 minutes thinking that, surely, this person would have hung up the phone. I ate my salad. Much to my surprise, when I picked up the receiver, they were still waiting.

Me: Hello?

AT&T: Is this Mr. Townsend?

Me: May I ask who is calling please?

AT&T: Yes this is AT&T...

Me: Is this *the* AT&T?

AT&T: Yes this is AT&T...

Me: The phone company?

AT&T: Yes sir.

Me: I thought you said this was AT&T.

AT&T: Yes sir, we are a phone company.

Me: I already have a phone.

AT&T: We aren't selling phones today Mr. Townsend. We would like to offer you 10 cents a minute, 24 hours a day, 7 days a week, 365 days a year.

Me: (I started to jot down the numbers and got the calculator out) Now, that's 10 cents a minute 24 hours a day?

AT&T: (getting a little excited at this point by my interest) Yes, sir, that's right! 24 hours a day!

Me: 7 days a week?

AT&T: That's right.

Me: 365 days a year?

AT&T: Yes sir.

Me: I am definitely interested in that! Wow!!! That's a great program!

AT&T: We think so.

Me: That's quite a sum of money!

AT&T: Yes sir, it's amazing how it adds up.

Me: OK, so will you send me checks weekly, monthly or just one big one at the end of the year for the full $52,560?

AT&T: Excuse me?

Me: You know, the 10 cents a minute.

AT&T: I'm sorry, I don't understand. What are you talking about?

Me: You said you'd give me 10 cents a minute, 24 hours a day, 7 days a week, 365 days a year. That comes to $144 per day, $1,008 per week and $52,560 per year. I'm just interested in knowing how you will be making payment.

AT&T: Oh no, sir, I didn't mean we'd be paying you. You pay us 10 cents a minute.

Me: Wait a minute, how do you figure that by saying that you'll give me 10 cents a minute, that I'll give you 10 cents a minute? Is this some kind of subliminal telemarketing scheme? I've read about things like this in the Enquirer, you know.

AT&T: No, sir, we are offering 10 cents a minute for...

Me: THERE YOU GO AGAIN! Can I speak to a supervisor please?

AT&T: Sir, I don't think that is necessary.

Me: I insist on speaking to a supervisor!

AT&T: Yes, Mr. Townsend. Please hold.

At this point I begin trying to finish my dinner. About a minute goes by.

Supervisor: Mr. Townsend?

Me (with a mouthful of food): Yeth?

Supervisor: I understand you are not quite understanding our 10 cents a minute program.

Me: Id thish Ath Teeth & Teeth?

Supervisor: Yes, sir, it sure is.

I had to swallow before I choked on my food. It was all I could do to suppress my laughter and I had to be careful not to produce a snort.

Me: No, actually, I was just waiting for someone to get back to me so that I could sign up for the plan.

Supervisor: OK, no problem, I'll transfer you back to the person who was helping you.

Me: Thank you.

I was on hold once again for about 20 seconds and managed a few more bites of dinner. I needed to end this conversation. Suddenly, there was an aggravated but polite voice at the other end of the phone.

AT&T: Hello Mr. Townsend, I understand that you understand our offer and are now interested in signing up for our plan?

Me: No, but I was wondering – do you have that "friends and family" thing? Because you can never have enough friends and even though I have a younger sister, I'd really like to have a little brother...

AT&T: (*Click*)

The sales rep just wasn't able to maintain his positive attitude after all my tomfoolery, but I give him credit for putting up with a difficult customer for so long. He understood that in order to succeed in his job, he had to make a sale. Sometimes the people you are selling to can put obstacles in the way (I certainly did for Mr. AT&T). It is up to you to overcome those obstacles.

So far, I have spent a good deal of time preparing you in the basics: developing the right attitude for success and researching the market to ensure that you will have customers for your product before you invest time and money into the product or service itself. It's now time to talk about how you will actually start your own business. Now that you know your product is a great idea and that there really are people out there who will buy from you, we are ready to turn your ideas into a successful company.

You will be starting out with a very limited budget. You are living on $2,000 a month or less and your new business does not have millions of dollars behind it. In fact, as you've seen, there are numerous companies that have had millions upon millions of dollars put behind them only to demonstrate that heavy capital investment does not solve the problems of getting a new company off the ground. Remember Steve Jobs, that high-tech whiz kid from Apple Computer? Steve sunk over seven million dollars of his own money into a venture called NeXT, Inc. Compared to the success of Apple, NeXT was a failure. Now you can buy NeXT computers on eBay under the "vintage PCs" heading for as little as $40. The technology was brilliant but the sales didn't support the company. Steve could afford the kind of money he put behind NeXT. You can't.

In all likelihood, you are starting a small business where the word to remember is *small*. Don't trap yourself with high overhead before you have made your first sale. It is worth repeated, that you should forget about buying a copy machine, fancy furniture, or coffee makers. All you really need, as far as equipment, is probably right in your kitchen this moment: a table, chair and telephone. Add to this a computer, printer, and Internet access and you now have the tools needed to source and sell anything to anyone around the world.

Let's look at a business that is probably the easiest to start: becoming an independent agent for an already established company. Remember Manuel? This is precisely what he did when he formed his export firm. He represents companies seeking to reach the Hispanic market. Another person who took that route is Tamara Johnson, a divorced mother of three from the Midwest who decided to sell some attic items via the online auction site eBay in 2003 and turned that experience into a profitable career.

A Simple Business Model:
Becoming a Manufacturer's Representative

Tamara made $400 from the first batch of auction items she sold, $650 from the second set, and $1,600 from third. She then approached her sisters, brother, and parents to sell their "junk." In two weeks she made $6,000. Then she identified a couple manufacturers and became a manufacturer's rep selling exclusively through eBay. Last year she made $104,000!

What special educational and job experience skills did Tamara possess that let her create a successful online business? She left high school halfway through 11th grade when she became pregnant. She was married at 20, had two more children, and was divorced at 24. She never attended college, but she did take a community college course on how to become an administrative assistant. She worked at a day care center where she listened to the needs of mothers, but she never gave this acquired knowledge much thought. She learned how to use a computer by using the public library's computers. She learned how to use eBay by reading the FAQ (Frequently Asked Questions) section of the site and by reading two books (again, at the public library) on how to sell on eBay. So you see, Tamara had no specific experience that would guarantee her success. In fact, if you read her résumé, you'd probably conclude that Tamara was destined to be a waitress or check out girl at the local grocery store. There was nothing in her past to indicate she could be successful.

What wasn't visible is exactly what made Tamara successful: she had a burning desire to make a better life for herself and her children.

"I listed my first items on eBay by using the community library's computer, said Tamara. "When I made enough to buy a computer I did so and started selling friends' and neighbors' unwanted possessions, and split the profit with them. When I found my manufacturers, they were excited to have me selling for them. Now my business is going great and I have made more money in the last two years than I ever imagined."

Tamara outfitted her office with all the lavish indulgences she needed to start her company. She placed a folding card table and chair in the corner of the living room; bought a $28 telephone with built in answering machine from Sears; financed an $800 computer and $200 digital camera through the manufacturer's web site; and added broadband access from her cable television provider.

How has life changed with Tamara's newfound success? The folding table remains, but she splurged on a high quality chair and upgraded to a wireless phone. She pays her sister to manage product listings, which costs $2,500 a month, but readily admits she could do this herself. "I hired Rhonda because she needed a job and the time I save not having to manage listings lets me spend more time with my two girls," beams Tamara, clearly happy with her situation.

Anyone can make a sale on eBay. But not everyone can make a business out of it. Today, more than one million sellers are using eBay for a primary or significant source of their incomes. They are all small business owners and most of them would be classified as manufacturers' representatives.

So where do you start? A good search engine like Lycos, Yahoo! or Google can help you find hundreds of companies who can provide products for you to sell. Using search terms like "wholesale merchandise," "drop-ship services," "closeout dealers," "job lot traders" or "liquidators" will bring up thousands of sources.

Matching a supplier to your own interests or expertise is an effective way to find products that you have an interest in for your new venture. It is certainly easier to sell something you believe in than something you're just trying to move to make a profit. Having owned several Honda, Acura and Jaguar cars, I could sell those cars in my sleep because I believe in them. On the other hand, I probably wouldn't be a good salesperson for a BMW because the one I owned had so many mechanical problems I traded it in within a year. You might make a list of all the products you believe in and use that as a basis for what type of manufacturer you'd like to represent. This could include tubas, financial services, golf balls, hula-hoops, grafted cacti, children's clothing, motorcycle leathers, wine, nesting dolls from Russia, or any other product that there is a need for. Off the top of my head I can think of dozens of product lines I would have knowledge about and could probably find a manufacturer to represent: motorcycle accessories, violins, guitars, amplifiers, drums, olive oil, candles, soaps, tennis gear, radar detectors, computer supplies, children's clothing...the list goes on and on.

Once you have a product line in mind, conduct some research to determine if there is a market for the product. If so, find the manufacturers you want to represent and offer to work as the manufacturer's agent for ten to fifty percent of net profit, depending on the product. Once you have done this, and the manufacturer agrees, you can then turn to the job of actually selling and establishing yourself as your own company.

At this point, your primary goal is to make that first sale. This must be your goal, but not just because you need the money. As a new company, you need to establish both a good reputation and a lot of credibility. Having a paying customer as a reference goes a long way toward convincing your prospects that you are serious about your business and theirs and are going to serve them in the best, most reputable manner possible. If you are launching an e-commerce company, get your product online ASAP and start spreading the word that your store is open. If you're selling in a more traditional manner, I suggest you start with two fundamental tools of business: direct mail campaigns and telemarketing. Both of these techniques will prove invaluable to you as a small business owner, and for that reason, the following pages will stress their importance. Although a direct mail campaign precedes telemarketing, I'd like to first explain the importance of that most wonderful piece of marketing equipment that teenage girls have known about for decades – the telephone.

The Importance of Telemarketing (yes, you have to do it!)

It seems the telephone has been relegated to a second-class citizen when compared to e-mail. E-mail is quick, easy, and efficient. But e-mail doesn't give you the personalized touch of having a live person on the other end of the line. In business, time means money. No successful businessperson can afford to waste time. This is just as true for you, the new entrepreneur, as it is for the CEOs of Boeing, General Electric, and Yahoo! The best way to search for customers and contacts is not to dress up in your best suit, plaster a frozen smile on your face and knock on doors. That might work for Greg and his lawn care business, but you have a product that needs to be sold to a specific audience. To knock on doors would be wasting your time. Ninety-nine percent of the people you would want to spend time seeing in person are either too busy to talk to you, in a meeting or are simply not interested in wasting 30 minutes looking at your smiling face. In addition, half of your time would be wasted talking to receptionists and other people who have no interest in whatever it is you might be selling. You can't waste your time and money driving all over town in the hope that someone will listen to you. The telephone will save you time, aggravation, frustration, and ultimately, money.

When I was managing new business at Ketchum, I developed and maintained a contact list of 700 prospects at over 300 companies. I say "maintained" because you cannot simply create a list and forget about it. People change jobs and positions, and the list, being your lifeline to prospective clients, must be kept up-to-date. These 700 people were my prospects and I divided the list into groups of 100 in order to effectively communicate with them each week. I worked 100 prospects one week, the next 100 the following, the third 100 after that, and so on. By the time the eighth week came around I was back to the original 100 prospects. All these phone calls taught me valuable lessons about communicating via telephone, and they reinforced the power of Alexander Graham Bell's invention, especially for the small business owner.

Before you dial a single phone number here are some tips to make your phone time more effective.

If you have a computer, invest in contact management software. At Ketchum I used Telemagic, but ACT, Salesforce.com, SalesLogic, and Microsoft Business Contact Manager are all good programs. Even Microsoft Outlook can be used to great effectiveness. These programs allow you to keep a prospect's name, title, company, address, e-mail, fax, and other personal information at your fingertips. You can even track the progress of each contact electronically and print reports for weekly evaluation.

Pull up a contact's name and quickly review the details prior to dialing their number. What is their title? If you've spoken to the contact before, what did you talk about? What did you profile the prospect as? What other notes have you made about the prospect?

Todd Markley, a manufacturer's rep from the Southeast, keeps a database of 40 companies and 130 people who work for those companies. Todd's product is a multi-million dollar tooling machine that has a very defined audience of about 200 companies around the world. His goal is to sell one machine a quarter, which nets him a yearly salary of about $250,000. Because he has a finite number of prospects in his region, he spends time reading about the companies and researching the executives. He conducts online searches of executive names to learn more about his prospects and attempts to create a dossier on each prospect so that he can interact with the prospect as if he's known them for years. He relies on the telephone for 75% of his customer contact.

With the advent of voicemail, it is often difficult to get a decision maker on the phone. Don't leave a voicemail message. It's too easy to delete. When I reach Mr. Prospect's voicemail, I immediately dial "0." This most often connects me to a live operator whom I can then ask to direct me to the person I was attempting to reach.

Another trick I use is when an operator answers the phone, I will always introduce myself and mention that I dialed Mr. Prospect's line but got voicemail. Then I ask if I could leave a message with his assistant, and could the operator give me her direct phone number? Once you have the assistant's name and direct dial number, don't ask to be connected. Hang up. Wait a few minutes and then call Mr. Prospect's assistant. You'll find most conversations will go like this:

"Mr. Prospect's office."

"Oh, hi. Is Mr. Prospect in?"

"Who may I ask is calling?"

"This is Rick Ross with ABC Widgets."

"And what is this call regarding, Mr. Ross?"

"I want to talk to Mr. Prospect about my new products."

"I'm sorry, but Mr. Prospect is in a meeting. Can I take a message?"

As you can see, a red flag was raised with the assistant within the first few seconds of the conversation. It was easy for her to peg Rick as a cold call. Now let's look at how I handle these situations to dramatically increase the odds of getting through to my prospect. You can use the same tactic. Remember, we've already spoken to the operator and know Mr. Prospect's assistant's name.

"Hello, Mr. Prospect's office."

"Hi Sue. This is Bill Townsend, is John in?"

(Sue's now thinking, "he knows my name, he told me his name, and he knows my boss's first name. He must know my boss." At the same time, if she didn't catch the caller's name she may hesitate to ask for it for fear of appearing stupid).

"I'm sorry," she says, "Whom may I ask is calling?"

"Bill Townsend over at The Amati Foundation. Is John available?"

(Notice the use of "over at" instead of "from" or "with." This gives the assistant the impression that I've already spoken with her boss in the past and she should know who I am.)

With the former method of cold calling, you can rely on the old adage of make 100 calls, reach 10 people, sell 1 item. When using my technique, I've found I can get through to my prospect, in excess of 60% of the time. Imagine talking to 60 of every 100 people you call. That equates to 6 sales instead of 1, all because of your ability to get past the operator and assistant. By being proactive with knowledge of whom you're calling you can increase your odds of success dramatically.

Now let's suppose that Sue didn't patch me through to her boss but she did offer to take a message. A tactic I have used with great success is to type a letter to Mr. Prospect with a handwritten compliment about his assistant just under my signature. Be forewarned though, you can compliment the assistant *only if she or he really deserves it.* A typical note may be written like this:

Dear John,

I attempted to reach you last week to talk about how sponsoring The Amati Foundation's programs can help your company reach its goals while supporting education for underserved children. I have some great ideas I think you'll enjoy hearing. I will call you Friday morning to discuss.

Best regards,

Bill Townsend

Chairman

P.S. When I called your office I spoke with Sue. I just wanted to tell you that she is one of the most professional and pleasant people I've dealt with.

Mail this letter to Mr. Prospect and you are virtually guaranteed that Sue is going to make sure he reads it. Think about it: if you received a letter addressed to your boss and it complimented you in it, wouldn't you make sure he or she saw it? Your handwritten note (don't type as it's too impersonal and never send e-mail) has two consequences; it gets your letter in front of your prospect and it makes Sue more willing to help you reach him.

The next time you call, in this case, Friday morning because that is what your letter stated, you may be surprised to find Sue is friendly and eager to assist you. In fact, she may very well tell you how thankful she is for your compliment. Be sure to tell her you meant what you wrote.

Notice the importance of identifying when you intend to call back. Don't expect your prospect to call you. They won't. You have to call them and you will want to do so because by doing so you are being helpful to the prospect, opening the door to a sale, and putting you one step closer to your goals.

The ring tone on my cell phone proclaims, "You have 937 messages…all of which are marked urgent." It cracks people up when they hear it. I saved it after returning from a trip to Italy where I had not taken my phone. Apparently, there were quite a few people who had left me messages during that time. I wasn't about to listen to all the messages so I simply deleted them. And guess what? I didn't miss anything. If someone had to reach me, they tried calling me upon my return or they sent an e-mail. I converted the message to a ring tone because it reminds me that you must call people until you reach them. You can't rely on prospects to return your call. Once the message is lost in an electronic voicemail system it may never see the light of day. So remember, to open doors, call, call, call.

When you do connect with a live person, I can't stress the importance of being friendly sounding on the phone. An effective tactic to ensure that you sound good is to keep a small mirror next to the telephone and look at yourself while calling prospects. Smile while you speak and the pleasantness in your voice will translate well over the phone lines.

Let's hang up for a while and get back to using direct mail to open customers' doors. Before you pick up the telephone you need to establish your own identity within your group of prospects. The most effective way of doing this is by direct mail.

Create Your Own Direct Mail Campaign

The first letters you want to send out are designed to accomplish two things: introduce yourself and introduce your company. Actually, these are one and the same thing. Your company *is* you! You are the brand! I can't stress enough the importance of believing in yourself and making sure that this belief is reflected in everything you say and do. To get a prospect interested in your business, you will have to let your confidence and enthusiasm shine through in your direct mail letter and your follow-up phone call. Everything you say and do is a reflection of your business. This is so important that you should copy this page and cut out the line below and tape it to the front of your phone.

Everything I say and do is a reflection of my business.

If a customer thinks you sound desperate, it will make the company look desperate. If you sound weak or dishonest, the company will look even worse. You are the company and you must be the most virtuous and confident role model for your new company.

A good way to begin your direct mail campaign is to compose a personalized introductory letter. Make sure your letter is neat, professional and to the point. One page is enough. Personalize it to your prospect. With today's word processors (ex. Microsoft Word) you can take your database of prospects and insert company names and product names into the letters automatically. A sample letter might fall along these lines:

Joseph C. Reader, President
Reader & Sons Corp.
P.O. Box 340552
Austin, TX 78734

Dear Mr. Reader:

I know the reason you are in business is to make a profit. As the president and owner of XYZ Corp., I take great pride in providing my clients with competitive pricing coupled with exceptional service before, during and after the sale. I have found the companies that appreciate fair pricing and exceptional service are the ones who most likely hire me as their supplier.

I would like to call you next Tuesday to tell you about XYZ Corp. I will take less than 10 minutes of your time. If you don't agree that what I offer can assist your company, then nothing is lost. But if you like what you hear, the long-term benefits of our working together will make that 10 minutes seem like the best bargain of your professional life.

Sincerely,

James X. Bancroft
President & Owner

Send out a lot of letters: 100 letters a week followed by 100 follow-up phone calls the following week will get you started. Mail your letters on Tuesday and begin calling the following Monday. Mail an additional 100 letters the day after you begin your calls (Tuesday), to which you'll begin calling the following Monday. You won't be bombarded with replies, so it is much safer for you to send hundreds of letters to increase your chances of getting those replies. Past experience has shown me that at any given time, 25% of the prospects you are calling have a need for your services. Of these, half are ready to switch suppliers. Out of 100 prospects, roughly 12 prospects a week are actively seeking a new solution to a problem they have. It's up to you to identify which prospects are hot and which are cold. Those that contact you after receiving your letter are automatically lumped into the *hot* category because if they called you they must have an immediate need. Don't let them get away without a meeting and be prepared to ask for the order while you are there.

You might want to send two different letters of introduction to prospects. One to people you know and one to people you don't know. If we assume that you are starting your business in the same field as the one you've already worked in, you should already have a list of people that know you. It is a good idea to send these people even more personalized letters. Your list of letters will grow as you think back on all the people who know you and as you search through trade journals and such to find people who don't. Keep adding to your list and keep it manageable by dealing with 100 prospects a week. Each letter you write could be the one that will lead to your first sale. Don't be discouraged at the prospect of writing multiple letters geared toward different company types or industries. If need be, get someone to help you. Pay for word-processing and copier services, get your Aunt Jean to type, have your kids lick stamps, but write and mail those letters, then follow up with phone calls. Through these actions, you are taking a vital step in establishing yourself as a business.

There is no rest for you even after you've mailed one thousand introduction letters. The entrepreneur does not sit on his can and wait by the telephone for the one thousand phone calls he thinks his letters will bring. As Dana Carvey would say doing his impersonation of former President George H.W. Bush, "Ain't gonna happen!"

You must try to imagine yourself as the person who receives your letter. They are busy and receive dozens of solicitations each day. You have to face reality; no matter how beautiful your letter is, some people have probably either not read it or worse yet, have thrown it in the circular file, otherwise known as the trash bin. But someone may have read it and is waiting for the next step: your telephone call.

Since you've got quite a lot of calls to make, you might want to divide your list into the two categories of those people who know you and those who do not. Keep in mind that your goal is to get that first order. Do whatever it takes to get that order as long as you are honest. The best calls to start with are the people who know you. With these prospects you should feel comfortable enough to ask for the order over the phone.

When making follow-up calls to people who know you, it is important to be honest and up-front with them. After the preliminary "hello" and "how are you," state flat out that you need their help. Tell them that you are just starting out and really need an order. But don't be discouraged if you don't get one. Even if you saved Eddie's life in a freak jet ski accident, he might not be able to help you. But Eddie may know someone who does need your product or service and perhaps he'd let you use his name when you called that person. You should never give up. Keep making phone calls and eventually, you *will* get that first order.

When calling people who don't know you, the most important

thing to remember is to ask questions and listen to the answers. The three key questions to ask are: "Tell me, how I can help you?"; "Tell me how can I serve you better?"; and, "Tell me about what problems are you having?" Use the "Tell me about…" technique to get to the bottom of these questions. You don't want to come across as pushy or arrogant. You want to be honest and helpful. Always be polite and courteous on the phone and in person, no matter who you are talking to – you might wrongly assume that you are talking to an unimportant secretary or clerk when you are really talking to the vice president of the company. You can't risk taking those kinds of chances. Keep that mirror in front of you and smile while you talk. Even if you *are* talking to a secretary or clerk, *do not* treat them any differently than you would the owner of the business. Remember that everything you say and do is a reflection of you and your company.

What Did You Learn?

1. The easiest business to start is that of manufacturer's representative. There are thousands of companies that would love to have you pushing their product to customers. Find a product line you connect with and determine if you can make a go at selling it.
2. You don't need an advanced degree, tens of thousands of dollars, or a fancy office to start your own company. Tamara Johnson started her company at a public library and then moved into her living room. Today she is in the top 5% of all wage earners in America. What stops you from doing the same?
3. The telephone and direct mail are two powerful tools for seeking customers. Learn to use them to your advantage, and persevere with these techniques. Don't become discouraged— you will need to make many calls and writes hundreds of letters, but you will succeed.

4. Always act graciously and with integrity; you are a constant reflection of your company.

CHAPTER 17

Yes You Can: Sell, Sell, Sell.

You can't succeed if you don't try.

T HIS CHAPTER IS FILLED with tactical advice on getting clients. At first glance it may seem too mired in detail, but I encourage you to read through it and absorb the tactics outlined as they will help you become a better salesperson, and thus, more successful. A former employee of mine used to say, "Bill you talk about selling the steak by highlighting the sizzle. These tactics teach me how to prepare the steak so as soon as the customer sees it, he's already salivating to eat it."

After having researched the product or service and the financial requirements to start your business, you are really close to being in business. Let's suppose you've bought some inventory and you're ready to go land that first customer. There is an essential skill you need, and that is the ability to merchandise the product or service. Dictionaries define *merchandise* as "to buy or sell goods." In this case you're going to sell goods, be they a product or a service. Selling is a skill that you will master largely through your own enthusiasm which will continuously grow because it is your business you are building. You can get a head start on selling by purchasing a book on the subject, such as *The Little Red Book Of Selling: 12.5 Principles Of Sales Greatness* by Jeffrey Gitomer, or an audio CD like *5 Steps To Successful Selling* by Zig Ziglar. Regardless of the approach you take, one thing is sure, selling a product requires super salesmanship and you *must be* a super salesman!

There are many forms of selling, but for the most part, the various types boil down to two kinds: direct selling such as in person or by telephone, or indirect selling, such as through catalogs, direct mail, and the Internet. All are separate yet related to each other. The important thing to remember is that ***selling is helping,*** and that message of helping must be conveyed to the customer or client, be it a product or a service. Through your selling, you help customers solve problems, fulfill needs, become more competitive, and even realize dreams.

Author and motivational speaker Zig Ziglar said, "Every sale has five basic obstacles: no need, no money, no hurry, no desire, no trust." The next few pages will show you how to overcome these obstacles.

Understanding the Four Primary Aspects of Selling

Selling is primarily made up of four parts, which I call "P2C2" (not be confused with George Lucas' little droid, R2D2). P2C2 includes *Prospecting, Presenting, Closing,* and *Commitment.*

Prospecting is simply identifying who can and who will buy your product or service. This is often as easy as looking in the phone book and finding companies that need what you sell. You can use the Internet to search for prospects, and there are numerous websites that offer not only company names but contact information and personnel listings. If your product is to be sold to consumers, you can identify likely buyers and determine the most effective means to reach them through advertising, direct sales, or selling through retailers. Regardless of the approach, you will be prospecting for men and women who have an interest in your product or service.

In nature, there are not more than three primary colors (blue, yellow, and red) plus white (pure light) and black (the absence of light), yet in combination they produce more hues than can ever been seen. People are much the same, with different personalities and idiosyncrasies. You can define – or profile – a potential customer in a matter of minutes, even seconds. What's this got to do with selling? Everything! You've heard the adage "People buy from people they like." By profiling your prospect you'll understand how to interact and relate to different types of people much quicker than if you didn't know anything about them. This will assist you in making an effective presentation to the customer and will be helpful in negotiating a sale.

Identify the Type of Client You're Dealing With

Almost every person on the planet will fit into one of four profiles: headline, illustration, body copy, or logo. So what are these? Think about an advertisement in a magazine. The headline shouts out what the ad is about. The illustration is the cool, hip, creative element. The body copy gives you the details, explaining every little thing about the product. And last but not least, the logo lets you know who the ad is for – the people behind the product. Now relate this to people:

The Headline: He or she is demanding, fast-moving and quick to decide. Headlines like bullet points: short, sweet, and to-the-point. Whatever they say, they stick to it. You'd best be prepared to state your case in less than 30 seconds to any person who is a Headline. When you find yourself dealing with a Headline, all you need to do is quickly state what this person would lose (fear motivator) or gain (reward motivator) by using your product. Lots of CEOs are Headlines. They are strapped for time and want you to get to the point. "What is it you sell? What does it do for my company? What does it cost? When can I have it? Good! See Jane and let's get some of your widgets in here right away!" Headlines don't have time to waste, and giving them a to-the-point presentation – even a one page bulleted list of benefits – will go a long way toward making them comfortable with giving you an order.

After your meeting, send the Headline a short, hand-written note thanking them for their time. Keep it simple, such as, "Mr. Taylor, Thank you for your time Tuesday. I look forward to supporting your company with our product. Regards, Sandy Robinson."

The Illustration: This person loves being the center of attention and involved in anything else that's happening. This social butterfly is typically very opinionated. They like the latest and greatest. They visit the hip new coffee shop downtown, have the latest cell phone strapped to their side, and know all the current "happening" places around town. Name-dropping and thinking big will impress this prospect more than anything else. It's best to provide plenty of social proof about your product with reprints of articles and pictures of some "mover and shaker" standing in front of your product, or magazine or newspaper clippings about your firm. The Illustration likes adventurous ideas, impactful products, and anything that will stroke their ego. You may say, "By using our widgets you'll save your company $50,000 a year and be seen as a hero," and the Illustration will eat it up! Illustrations often display their degrees, awards, and other mementoes of importance in their office. They often have stacks of paper lining their desk, assuring themselves they know where every little scrap is. They will often prefer to hold the initial meeting at their office and subsequent meetings at a restaurant or coffee shop.

After meeting with an Illustration, send them a handwritten thank you note on a nice cotton-based note card with your company name or initial embossed on the cover. You can really knock the Illustration out by enclosing an article about some upcoming event they may be interested in such as a new art gallery opening or concert series. "Dear Joe, Thanks for your time Thursday. I think our companies can do great things together. By the way, I am enclosing an article about the William H. May photography exhibit next month. Thought you might find that interesting as he's one of the best photographers to ever exhibit in our city. Let's talk soon, Sandy."

The Body Copy: He or she is the consummate analyst. They need facts and figures, statistics, research and trends with plenty of proof and demonstrations. They are very methodical in their decision-making process. In fact, they love process. They'll demand proof for everything. Your offer to demonstrate your product's capabilities would knock the socks off this prospect if you walk them through the process of how your product solves their needs. Body Copies like conversations that flow along these lines: "This, then that, produces this, therefore that."

Whereas with a Headline you might start a conversation by saying, "My widget is made better than the widgets your company is currently using, and I can deliver them for $1 less than your current supplier saving your firm $50,000 a year," with the Body Copy you'll present the information in a totally different way. For example, you might say, "My widget is made of extruded titanium, which is stronger than the steel alloy used in the products your company currently uses. By creating our product in titanium we can produce them less expensively because we have fewer defects. This means we can provide your firm with units $1 less than what you're currently buying; therefore, we can save you $50,000 a year while providing a higher quality, more durable product resulting in fewer breakdowns on the assembly line." All that "this, then that, produces this, therefore that" sounds like a mouthful, but the Body Copy appreciates the details.

After your meeting, send the Body Copy a handwritten thank you note or letter on your stationery restating the next steps in the process: "Dear Joe, Thank you for your time Tuesday. As a follow-up to our meeting, we discussed that we would provide you with cost estimates on 5,000 widgets. I will send this to you no later than Tuesday of next week then call you to discuss. Regards, Sandy Robinson."

The Logo: Logos relish relating on a personal basis; family and friends come first, business is secondary. Think warm and fuzzy stuff. When approaching this type of person, keep everything low-key, safe and secure. They move slowly and resist change. They need to have a good relationship with their supplier and trust that the supplier is always looking out for their best interests. A Logo's office usually has a lot of photos of their kids, spouse, softball team, Aunt Pearl, etc. They will invite you in and talk about their lives and your life before beginning to talk about business. They thrive on personal relationships and you can adapt your selling pitch based on that knowledge. Phone conversation may go like this: "Hi Joe, how are you? How are the kids? Is Allison enjoying soccer camp? Great. Great." Sometimes you will spend 5, 10, or 20 minutes talking about family and friends before the Logo is ready to talk business. When they're ready, they'll tell you and that's when the relationship you've built with them pays off.

After the meeting, send a handwritten thank you note that is personal and friendly, such as, "Joe, It was my pleasure to meet you Tuesday. I look forward to establishing a long relationship with you and your firm and feel we can be of great service to you for years to come. With best regards, Sandy."

It's not hard to see that your product pitch and approach must be different with each of these four styles. A "one size fits all" way of thinking is what your competitor is going to do when they walk in the customer's door. While prospecting, you will begin to determine their profile by the way they interact over the phone or in face-to-face meetings. You'll have already profiled the customer and will continue to do so, and then alter your approach based on what you know about the type of person you're selling to. Knowing your customer's personality profile will make the sales process easier and will give you an unfair advantage over your competition.

Presenting is simply knowing your product inside and out and showing it effectively. Practice your pitch in front of the mirror or your spouse or significant other. You want to get across a couple key points, including that your product is better than others; that it solves the customer's needs; that your company is dependable; and that serving the customer is your number one priority. You can present by placing a product on someone's desk and talking about it or creating a presentation on your computer, or buying a flip book and filling the pages with important selling messages that address the product, customer, and fulfillment of that customer's needs.

The benefit of creating a presentation on your notebook computer is that you can create individual presentations for every type of customer you might meet. The Headline presentation will be 4-6 slides and feature 3-4 bullet points on each slide. The Illustration presentation will be more graphics intensive with product shots, scans of newspaper articles, bold colors, and charts and may be 6-12 slides in length. The Body Copy presentation, about the same length, will feature charts and graphs and highlight the process of working with your firm. There may be 4-5 bullet points on each slide – whatever it takes to convey the details of your product and how you'll support the customer. The Logo presentation should be shorter, 4-6 slides, and talk about product benefits and how your firm can support his or her company. Logos will like it if you use the presentation as a reference source only and keep the discussion primarily between the two of you.

Another key element of Presenting is understanding when to speak and when to listen. It's really difficult to sit back and listen to a prospect tell you about their problems. It's human nature to want to jump right in with an answer. But if you start each meeting off with the phrase, "Tell me about…" and complete it with the following inquiries: "Tell me about your widget needs"; "Tell me about what you don't like about the gizmos you're currently using"; "Tell me about what your current supplier could do better," you'll be pleasantly surprised to learn that your customer will tell you everything they like and don't like about your competitor's services and products. Once you know what they don't like – what their pain point is – you can tailor your presentation to address that topic.

There is a story about a guest who appeared on *The Tonight Show* when Johnny Carson was the host. The guest was billed as the greatest salesman who ever lived. Johnny started by saying, "You're the greatest salesman in the world: sell me something."

Johnny expected a big sales pitch, but instead, the man said, "What would you like me to sell you?"

"I don't know," Johnny replied, "How about this ashtray?"

"Why, Johnny?" asked the guest. "What is it that you like about that ashtray?"

Carson listed the things he liked: It matched the brown color of his desk, was octagonal and fulfilled the need for someplace to put his ashes.

Then the guest asked, "How much would you be willing to spend for a brown octagonal ashtray like that one?"

"Maybe $20," said Johnny.

"Sold!" said the guest.

"Tell me about..." is the ideal tactic for understanding your customer's needs and concerns. The secret lies in persuading the customer to state her own needs and then getting her to sell herself. By asking detailed questions, you can often uncover the prospect's problems and won't have to guess what they are. If you don't take the time to ask about their business and use the "Tell me about..." question, you may never learn what their concerns include.

Another way to think about this is like a visit to your doctor. When you see your doctor, do you let him sell you on all the wonderful things he can do, or does he start by asking something along the lines of, "Tell me about what hurts?" You're doing the same thing with your customer, only by using "Tell me about..." you present the customer with a wide open door to tell you everything you need to know to get to the C2 part of P2C2.

The first part of C2 stands for **Closing**. In closing you are winning the sale. You can't win the sale if you don't know what the problem is you're solving, but since you found that out in the Prospecting and Presenting phase, you now only have to ask for the sale to close it. Closing the sale can be done in a hard sell approach or a soft sell approach. Sometimes being aggressive is the only way to get a prospect to place an order. At other times, a soft sell approach is the better way to go. You have to decide which tactic is appropriate. Regardless of your approach, you must remember that your customer is not your enemy. Rather, he or she is simply someone you are trying to provide a good product and service to and they are trying to ensure they get what they pay for. In the end, it has to be a win-win situation for both parties.

Personally, I prefer the soft sell approach. I believe that in most cases people buy products or services based on a need that can be addressed through their head or their heart. Hard selling is mostly about the head: "what are the data points, how does it help my bottom line?" Soft selling is mostly a combination: the head wants to know the facts but the heart wants to feel good about the transaction. You can often close a deal based on simply meeting the needs of your customer; and by ensuring them you are going to commit yourself to delivering.

Dealing With Your Customer's Objections

There are three steps to effective soft selling that you can utilize when the customer comes at you with an objection:

First, listen and observe. You want to know not only what the person is saying, but also how or why she is saying it. Establish eye contact and create a bond that can lead to a strong relationship. Mimic the way the customer sits and use some of the same gestures they use to make them feel at ease. Now, if the customer is leaning back in their chair with their legs crossed, that's not an excuse for you to slouch, kick your legs out and cross them, but you can sit up in the chair, cross your leg, and gently lean in to the customer. This shows that you are interested and attentive to their needs.

Be yourself at all times. You don't have to become friends with a customer but you do need to be yourself. Some relationships will develop quickly while others will take time. Some are purely professional while others may become more personal. Part of building this relationship is adapting to each other's personality, and if you aren't being yourself, it becomes impossible for your customer to trust you.

I used to sell online advertising to a brilliant media professional by the name of Karen Anderson. Her firm, Modem Media, represented several of the larger clients advertising on the Lycos web site. Karen and I developed a great personal relationship which we have sustained for many years since our working together. Even though we are friends, when it came to business, we kept our work at a highly professional level that created a win/win situation for Modem Media, their clients, and Lycos. Our relationship was based on trust and mutual admiration for doing what was right. On the other side of client relationships, when I managed Digital Equipment Corporation's printers division's advertising account, my relationship with the client was purely professional. There was never any talk of family or vacation or even grabbing lunch together. It was 100% business, 100% of the time. That's not to say we didn't have a good relationship, it just means that our relationship was strictly business with no room for personal interaction.

Second, question the prospect's objections. You can't provide a good answer to an objection unless you understand exactly what it is and where it's coming from. Only then can you see the possibilities available to make your product or service fit with your customer's needs. You should have already used the "Tell me about…" technique to get the answers to most objections, and if a new objection arises, use the same technique to better understand her concern. Ask the customer to explain, expand and elaborate until you fully understand the situation. Be patient and the answer may present itself.

I once asked a client of my consulting firm Interminds to meet with one of his largest customers. There was something preventing the customer from ordering more from my client and I wanted to try to uncover the answer. We made chit chat and I quickly identified the customer as an Illustration. My client was a Body Copy. Right away it was clear that someone who was looking for big idea concepts wasn't going to get them from a process driven individual. I used "Tell me about…" to inquire as to what the customer wanted from my client. She responded by saying, "I wish I got more aggressive ideas from them. Everything they present is well thought out but safe. I need to make big changes in here and one of their competitors is promising solutions that far outshine what we're being offered." I then asked her to tell me about the other solutions. She replied that the cost savings of a competing software application was supposedly four times the level of my client's, and could be implemented in half the time. I knew the product, and while it did offer initial cost savings, I understood that long-term costs would likely erase any initial savings within a year. I also knew that the implementation time for the competing product was shorter than my client's, but it also required the purchase of other software (in this case, database software) that wasn't entirely compatible with the customer's current systems. I suggested I return the next day with my client to discuss how their product compared with the competition.

After the meeting I explained the situation to my client. His customer was hearing aggressive claims by competitors, and because of the personality of my client, he wasn't going to make statements that were not entirely true. I helped my client understand the personality of his customer and together we crafted a pitch that addressed the customer's concerns. My client spent an hour the next day explaining to the customer that his company would never embellish what his software could or could not do, and the reason for doing so was to guarantee that his customer would be confident that what was promised was delivered. Within one quarter, the customer increased her use of my client's software, increasing spending 130%.

Thirdly, when your customer has an objection, you need to address his concerns. Use your customer's own objections to deflect their concerns and lead them to a positive conclusion that buying your product or service is a good step to take. Take what you learned from the "Tell me about…" technique and say something along the lines of, "You mentioned this was your real concern about using widgets. Here's what we can do for you to make sure that all your needs are met."

Sometimes it is necessary to take a more aggressive sales approach to closing. When you need to employ the hard sell, here are two tips to make it easier:

1. Let your passion and enthusiasm for your product show. Let customers see that you believe strongly that there is a match between what they need and what you have to offer. The famous Asian general, Sun Tsu, wrote in *Art of War* about five essentials of victory. One of them is, "He will win whose army is animated by the same spirit through all its ranks." It means, if you fully understand the benefits of what you are selling and understand the needs of your customer, and you feel confident and assured in your beliefs, then you will come away with a victory.

2. Be able to support your belief. In closing a sale, belief and enthusiasm must be supported by knowledge and understanding. Have all your facts and figures at hand, and have at least three or four strong reasons illustrating how your product or service stands out from the rest.

When you're closing a sale, you have to know what to do when an objection comes at you from left field. To make the strongest close, you have to be ready to use what you've learned about your customer, what you know about yourself and your product, and how much you believe in what you're doing.

Don't Forget to Get the Order!

In all the years of running sales organizations for both products and services, I have been repeatedly dismayed at how many salespeople miss the opportunity to make a sale because they don't ask for the order. Usually, they're afraid the customer will say no. But you will hardly ever get a flat "no." And remember, we're not afraid of hearing the "N-O" word. What you usually get during a sales pitch is an objection. And once you discover a solution to your customer's objection, you simply state the solution and add your closing line of, "Why don't we go ahead and get you the widgets you need?"

You can even try closing lines centered around payments. I once closed a $900,000 sale by asking in a matter of fact manner, "Would you like to put 50 percent down, or is 20 percent easier?" The client wasn't even completely convinced he wanted to make the order, but by assuming he would, I pushed him to close. It worked because I had listened to him, discovered his needs and asked for the order. Notice I wasn't asking, "Do you want to buy this or not?" which gives the customer an easy out. I was *assuming* he would buy it and had already moved forward to asking how he was going to pay for it.

Part four of P2C2 is **Commitment**. You've closed the sale and made a commitment to deliver on that sale. Whether the sale is recorded on an order form, a contract, or even a handshake, once you've closed the sale you have made a promise to the customer to deliver. Do so! If it means staying up all night the day before the order is due, do it. If it means driving four hours to pick up the products and then another four to deliver them on time, do it. Your commitment to deliver your customer's order is your bond. You must fulfill the order no matter what.

The responsibility of delivering on your promise lies with you. As the company owner and salesperson, you have to ensure that all details of the deal are fully concluded and implemented. Though perhaps a bit dull and mundane when compared to the emotional high derived from pulling off a big sale, it is crucial that this step be fully concluded. Once again, it can't be stated too often that you drive this process. It is your responsibility to make sure that administration, ordering, accounting, delivery and all other steps in completing the transaction take place, even though others may actually be doing the work. The job cannot be considered complete until this is done. It is said, "It ain't over 'til it's over," and that means that everything that was agreed to is delivered. Your success depends upon it, so make it happen.

Why is this important? Let me share a story with you.

My father was the General Manager of The Meadows racetrack in Pennsylvania for many years. In the 1970s, The Meadows was considered to be one of the premiere harness horse tracks in America, often attracting 8,000 to 12,000 people to the races on any given night. Dad would often relate to me stories of great salespeople and superb employees. He used to tell me that he had three employees he never had to worry about: Tom Rooney in public relations, track announcer Roger Houston, and facilities manager Quinton Patterson. Dad knew that if there were a problem in any of their respective departments, Tom, Roger and Quinton would solve it. They owned their part of the business and were responsible to drive it. They took responsibility to ensure that they delivered what was supposed to be delivered. They made their departments successful by managing them as if they were their own businesses.

When it came to outside suppliers, my Dad would seek the same type of people: people who would actively manage the business between their company and The Meadows. This meant that my father didn't have to worry about orders being filled and assignments being completed. He thus had more time to concentrate on more pressing concerns. It meant these suppliers were helpful. Keep that in mind, as your role as a business owner is to make your customers' lives easier so that they can focus on their business instead of worrying about yours. Nothing worthwhile comes easily. Continuous hard work is the only way to accomplish results that last. As a supplier, your efforts should make your customer's job easier, not more difficult.

Of all the advertising and public relations agencies that The Meadows had hired over the years, one person in particular stood out in my father's mind. Paul Alvarez was the account representative for Fahlgren & Swink. He was the only person who continually brought ideas to The Meadows' management. He came up with promotions before the track management knew they needed a promotion. He helped his client by understanding The Meadows' business as well, and maybe even better, than many of the track's own people did. His skills as a public relations and advertising professional, while evident to my father early on, became apparent many years later when Paul Alvarez became Chairman of the $1.3 billion advertising and public relations firm, Ketchum.

The other person my father often spoke about was a man who sold IBM Selectric typewriters. Before ever approaching my father for an order, this salesman – this super salesman – had gotten to know all the people in the secretarial pool and understood their work habits and challenges as well as they did. (Remember Frank Federer's comment that he can learn everything about a company by talking to the guys on the loading dock? This salesman was doing the same thing with the people who ultimately would use his products.) When it came time to present my father with the opportunity to purchase several IBM typewriters, this super salesman had the collective support of everyone in the secretarial pool, plus knew exactly how productivity could be increased in each department by the features offered in his product. He became successful and closed the sale because he wasn't just selling a product; he was selling a product that would solve his client's secretarial pool challenges, even if his client didn't yet know he had a problem that needed to be solved. This example of "Customer Connection" proves that you too can understand your customer's issues better than he or she does. You simply have to do your homework. Once the IBM Selectrics were installed, the features of these machines assisted in a rise in productivity and employee morale.

Honesty Really Is the Best Policy

While we're discussing being helpful to your customers, I believe there is another essential fact that the entrepreneur must know, and that is that cheating is not in the true spirit of the entrepreneur in serving customers. By this I mean deliberately misrepresenting the product or service for the sake of profit. Cheating is not winning, and the successful entrepreneur cannot lose sight of that philosophy. Lying, cheating and stealing are all one and the same.

The truly successful entrepreneur builds his business on the bedrock of honest dealings. As Mark Twain said, "If you tell the truth you don't have to remember anything." Be honest in your dealings and most everyone will be honest with you. Cheat someone and you not only offend that person and lose their business, but you'll lose the potential business of every person that your ex-customer comes in contact with. Put simply, be honest because cheating for the benefit of a little more profit today isn't worth it in the long run.

What Did You Learn?

1. Prospecting, Presenting, Closing, and Commitment are the four primary steps of selling.

2. Every prospect can be categorized into one of four personalities: bullet point Headlines; big idea Illustrations; process oriented Body Copies; and relationship centric Logos. Learn to identify these people and adjust your sales strategy to match their desires.

3. Utilize the "Tell me about…" technique to zero in on your customer's needs. To overcome a customer's objections, there are three important steps you can take: listen to your customer's words and observe his body language; questions his objections; and address his concerns directly.

4. In some instances, you may need to employ a hard sell approach to closing a deal. To make hard selling easier, be passionate about your product or service and have all the facts at hand to support why what you offer is the best.

5. Once the contract is signed you must do everything in your power to deliver what you promised.

6. Taking the high road will always make for a more rewarding journey.

CHAPTER 18

Yes You Can: Professionalism Commands Respect

Respect for ourselves guides our morals;
respect for others guides our manners.

I WAS STANDING in the back of an elevator, on my way to put the finishing touches on a $26 million contract with a large government contractor, when into the elevator walks a man with oil-soaked sweat pants, a stained shirt, and filthy hands. I knew who he was and nodded "hello." In front of me were two sales reps that were bantering back and forth about what a pain this company was to work for and how the president was supposedly a real jerk. (They actually used a word that began with "a," but since this is family book I won't repeat it here.) The four of us exited at the same floor and the sales reps and I went to the reception area. Within a few minutes, the president of the company, still wearing the oil-soaked sweat pants and dirty shirt, walked into the waiting room and introduced himself to the reps. He turned to me and said, "Hi Bill, sorry for my appearance. I went for a bike ride at lunch and, wouldn't you know it, the chain broke. That's why I'm mess. I was supposed to meet with these two but I decided to cancel their meeting. Good-bye gentlemen. Come on back, Bill." In his office, we had a good laugh about the two unlucky – or should I say unwise – salesmen who would never do business with his company.

To succeed in business, you must always keep professionalism at the forefront in your contact with your customers. The customer is always right. Never forget it. When dealing with people in business, personalities are irrelevant. So what if the guy who comes to your office is wearing overalls, smells like a barn and has no front teeth? He is a customer and must always be treated with respect. When I was growing up, the man who owned the farm next to my parent's farm would often stop to ask how school was going. Many times he'd be wearing a suit and tie while donning a ratty old baseball cap. If you ran into him at the post office you'd think he was just released from the loony bin. Who in their right mind mixes a classy suit with a tattered baseball cap? Of course I knew better. I knew this gentleman as Mr. Ryan, a tremendously smart, caring, generous, and wealthy individual who would always take time to stop me to inquire how school was going or how my parents were or what my sister was involved in. Millions of homeowners and thousands of his employees knew him as Edward Ryan, founder of Ryan Homes, one of the largest homebuilders in America. If Mr. Ryan wanted to wear an old grimy hat, well by golly, he was going to wear it. You really can't tell much about a person by looking at them, so be warned: looks can be deceiving, and your initial impressions may be wrong.

Follow the Golden Rule and Set the Standard for Professionalism Throughout Your Company

Always treat every prospect as you'd want to be treated yourself.

Marvin Bower, a long-time partner at the highly respected management consulting firm McKinsey & Company, wrote about how adhering to the Golden Rule is essential to being a successful consultant. In case you forgot, the Golden Rule has been endorsed by all the world's great religions and is best interpreted as stating, "Do unto others as you would have done unto you." In other words, treat others only in ways that you are willing to be treated in the same situation. To apply this to your business life, imagine yourself in the exact place of the other person on the receiving end of the action. If you act in a given way toward another, and yet are unwilling to be treated that way in the same circumstances, then you violate the rule. Bower's comments demonstrate the importance of maintaining professionalism, and his firm has adhered to the utmost levels of professionalism and ethics since its founding by James O. McKinsey in 1926.

I led a McKinsey & Company engagement at our company, Pay By Touch. A team of eight pricing, consumer adoption, and international business professionals were assigned to the company for a period of eight weeks. Each day, they were among the first to arrive and the last to leave, displaying utmost professionalism during every aspect of the engagement. When they didn't have an answer to a problem, they reached out to other members of their firm to find the answer. "Can't," "Won't", and "I don't know" are not part of their vocabulary. Instead, I heard "We can," "We will", and "We'll find out." The professionalism displayed by every member of the team was a reflection of the same professionalism that can be found at the highest levels of McKinsey.

Your professionalism will be conveyed throughout your company. As it grows, every employee will look to you for leadership. If you cheat customers, they will too. If you use corporate supplies for personal use, your employees will too. If you bill customers for more than they receive, so too will your employees. This is no way to run a business, and those that do so are doomed to fail.

Let's imagine a car dealership owner who holds firm in the belief that all women know absolutely nothing about the mechanical workings of automobiles. To him, female customers are fair game for his dishonest business policy. Women are never treated with respect when they arrive at the dealership. If they pull in for a squeaky wheel, they pull out with a bill for a new radiator hose, oil and transmission fluid, none of which was needed. For good measure, the dealership owner probably adds a warning that they best return to him later that week for new brake pads before they fail and the car smashes into a tree. Mr. Auto Dealer thinks he is doing great business because he is making lots of money servicing customers for unnecessary repairs. But he is *not* doing *good* business. For one thing, he is totally wrong to assume that all women know nothing about cars. Many will complain to all of their friends about how the dealership is nothing but a rip-off. Pretty soon, the whole neighborhood will know about the dealership's shady dealings and people will buy their cars elsewhere. The dealership has earned the reputation it deserves and the owner has sacrificed years of business for dishonest profit in the short run.

One of the German dealerships in my area has just such a reputation, and even though we like the automaker's products we won't buy one because of the dealer. As a businessperson, you can *never* afford to tarnish your reputation. You will get much further in business if you are painstakingly honest and hold professionalism to the highest standard. Never sacrifice your future for a quick buck. Stay true to yourself and true to your customers. Be professional and become successful

You Must Deliver! No Excuses Allowed!

Along with professionalism, it is always important to make sure that your business *can* and *will* live up to its promises. It has to have integrity. Sooner or later, you will be talking to someone who is interested in your product. If you have a potential customer on the telephone, pin her down to determine what it will take to earn her business. If you remember to ask the right questions and listen carefully to the answers, you will hit pay dirt. You will reach someone who answers with "Yes, I am unhappy with the product I already use," and they are interested in either talking with you in person or ordering your product right then and there. When this happens, you must be prepared for it. From the first phone call you make, you must be ready to deliver. If a customer asks for you to see him tomorrow, you must go. If they want the product tomorrow, you make sure that they get it. You are just starting out and you must work faster, smarter, and harder than the competition. You'll do this for two reasons. The first is that you must become successful, and, as I have stressed previously, the only way you'll be successful is through hard work, professionalism, and integrity. Secondly, your prospects will recognize your commitment to excellence and will likely reward you for what they perceive as your good efforts. Most of your competition has been doing the same job for years and they have gotten lackadaisical. Their fire isn't burning as hot as it once was. They rarely jump in the car and rush over to help a client, instead scheduling a meeting for tomorrow or next Tuesday. There are no excuses as to why you can't get to your customer. If your car is in the service station, rent a car or take a taxi. If your kids are sick, get someone to watch them — your spouse, your mom, mother-in-law, or babysitter. You can't afford to lose this first order! If you do, you have probably lost a customer forever.

When I was in college, my friend Salvatore Midolo and I decided to start a delivery business for a local pizza shop that did not deliver. We perceived a need, and after quizzing a couple dozen students if they'd be interested in getting pizza delivered to the dorm, found there was a huge market for pizza delivery on campus. We believed we could build a solid, repeat business that would put money in our pockets to buy textbooks, fund our spring break excursion, and provide a great means to meet girls. Little did we realize but we were in fact becoming manufacturer's reps for Matso's Pizza. We passed fliers around campus and the calls started coming in. Of course, it helped that Sal was really good looking and the women on campus would swoon whenever he knocked on their door (you have to have a marketing hook and Sal was mine). We were not prepared for the overwhelmingly positive response we received. We had to deliver dozens of pizzas each night and we ran our butts off from dorm to dorm, up and down stairs, all across campus. It was exhausting. Our goal of making a delivery within 30 minutes soon slipped to within 45 minutes, then to 60 minutes. By this time the pizzas were getting cold and our customer base was getting frustrated. "If Dominos can deliver in 30 minutes, why can't you guys?" we'd hear. We had a wonderful business opportunity with a captive audience, but we had not figured out our distribution process, and in the end we couldn't keep up with the orders. It was a failure. The same can be said for you and your business. If you are not prepared to react to customer demand, you may lose everything. Does this mean you have to hire a fleet of trucks? No. But you do have to be aware that the customer comes first and if your customer base grows and you are making a profit, you may have to hire someone to help you. It's always good to have a new hire in mind, but don't make that commitment until you are 100% positive that you can afford it and that it is absolutely needed.

Here's another story of how an opportunity arose in another one of my business ventures.

A few years after I got my start in advertising, I found myself in the position of receiving an order from a customer who needed an advertisement designed and written for submission to a publication the very next day. The day after would not do, it *absolutely had* to be tomorrow. I had other work in progress and my plate was nearly full, but the customer was willing to pay me extra to meet the deadline, if they could have their ad completed by the close of business the next day. If I missed the deadline they wouldn't pay me and I'd never see another penny of their money. Previously, I had succeeded in offering this client the best price, availability and service. That's what hooked him as a client. But now I was faced with the challenge of living up to my promises on a very tight deadline. My professionalism and integrity were at stake.

This was in the days before PCs and Macs, Adobe Photoshop and InDesign, digital cameras, and all the other great tools we now have that allow advertising agencies to quickly generate and deliver ads in a matter of hours instead of days.

After I got off the telephone, I called my typesetter and explained my predicament. Within 15 minutes I was on my way to her office to oversee typesetting the text of the ad. I have always kept a little pocket tape recorder handy to take notes, and used it to draft the copy for the ad while driving down the road. Luckily, my typesetter was available, but if she weren't, I would have sped to another typesetter further up the road. While she set the type, I called a local photographer whom I had often worked with and scheduled a photo session for 7 pm that night. He'd develop the photos that night and have them to me by 8 am the next morning. My typesetting was ready by 5 pm, so between 5 pm and 6:30 pm I mocked up the ad. I called the client and told them

I'd have something in their hands before 7 pm. I faxed the completed copy and mockup to the client around 6:30 pm, and they called me at the photo studio just after 8 pm to make two small changes. I had built enough trust with the client that a second viewing of the ad wouldn't be necessary as long as I made the two changes. I called my typesetter and she made the changes, then met me at the photo studio to give me the new type. It was just after 9 pm when I the completed the layout. All I needed was a good photograph to insert and then get color separations done in time to deliver the ad to the magazine. I had called my color separator and arranged to bring him the artwork and photograph by 9 am the next morning, and he promised me that four-color film would be ready by noon. I begged and pleaded for him to have it by 11 am. At 11 o'clock I sat in his office waiting on the film. I got it about 20 minutes later, jumped in my car, and drove four and a half hours to the magazine to deliver the finished ad to the publisher. I must have pushed my little Honda Prelude to the limit on that drive, collecting a speeding ticket from a vigilant Pennsylvania State Trooper, and arrived 35 minutes before the deadline. I turned around, drove home and was in bed by midnight.

Whew!

Two whirlwind days resulted in my client's ad making it into the publication on time. He paid me double the going rate. I paid my suppliers their invoices within 10 days. They helped me in a time of need, and I rewarded them with prompt payment of their bill plus a gift certificate for two to Cliffside, one of Pittsburgh's best restaurants, all enclosed in a handwritten thank you note. I ran into the owner of the color separation firm several years later and he told me that he never forgot that handwritten thank you note and gift certificate. He said it showed how professional my firm was.

Find Suppliers Who Can be Flexible When You're in a Time Crunch

You too will need to have at least two back-up manufacturers and suppliers, since it is bad business to have to call a customer and tell them you can't deliver because you are out of stock or your suppliers can't supply products to you. Don't *ever* let that happen. I always explain to my suppliers that there may be times when last minute-jobs will come in, and if they're willing to bend over for those, I'll be loyal to them. The arrangement works because both parties win. Seek out the same type of suppliers. You will find that most business owners want to make money and will work with you in time of need to solve your customer issues. That doesn't mean you can take advantage of them, but it does mean that if they value your business, they will work with you to make sure you succeed. For when you succeed, they succeed.

No matter what it takes: driving all night, collecting speeding tickets, begging and pleading with suppliers, you must live up to your promises of *price, availability and service*. If you remember that you can never let a customer down, your business will succeed. Remain professional, act with integrity, don't promise what you can't deliver, and you will be rewarded with a successful business.

What Did You Learn?

1. Operating your business with professionalism is imperative to building trusting relationships with customers and suppliers.
2. Never compromise your integrity. If you say you'll do something, do it. If you promise a customer you'll deliver, then deliver.
3. Be willing to go the extra mile for your customer even if it

means working round the clock, and show your gratitude to the suppliers who are also willing to go that extra mile on your behalf.

4. Identify at least two additional sources for your product so that if your primary supplier fails you have backup avenues to fulfill customer orders.

CHAPTER 19

Yes You Can: Stay Focused

The temptations of becoming successful.

NOW THAT YOU have read the first seventeen chapters of this book, you know all you need to know about becoming a successful entrepreneur. Really! It's true. You have learned that it is a myth that it takes money to make money; that only those with proper family ties or other connections and degrees from the Ivy League schools can make it; or that all it takes is luck to succeed. You've learned that people like Tamara Johnson, born and raised in poverty, unwed with two kids, and facing a life of uncertainty, turned her life around to join the top 5% of all U.S. wage earners. You've learned the importance of motivation, ambition, self-improvement, professionalism, and integrity. You've learned which traits make a good entrepreneur or employee and which ones constitute a bad entrepreneur or employee.

Perhaps you still question whether you can make your life successful.

If you stop dwelling on your lack of luck, family ties, old-boy networks, and money and take a positive attitude toward yourself and your abilities, you can become a success. If you sit around moaning about the things that you don't have or the people you don't know, then you are just feeling sorry for yourself and wasting your time. That kind of woe-is-me attitude will get you nowhere. There are plenty "if only I had blah-blah-blah" people in the world. It's easy to give up and be negative toward life. It's easy to nestle into that 9-to-5 routine and spend your life dreaming about other people's success stories. But that kind of thinking has nothing to do with the entrepreneur. The entrepreneur is never satisfied with a humdrum, routine existence. And no matter how successful he or she is, the entrepreneur *never* stops striving to reach his or her goals.

Throughout this book, I suggest many different types of traits that are shared by those who have risen to the top, but for now, I want to tell you what it is not. It is not greed for money or material gain. Unfortunately, much business philosophy revolves around making money no matter what the price. Honesty, professionalism, integrity, quality workmanship and the like are all too often sacrificed as the race for the almighty dollar supersedes all else. Of course money is great. I love money! But you must never fall into the trap of thinking that money is the only thing that matters. What really matters, more so than money, is knowing that you have turned your personal resources into a successful entrepreneurial effort. This sense of accomplishment is worth more than any check someone will write you. You might make more money in the short run with unethical business practices, but ultimately, you will lose. Pride is a main component of the spirit of the entrepreneur, but if you cheat your customers you'll never feel pride, only shame. Cheating customers is not an accomplishment. An accomplishment is serving customers fairly, honestly and ethically, and watching them reward you with their continued business.

Don't Let Money Ruin Your Business—Or You!

You will face certain dangers as your business becomes more and more successful. Ironically, the biggest danger is that you will now be making money. It's a cliché, but money often does change people. When Lycos went public and employees were sitting on stock options worth tens of thousands of dollars, if not millions, many of them spent more time watching the stock ticker than doing their job. I used to tell people, "do a great job and the stock will take care of itself." If you watch how much you are worth and only react to it when it drops, it's too late. The accumulation of money, especially if it is sudden, changes both the person who has the money and those around him who see that he has it.

An acquaintance of mine started a high tech company in the late 1990s. With the help of 12 employees and angel investors, he built it into a firm that was likely to become profitable within two years and would have been a good IPO or acquisition candidate. Unfortunately, the venture capitalists and angel investors came in and wrote a check for over $7 million for part of the company. All of a sudden, the managers moved the company into expensive office space, installed a fabulous built-in kitchen, a gym and locker rooms, began leasing cars, bought $60,000 worth of conference room furniture, a 42" plasma television, and installed one of the biggest fish tanks I've ever seen. During all this exposure to money, they forgot about their business. Their deep pockets made them forget what it was like to be scrappy and work hard for their next dollar. They got fat and lazy. Today, the company is a bust, a tragic and unnecessary victim of mismanagement. It is one of many such casualties from the 1990s. Did these managers need an MBA to know what they were doing wrong? No. They simply forgot that they were in business to sell products, not to sit in the lap of luxury. Having money can ruin a business just as easily as it can make it a success.

The most dangerous person to change now that you are succeeding is, of course, you. Earning money cannot mean that you toss all caution to the wind or let your head swell. If you were eating lunch at Subway prior to making money, don't feel that you have to start eating at a five-star restaurant. I've seen too many people begin to believe that where you eat, what you drive, what watch you wear, or what neighborhood you live in, defines you. It doesn't. If you let material things take precedence in your life, you will undoubtedly fall flat on your face. Carelessness, cockiness, inflated self-importance and living for the status quo are sure ways to destroy the spirit that brought you success. Just like in the beginning, common sense must dictate what to buy, when and where to buy it, and even whether or not it is wise to buy at all.

You will be faced with many temptations. Some are personal and some relate to business. You are going to make mistakes, but you will make far fewer of them if you are aware of the dangers ahead. Since you are, and will always be, your most important resource, you must realize the temptations that lurk out in the world as you become more and more successful in business and life.

Be Wary of Developing a Status-Oriented Lifestyle

The notion of success is often wrongly defined by showy material acquisitions, hobbies, clubs and exotic travel experiences. Trust me, I know. I spent two years living the high life in the Upper East Side of New York City. I had it all: a luxury condominium on the Upper East Side, nightly dinners with the "in crowd," first class travel, and a $90,000 sports car sitting in a $400 a month parking space. I wore

Brioni and Zegna suits, custom made dress shirts, and the finest Italian dress shoes. I had so many material possessions that I must surely have been viewed as a huge success. But I wasn't truly happy. All these material possessions gave me the appearance of success, but I didn't feel as if they truly represented who I was. Truth be told, I'm a blue jeans and T-shirt kind of guy and putting $2,000 worth of clothes on each day just didn't jibe with my inner self. I know dozens of successful entrepreneurs who feel the same way, and what took us years to realize, you have just learned in a few sentences.

It wasn't until years later that I understood that all the material possessions don't mean a thing if you can't wake up each morning and be happy and content with the person you've become. I sold the sports car and the suits were given to charity as I now prefer jeans, a sports shirt, and a pair of comfortable shoes. I donated the Rolex to a Goodwill auction a few years ago and I'd rather eat dinner with my family and friends at Opie's BBQ in rural Spicewood, Texas than some schmaltzy, trendy restaurant while hoping to "be seen." The true spirit of the entrepreneur comes from the joy of doing, and it is not exemplified by forms of compensation, rewards, or creating the impression of being successful and wealthy.

Americans are mystified by great wealth and have crazy expectations of what defines it. For the most part, society defines wealth by material standards such as automobiles, swimming pools, expensive clothing and other baubles. Just look at the TV shows highlighting celebrities and their fancy homes. It's all about possessions; about the bling. Yet my experience tells me that most times, the person with the most baubles is not the richest kid on the block, but the one most in debt. I've worked with too many people who felt they had to own a BMW or Mercedes, dress in expensive Italian clothing, and belong to the country club in order to appear more successful than they are. At the same time, I know several multi-millionaires who wear Wrangler jeans and drive 10 year-old cars. Falling into the trap of consumerism is the first danger to watch for as your own monetary wealth increases.

Don't get me wrong; I am not against enjoying the finer things in life, but making a big show of material wealth is not a measure of success. Owning a Rolls Royce may give you a wonderful feeling of self-worth, but it is not an accomplishment in itself. The Rolls Royce will eventually stop running, but your sense of personal accomplishment never has to end. If you feel that by owning a Rolls Royce you have made it to the top, then you've lost your spirit. There is no top and the entrepreneur knows it. You cannot define your success by material possessions. There is always more. Very often, people with misguided goals find that they're unhappy, even with a garage full of Rolls Royce automobiles. I've concurrently owned a home in Texas, a condo in New York City, and a townhouse in Florida and can tell you that I never felt settled. So many times I'd ask, "Where is that thing?" and it was at another home. This became so frustrating that I sold everything and simplified my life into one location. What a relief that has been! If you think you are only successful if you own two or three homes, then your definition of success is too rooted in material possessions. You may eventually own all the homes you want, but I'll bet you'll still feel empty inside if you don't fulfill your life's work.

When I was in Aspen, Colorado a few years ago I had a conversation with the actor Kevin Costner whose kids were golfing at Maroon Creek Country Club that day. I happened to be sitting at the bar and Kevin walked in and sat down next to me. After talking about films, Aspen, beavers, and a host of other topics, I asked him what made him the happiest. His answer wasn't a fancy car, the jet set lifestyle, or the awards and accolades. He said what made him happiest was being at home, spending time with his kids and girlfriend (who is now his wife). Here is a guy who has tasted success throughout his career with films like *Dances With Wolves, The Bodyguard, JFK, Tin Cup, Field of Dreams,* and *Bull Durham,* and yet the thing that made him happiest had nothing to do with money and everything to do with family.

If you keep a firm grip on the true meaning of success, you will gain enormous satisfaction just by doing and not only by having. Reward yourself with a nice car if you must, but always remember that it is only a by-product of your success and not a definition of that success. Satisfaction comes from within, not from a department store, automobile showroom, jewelry shop, or real estate agent's office.

Don't Sacrifice Your Business for Your Family or Vice-Versa

In keeping with the theme of personal dangers, one must never forget the importance of being influenced by friends or loved ones, particularly by that all-important person, the *spouse*. My Grandfather used to say, "Marriage is like a three ring circus: first comes the engagement ring; then the wedding ring; and then the suffering." He was happily and lovingly married for over 60 years. All kidding aside, marriage can be a highly rewarding relationship, but one must never allow one's partner to determine the goals of the entrepreneur. The ideal mate for the entrepreneur is one who shares the entrepreneurial spirit, not the country club spouse. Your husband or wife may be the closest person to you, but your marriage is destructive if you find yourself living only to pay for the lifestyle chosen by your spouse and/or children. There is too much pressure on you if your family is living beyond its means and always lining up to you with palms extended. Earning a successful income means that one can have the better things in life. However, you are in big trouble if you are saddled with a spouse that defines your success only in terms of monetary gain. Your business will then be sacrificed to meet the needs of your family. Don't get yourself in a hole because you spend too much on the spouse and kids. If you do, you will soon find yourself borrowing from your business and that is a destined road to failure. Your business exists because it is the means to your goal. You haven't gone through the pains of starting the company to become a slave to paying the bills for your family's expectations. Your spouse must also understand that the symbols of success are not material possessions but finding happiness in your work and being proud of what you do. I know many people living in $500,000 to $2,000,000 homes, driving expensive automobiles. Many of these luxurious homes are filled with cheap, tacky furniture because the owners are so house-poor they cannot afford anything beyond their mortgage and car payments. You will be much happier if you and your loved one have the same material wants and needs and focus on what can make you comfortable, instead of what will make you *appear* successful.

On the flip side of this, it isn't really fair to put your home up as collateral to fund your business. To do so is to ask your spouse to risk a roof over their head for a business to which they may not be 100% committed. If you think your spouse bugs you now about business, imagine having your most valuable asset on the line. The tension this will create will distract both of you from the important things that must be accomplished in life. Love blossoms best when a man and woman respect each other. If one spouse's actions are driving a company into the ground and the other sees their home being foreclosed, then respect will quickly vanish, likely followed by love and ultimately, the marriage.

Enjoy the benefits of your success, but never think that money is the be all and end all. It is true that some of the best things in life are free, but there are quite a few of them that do cost money. Develop healthy priorities and always remember that these finer things are but a partial reward for your efforts. Never lose sight of your real goals. The only thing that can interfere with your goals is death, and hopefully one day that, too, will be negotiable.

Throughout your life, you will continuously be challenged to keep your personal life in order. The more organized you keep your life outside of business, the more smoothly your business career will run

.

Keep Your Personal Finances Organized

I once had an employee who paid her bills the day after they came in. It used to drive me nuts to see her spend every other day's lunch hour writing checks. I couldn't understand why she wouldn't just pay her bills on the 20th of the month, five days before they were due. She said she couldn't stand the thought of having an outstanding bill and felt a need to pay them immediately. Only after I explained to her how much interest she lost each month by paying her bills in full early and not taking advantage of the grace period, and also how much easier it was to pay everything at one time, did she change her ways. Along the line, I helped her set up an IRA, a money market account, and showed her the importance of securing life insurance early in her life. I ran into her about four years later, and one of the first things she said to me was how grateful she was that I helped her get her personal life in order. She couldn't believe how much time she wasted each month writing out checks every other day. She now has her priorities right and focuses on making herself a successful person in her home life and job. She no longer lets little things like paying the bills interfere with her bigger goal of being happy and unstressed. If you need help getting your household finances in order, seek it out. Ask a friend or your tax preparer to assist you in creating a budget. Start using software to track and pay expenses. You need to be able to focus on your business, and straightening out your personal finances will give you the peace of mind to do so.

Maintain Control Over Your Business

Once your business is making money, there are myriad ways in which you can find yourself losing control over both your money and your business. The small business owner should never forget that he or she is just that: SMALL. As you grow, those who want to convince you that you alone cannot run your business will no doubt approach you. You'll hear this from attorneys, accountants, and any person whose title contains the word "consultant." It might make your chest swell with pride to imagine that such esteemed individuals deem little ol' you worthy of their services. You may get giddy and light-headed at your own importance when these people flatter you in their attempts at selling what are usually unnecessary and over-priced services. Lawyers and accountants do fulfill a purpose, but don't forget that they exist only to help you when you truly need their assistance. An attorney or accountant should never know more about your business than you do. If you aren't careful, you could find yourself giving over your control of the company to strangers.

The success of people in service industries such as legal and accounting depends a great deal on how well they succeed at convincing you that you need them 24 hours a day. I really can't knock them for it, as they are only trying to compete in the free enterprise system, and their choice of profession is what is leading them to reach their own goals and definition of success. But just like making purchase decisions about anything else, you must follow the "buyer beware" policy when seeking the advice of any business professional.

Here are some key questions to ask yourself over and over again: How will this service benefit my company and me? Are these people *really* able to do more for me than I can do for myself? Will I be able to make more money with the advice that these professionals give me? It has always been my experience that when asking these fundamental questions, you will most often discover that you really do not need as much outside help as others will claim. Twenty years ago it was often necessary to pay $100 an hour for professional services. In 1989 it cost $1,600 to form a corporation through a law firm. Today you can form a corporation online in less than 30 minutes and for under $400. You can file quarterly taxes online. You can manage the entire financial side of your business with programs like QuickBooks or Peachtree Accounting. You can purchase easy-to-use legal forms online or on CD-ROM at OfficeMax, Staples or Office Depot. You can even buy inexpensive software that will help you write a business plan, devise a marketing program, or manage employees. Sometimes, whether by stupidity, human error or accident, you will need professional help, but remember, you and you alone are the boss and this must never change. It is your company and you must remain in control.

When you do require the services of accountants, lawyers or other professionals, don't become dependent on the advice of anyone but yourself. People don't deliberately give lousy advice, but sometimes that is what you get. Use your best judgment to make the final determination if action is needed. My point is not to claim that attorneys and such are liars or cheats, but in any business, it is fundamental that you put absolute trust in no one but yourself.

I've been managing director of a management consulting business, so I understand the role consultants play. At Interminds, we had four guiding principles. They included: 1) Professionalism and integrity is the most important part of our business. Without it we cannot be viewed as impartial professionals who are seeking answers for our clients' toughest problems. 2) We will not undertake work for a company if we believe we bring no value to the engagement. 3) We will only engage in projects that are clearly defined in scope, timeline, and cost. 4) Because we may work for similar clients, client confidentiality must be upheld at all times, and no scent of impropriety must ever be suspected by clients or employees. These principles form the core of the business. We don't stray from them, and if we are asked to do so we politely decline.

There are many exceptional consulting firms in the world: McKinsey & Company, Boston Consulting Group, Bain & Company, Booz Allen Hamilton, and Mercer, to name a few. These firms wouldn't be where they are today if they cheated customers. Smaller firms like Interminds and our competitors do well to emulate what the larger firms have done to create professional practices. Even so, always remember that it is up to you to determine what type of consultants you want to use, if any, and what the parameters of any consulting engagement include.

I've seen a fair share of proposals from my competitors where they pressure business owners to sign an engagement that is not clearly defined either in scope or time. Only later does the business owner find that the consultants are in no rush to complete the project because they're earning $10,000, $30,000, or more each month. Some consultants will purposefully delay completing projects if they feel they can stretch it out into one more pay period. Other consultants will take on a project, learn as much about the inner workings of a company, and then when the project is complete, take that knowledge to a competitor and pitch them on an engagement. Still others have gone into clients and walked out with employees, scalping from the very people they are supposed to be helping.

Giving away too much control to others, regardless of their credentials, means that you put yourself further away from the heart of your business. For your business to succeed, it needs your firm hand to guide it. Be aware of all that is going on in your company. Not only does this make for a more efficient and better business in the short-run, but it saves you from the grief of having to pick up the pieces from a hopelessly lost puzzle should someone else make a mistake. Don't fool yourself into thinking that you need large payroll departments, purchasing agents or financial analysts to keep the business operating at a profit. If you reduce your paperwork to the minimum needed for smooth operation, you will find that you can keep in close contact with all facets of your business. Keep things as simple as possible, and one step to take in doing so is to realize that for the most part, assistants to this or that spend an awful lot of time on self-preservation. That is, the minute you hire a fleet of professionals, you can be sure that these people will do all that they can to create more and more work just to ensure that they keep their jobs. Employees who just agree with you all the time are redundant. Why do you need them? If you really think about it, you alone can do what is needed to run your business with a minimum of wasted time and a lot less useless paperwork.

As a small business owner, you should be able to manage all the billing and tax requirements of your business if you invest in a good computer and a good accounting program. If you dedicate one full week to learning the software, you will be able to operate it and generate most any report you may need. As your business grows, your time may be consumed with customers, prospects and working on new product lines. At this point you may wish to hire someone to handle the finances of your company. Read this carefully: *This may be the most important hire you ever make.* Let me put it another way. If you were to hire someone to write all your personal bills and you knew they'd have access to your personal checking accounts and credit cards, what type of person would you hire? It had better be someone you trust implicitly. If you have to hire someone as the result of a want ad, get a minimum of 10 references and check each and every one. You will entrust someone to manage your cash flow, your profits, your paycheck, and the financial security of your company. Be aware and beware.

Play it Safe: Keep Inventory and Expenses to a Minimum

Another temptation small business owners often succumb to is the ridiculous notion that one must increase inventory to the bursting point if one is to look successful. No one should get caught up in the trap of carrying hundreds or thousands of different items and automatically increasing your payroll and overhead costs because of it. Sure, it looks like you have a ton of products, but you will be scrambling each day to keep your business afloat. If you go down this path, I can almost assure you that you will end up with a storage room full of useless junk that isn't moving and probably won't. Only stock the items that you know will sell. The customer is only interested in what he wants to buy and is not all that impressed by huge storehouses of items he doesn't particularly care about. If he wants that, he'll go to Sam's Club or Costco. Focus on getting the products your customers want to them in a speedy amount of time, at a reasonable and fair price, and you will have all the inventory that you will ever need.

Another danger that you will encounter concerns changes in the marketplace and our ever-evolving global economy. Not even the head of the Federal Reserve can accurately predict the future, but one of the forty different hats the successful entrepreneur must wear is that of the economic forecaster. It isn't easy to do, but you must be able to sustain yourself through *any* unforeseen economic tragedy, loss of a customer, recessions, or whatever obstacle may come your way. The best assurance that you can weather any storm is to preserve your equity. Keep costs at a minimum, reduce that inventory, and never, never, *never* over-commit your equity. A good example of businesses that made these types of mistakes are those formerly involved in the Internet Service Provider (ISP) industry. Many of these ISPs collapsed entirely because they failed to admit that dial-up Internet access was dying and the large online providers like AOL, Earthlink, MSN, and RoadRunner were eating everyone's lunch. They were acting as if the reign of small ISPs would go on forever. In the end, they were left with tons of equipment, payments to make on servers, computers and other hardware and no customers. It didn't take a genius to see what was coming. But the failure to prepare for a changing information access market resulted in the bankruptcy of many Internet Service Providers. The bottom line is, cash is king. Cash is the only liquid asset you'll need to stay afloat in tough times. Inventory, be it of a personal or business nature, has little or no value unless you can find a buyer.

The buyer, not the seller, sets the value of a good or service. That is an important fact of business to understand. In my spare time I like to build violins. If I had my druthers my violins would sell for $25,000 a piece, but I don't set the prices on my instruments. I ask the person playing it to tell me what he or she believes it is worth or I sell through music stores that help assess the value. Usually, they sell for $5,000 to $8,000 (which in reality is a very fair price for buyer and seller). Your business has a value only if you can find a buyer. Remember the story of Mr. Smalis and his quest to pay less for a Coleman lamp? The value he placed on that lamp was less than the retail price; however, the storeowner, wanting to make a sale, reduced the price to that expected and acceptable to the buyer.

In summary, the most important things I can say to you are the following: trust no one but yourself, and preserve your equity. Don't let others tell you to grow, expand, produce, sell or buy. You can take their recommendation under advisement, but you must make the decision to grow, and you should only do so if you feel it helps you get closer to your goal. Use your own judgment about making decisions. Growth in business is great, but growth should mean growth in profits and not just bigger inventory, office space, more employees or more advisors. If you can double your sales without increasing the cost of operating your business, you are on the right path. If not, you are in danger of negative growth and possibly even bankruptcy. Stay alert to the dangers ahead and you will be prepared when they arrive, know how to deal with them, and ultimately, you will become much more successful and knowledgeable as a result of your preparation.

What Did You Learn?

1. Successful people share many traits, but stealing, cheating, and falling prey to the trappings of money are not among them.
2. Don't let newfound success get in the way of achieving future successes.
3. Since it is your business you are starting, you must stay in control and make the important decisions. Lawyers, accountants, and other consultants can lend their advice, but only you should make the final decisions.
4. Other key points: Hire someone you trust implicitly to handle your finances; keep your inventory at levels to suit only your immediate needs; and preserve your equity at all costs.

CHAPTER 20

Yes You Can: Take Time To Laugh

You should never take yourself too seriously.

IN CASE YOU think you might not be smart enough to run your own business, here are some examples of how stupid many people must be. Since I mentioned lawyers in the last chapter, I thought it would be a good time to step back and see some of the results of their work. Over the years I have been astonished by the lengths our litigious society goes to protect consumers from their own stupidity. In case you needed further proof that the human race is doomed through stupidity, here are some actual label instructions on consumer goods followed by my personal thoughts:

1. On a hairdryer: "Do not use while sleeping."

    [Gee, that's the only time I have to work on my hair.]

2. On a bag of corn chips: "You could be winner! No purchase necessary. Details inside."

[Uh.....]

3. On a bar of soap: "Directions: Use like regular soap."

[Oh, that explains everything.]

4. On boxes of frozen dinners: "Serving suggestion: Defrost."

[But it's just a suggestion.]

5. On a box of Tiramisu dessert (printed on the bottom of box): "Do not turn upside down."

[Oops, too late!]

6. On a box of bread pudding: "Product will be hot after heating."

[As sure as night follows the day.]

7. On packaging for an iron: "Do not iron clothes on body."

[But wouldn't this save time?]

8. On a bottle of children's cough medicine: "Do not drive or operate machinery after taking this medication."

[We could do a lot to reduce the rate of construction accidents if we could just get those 4-year-olds with head-colds off the forklifts.]

9. On a bottle of sleep aid: "Warning: May cause drowsiness."

[One would hope!]

10. On most brands of Christmas lights: "For indoor or outdoor use only."

[As opposed to what?]

11. On a Japanese food processor: "Not to be used for the other use."

[I have to admit, I'm curious.]

12. On a can of peanuts: "Warning: Contains nuts."

[Cans of peanuts now found to contain actual nuts!]

13. On an airline's packet of nuts: "Instructions: open packet, eat nuts."

[I hope their pilots are better trained.]

14. On a bottle of shampoo for dogs: "Caution: The contents of this bottle should not be fed to fish."

[And don't bathe your puppy in fish food.]

15. On a can of self-defense pepper spray: "May irritate eyes."

[Isn't that the purpose?]

14. In the manual for a microwave oven: "Do not use for drying pets."

[I kid you not: I know someone who tried to dry their kid's pet hamster that way. What a mess!]

15. On a case of hammers: "Caution: May be harmful if swallowed."

[I don't even want to know how they came to that conclusion.]

16. Instructions on an electric coffee pot: "The appliance is switched on by setting the on/off switch to the 'on' position."

[So that's how you get it to work.]

17. On a child's Superman costume: "Wearing of this garment does not enable you to fly."

[I don't blame the company. I blame parents for this one.]

What Did You Learn?

1. Are people really this stupid? Apparently some must be, otherwise we wouldn't have warnings like these. Now imagine how successful you will be if even 20% of the population is as dumb as these manufacturers and their legal counsels would suggest they are. This means you're really only competing with 80% of the population. Starting your own business is sounding better and better, isn't it?

CHAPTER 21

Yes You Can: Refuse To Retire

Getting high on enthusiasm and creativity
is a lifelong journey.

A S I HAVE INDICATED in the preceding chapters, there is truly no end to the success of an energetic, self-motivated and creative individual. It is possible to take an idea, mold it, plan it and turn that bright idea into a million-dollar business. Once this has been done, the creator can either take the money and run or continue to develop new ideas and try to turn them into real successes. I have known several people who have had one successful run after another. When I ask them their secret, they often say they focus on a niche, and then through sheer enthusiasm become determined to own that segment.

Nolan Bushnel hit it big as the founder of video game company Atari. Years later he scored again as the founder of restaurant chain Chuck E. Cheese. Then he started a new company called uWink, which offered an entirely new venue in entertainment and restaurants. While seemingly vastly different, each company focused on a similar business model and audience: entertaining young people. Nolan could have retired long ago, but he keeps coming up with new ideas to pursue.

When I was a young boy in Junior Achievement, our team built and sold jumper cables as our business. We chose this partly because one of my Junior Achievement teammates, Nick, knew a few things about electricity and wiring. Thirty years later, Nick was still focused on electricity, running a very successful lighting and electric business. It is now one of the largest in the state, with over 130 employees and $5 million in inventory. He took his enthusiasm for energy going across copper wire and made a career out of it by focusing on a niche market.

Five years ago, I spent an afternoon golfing with a gentleman named Gene, who during his career, founded one of the largest real estate companies in America, owned an aircraft manufacturing company, and eventually a chain of very successful restaurants. His secret: an uncanny ability to get high on the enthusiasm surrounding building a winning business in niches where he can apply his skills.

Of the founding members of Lycos' management team, none of us have retired. We're all working on new projects that are very different from Internet search technology. Bob Davis is a venture capitalist. Ben Bassi runs a company in the information technology and e-commerce space. I pursue multiple business opportunities each year, and launched Corvosi, a sports sponsorship firm with clients that include Suzuki, Rahal Letterman Racing, Michael Jordan Motorsports and others. And I still find time to dedicate to preserving the strings industry as chairman of The Amati Foundation, an organization I founded to expose children and teens to classical music, preserve rare violins, and help support violin makers, orchestras, and musicians.

You can develop the positive, enthusiastic attitude that will jumpstart your successful career and carry you from one successful venture to another. It is a myth that everyone reaches a point where it seems necessary to retire. There is more in life than a Social Security check at the end of each month. It is up to you to decide what you want to do with your life, especially if you have already reached some of your goals and are nearing the traditional "retirement" years. There is no reason why you can't devote your whole lifetime to an ever-changing arena of plans, schemes and dreams.

John Reed founded Sterling Radiator Company in 1946, and today, the firm known as Mestek is still run by Mr. Reed. In July 2005, the Boston Business Journal wrote that Mr. Reed, at age 89 and the oldest CEO of a NYSE listed company, was taking the company private with no intention of retiring any time soon.

If you looked at my résumé from a date of employment standpoint, you'd think I couldn't hold a job for more than a couple years. But if you read more carefully, you'll realize that since graduating from college I have been involved in launching more than 20 companies, including two that are publicly held. I've been exposed to all types of different business situations; learned to excel at running rapid-growth startups, where devising a creative business strategy and getting the most from people is critical to success; and managed to leverage each success or failure into a formula to create the next success. You'd also see that I started Interminds in 1998 and have created two spin-offs from that firm. You see, I get high on starting companies. I get high when I am able to use my creative side to solve problems. I get high when I see my employees reach their goals. I get high creating entrepreneurial environments where employees excel and see their dreams come true. I get high on telling you that you too can get high on your own enthusiasm for as long as you live! I hope, like John Reed, that I'm starting companies or helping companies excel when I'm 89.

Enthusiasm for your life's work never needs to end. I once watched

Ryan Homes founder Ed Ryan drive nails into the fencing on his farm. He made a game of it, seeing how many times it would take to sink the nail into the 2x6 boards that he and his farm manager were installing. Mr. Ryan, then in his mid-60s, drove almost all of the nails fully into the boards with only two hits of his hammer. Even after all the years of homebuilding, his enthusiasm and love of building things never waned. What I learned that day from Mr. Ryan was that enthusiasm and love of your craft exists not only in bodies that have lived for twenty years but also in those that have lived for sixty, eighty, or even one hundred.

William Hilton is a classically trained violinist from West Palm Beach, Florida. He runs a repair shop and holds a full schedule of violin lessons each week, primarily for younger students but also for more mature students. He is in his mid-80s and shows no sign of slowing down. He is high on life and enthusiastic about what he sees in his young students.

I ran into Johnny Carson at the Beverly Hills Tennis Club when I was in college. Having no fear of hearing the word "no" I walked right up to him and introduced myself. We spent 20 minutes talking. Carson was the host of *The Tonight Show* from 1962 to 1992, a phenomenal 30-year career where his preeminence in late night television was often challenged but never matched. 50 million people tuned in to his last telecast, proving once and for all that he truly was the King of Late Night. When I met him, he was in his 70s, I asked him what made him stay in his role so long? He replied that he never felt his age was a factor in how long he should stay on television. He said as long as his health was good and he was doing new things, he didn't see a need to retire.

Joe Hardy, the founder of 84 Lumber Company, could have retired after reaching 400 stores. Instead, when he handed the reins over to his daughter, he gave rebirth to his entrepreneurship and opened a restaurant, and then built an exclusive country club and resort called Nemacolin Woodlands, which now hosts one of the Professional Golf Association's leading competitions. What does running a successful lumber company restaurant and country club have in common? I have no idea. But Joe never stops creating. Neither should you.

Keeping It All in the Family

One of the benefits of running your own business for a lifetime is the opportunity to leave it to your children. For a relatively young country, America has incredible success stories when it comes to family-owned businesses that have passed from generation to generation. These companies prove that you can build a business that you can be involved with your entire life, then leave them to your children to continue on. At the top of my list of favorites are four companies still operating to this day. The first is the Zildjian Cymbal Company, started in 1623. This cymbal manufacturing firm was founded 14 generations ago by an alchemist named Avedis who was giving the name Zildjian by the Constantinople sultan. The family arrived in the U.S. in 1929 when Avedis Zildjian III established the firm in Massachusetts. Today, his granddaughter Craigie Zildjian serves as CEO.

The second is Tuttle Farm, started around 1638. The founder, John Tuttle, left England in 1635 and survived a shipwreck off the Maine coast. The 240-acre farm is now run by the 11th generation of Tuttle growing vegetables and strawberries. The family also runs a retail shop on the farm's grounds. There are several other farming operations that have passed through generations for years, including: Shirley Plantation of Charles City, Virginia (1638); Barker Farm of North Andover, Massachusetts (1642); Miller Farm of Frederica, Delaware

(1684); Nourse Family Farm of Westborough, Massachusetts (1722); and many more. My paternal grandmother's family, the Millers, ran a farm in Western Pennsylvania for over 200 years, a mere moment in time compared to these long established family run businesses.

In 1843, John Baumann opened a store in St. Louis offering trunks and supplies for pioneers who were setting out on the Oregon Trail. The firm later added safes to its line of business. Run by the founder's great-great-granddaughters, Baumann Safe Company has adapted to changing tastes and technology, and now offers video systems and home surveillance products as well.

Here's a business I'm dying to tell you about. It was started in 1769 by Johannes Bachman, a Swiss Mennonite who worked as a cabinetmaker in Lancaster County, Pennsylvania; his business eventually evolved to include coffin making. Eight generations of Bachman family have run the Bachman Funeral Home since then. Just look at what a steady stream of customers can do for a business!

If there is one thing I've learned from people like Ed Smalis, Ed Ryan, William Hilton, and others, it is that age is simply a state of mind. There is no reason you can't take a career into your later years. If you love what you do, why quit because you turn 65? Keep chasing your dreams and keep producing no matter your age.

Retiring is nothing more than waiting around for your Social Security check as a means to pass the time while you wait to die. Americans have a misguided notion that the ultimate reward for life's efforts is the glorified state of retirement. Aging is an unavoidable fact of life, but it is not and should not be thought of as an end to living. Dying requires little effort and certainly no practice, so it is senseless to spend the last ten or twenty years of life preparing for death. I live in an area that was designed as a retirement community. There are lots of "gray hairs" puttering around on their golf carts, playing doubles tennis, and meeting at the clubhouse for their daily lunch and card game. At the same time there are many older entrepreneurs in the community starting new businesses, continuing to work at their career, and enjoying their golden years by staying busy and keeping their minds engaged. These years can be happy, rewarding, productive, and full of energy as long as you are determined to make them so. My good friend Donn Wilson turned 87 in 2012. Donn has had an amazing career, becoming one of the early McDonald's franchisees, serving as past president of Wendy's Canada, and helping launch Blockbuster video stores. Today he serves on a few boards of directors, operates White Water Pizza in Boise, Idaho, and is launching an airline!

Always Continue to Improve

As you become successful you must continually nurture the creative spirit that was so instrumental in your initial success. The only way any business can insure of future success is to by continuing to improve on the product, price and distribution of that product. What if Bill Gates and the folks at Microsoft had stopped developing software after they released DOS? There would be no Windows 95, Windows 98, Windows 2000, Windows ME, Windows NT, Windows XP, Windows 7 or Windows 8.

What if Bernard Marcus had stopped after building his first hardware store? You couldn't pick up your hardware at one of the more than 1,400+ Home Depot stores across America. What if Paul Orfalea had been content running a single copy machine? You couldn't drive down the road to one of the 1,100 neighborhoods Kinko's (now owned by FedEx). What if Charles Martin Hall hadn't investigated a means to inexpensively produce aluminum? There would be no Alcoa. What if King Camp Gillette listened to the naysayers who said you couldn't create a disposable razor for men? There would be no Gillette. What if Christian Frederick Martin hadn't decided to focus on guitars instead of cabinets and move his company to America? There'd be no Martin guitars. What if Charles Alderton, a young English pharmacist working at Morrison's Old Corner Drug Store in Waco, Texas, hadn't experimented with sugared water in order to satisfy the taste buds of the store's owner, Wade Morrison? We wouldn't be drinking Dr. Pepper.

Will Keith "W.K." Kellogg once wrote, "Am afraid that I will always be a poor man the way things look now." Working for his older brother, Dr. John Harvey Kellogg, Will ran the brother's sanitarium, working 15 hours a day, 7 days a week. He wore many hats: bookkeeper, supply clerk, secretary, janitor, handyman, and sales clerk. He earned $6 a week and worked seven years before his brother gave him a vacation. In 1894, Dr. Kellogg gave his younger brother another chore: running experiments on boiled wheat paste. One night W.K. left the paste out overnight where it dried out. When run through rollers and then baked, it turned into crispy flakes that were unexpectedly tasty when combined with milk. W.K. Kellogg had inadvertently invented Granose, which was quickly eaten up by the sanitarium's patients. Altering the formula to a corn base, he created Sanitas Toasted Corn Flakes, the precursor to Kellogg's Cereal. Kellogg's continuous development of his cereal helped make Kellogg's the household name it is and helped make the Kellogg family wealthy beyond their wildest expectations.

Advertisers are not the only people convinced that "out of sight is out of mind." Companies that maintain their success are well aware of the need to forever improve upon their products and services. Successful companies nurture creativity and enthusiastically support new product ideas that can change and expand their business.

Think of yourself as a company, and continually improve upon your product and services, while expanding your knowledge. Trust me: it is not work; it is fun and it's something you can continue to enjoy pursuing even while your contemporaries are milling around the Old Folks' Home.

Many people retire hoping to spend their days on the golf course, putting away the last few years of their lives. Playing golf is a pastime; it is not truly creative. Once the rules and techniques are absorbed, one merely has to repeat them over and over to play the game. There is nothing wrong with spending your golden years playing golf, but too much golf and not enough creativity will never make the person with the entrepreneurial spirit happy.

It takes an enormous amount of creativity to turn bright ideas into successful business ventures. As long as your enthusiasm to develop new ideas remains, creativity stops only at death. And who knows, perhaps creativity even extends to the great beyond?

Keep Being Creative and You Will Always Feel Passionate About Life

Creativity can be defined in different ways, but for the entrepreneur, creativity is the desire to develop new goals and new ways to achieve them. Creativity is a planned effort. Truly creative people will find that there is always something new to work toward, even if it seems that they have accomplished it all. That is, the business has succeeded, the family has been raised and money has been made, but the yearning to do more, grow, earn more money, and generate new ideas never stops. There are always new goals to strive toward and one never reaches the top of the mountain. There is no financial reason for Clint Eastwood or Robin Williams to continue with their careers other than to satisfy their own creative instinct. Creativity will continue to keep you young, happy, and healthy, no matter how many candles are on your birthday cake.

Russell Waters recently stopped by my office. At 18, Russ graduated from high school and went to work for his uncle's construction company. He then became a facilities supervisor for a manufacturer with operations in a couple states. At the age of 33 he enrolled in a part-time community college and earned a degree in electrical engineering. He spent the past 55 years inventing gadgets and holds over a dozen patents. He receives over $400,000 a year from licensing fees derived from companies who pay him for use of those patents. He is 92 and works 4 days a week. His wife now makes him take Fridays off.

Russ strode into my office one morning and with a big grin on his face proudly proclaimed he had a creative answer to the challenges of quickly transporting people from Dallas to Houston, currently a 4 hour drive. Russ said, "When a cat is dropped, it always lands on its feet, and when toast is dropped, it always lands buttered side down. I propose to strap giant slabs of hot buttered toast to the back of a hundred thousand tethered cats. The two opposing forces will cause the cats to hover, spinning inches above the ground. Using the giant buttered toast/cat array, a high-speed monorail could easily link Dallas with Houston."

I replied, "Well, I don't know how practical this is, but it sure is creative."

Russ shot back, "You gotta keep thinking, Bill, you gotta keep thinking."

He was always coming up with ideas. It is what he often said, "keeps me young and keeps me going."

When One Phase of Your Life Ends,
Create New Goals and Objectives

There are plenty of ways for you to lose your creativity and enthusiasm. The easiest way is for you to reach a point where you decide that you have done everything, seen everything and reached all of your goals. I had an investor in one of my companies who had made in excess of $600 million during his career on Wall Street. Spelled out, that is $600,000,000, or the equivalent of more than 3,500 Ferraris. He was financially secure, yet at the age of 58 was bored with life. He had retired seven years earlier and had made so much money and focused such long, continued effort on the act of making money that he had forgotten how to have fun. Retirement was a chore for him and he didn't know where to turn to bring the joy back into his life. Golf didn't do it. Clubbing didn't do it. Chasing after girls half his age didn't do it. Nothing he tried gave him the joy that he felt when he was working on Wall Street. When I asked him what it was that he missed most, he replied that it wasn't the speed of the market or scoring a big gain, it was the creative side of analyzing trend lines and determining where an investment vehicle was headed. Even though he didn't need the money, he eventually started trading stocks and commodities for himself and for the first time in years he completely engaged in life.

The sports celebrity who suddenly finds his or her career ended by the age of 35 or younger demonstrates another example. It is a great personal tragedy for some of these people when they are unable to create new goals for themselves to replace the athletic pursuits that they are no longer fit to perform. Yet, it is ridiculous to think that one's life is over at 35, 40 or 50. Professional sports is a field where one's career is limited by age and health restrictions, but this does not mean that there is nothing left for the former sports figure to do but drink, take drugs or waste the rest of his life reliving past glories. The more rewarding attitude is to accept that while one phase of one's career has ended, there is still plenty of time to begin a new career, whether this means coaching others in sports, teaching or starting a small business. The point is that one must set new goals and strive to achieve them. Telling yourself that "life is over" or "there is nothing more for me to do" is self-destructive and will only serve to make you miserable. If life is what you make it, then surely it is better to make it exciting and worthwhile rather than empty and pointless. The most important thing in life is the satisfaction that comes from doing something worthwhile, and one must never assume that there is nothing more to be done.

I believe there are quite a few among us who see the same satisfaction as I do in pursuing life as a constantly changing series of goals and objectives. There are certainly plenty of reasons to want to retire from work and spend one's time fishing, playing golf, tending a garden or whatever. It certainly makes sense that a person who spends thirty or forty years inserting bolt A into nut B on an assembly line would want to quit and spend time pursuing more interesting and rewarding endeavors.

The reason I can afford to tell the new entrepreneur to forget retirement is that if you develop the type of business that I am advocating, you will have no reason in the world to want to retire. You will want to work forever because work is fun and fulfills your life. I can see myself running The Amati Foundation until I die. I am so passionate about bringing classical music to children and exposing them to the music of the violin that I don't ever see myself retiring from this initiative. Why should I? If I love what I do and can physically manage the demands of being chairman, I should work until my mission is accomplished, and then find a new mission to pursue.

I challenge you to shape your own creativity in such a way that you *are* your work: It is your greatest pleasure in life and your most satisfying hobby. If you succeed in doing so, you will have no need to stop. There is no obvious self-satisfaction in inserting bolt A into nut B; for the person who does so, retirement is a most sensible goal. But the goals that the entrepreneur starts with are creative and are achieved only to satisfy a desire within the individual.

Success means that you can continually be in control of your own destiny. Just as you gain freedom, independence and satisfaction early in your business, you will find as you grow older that you want to continue with your career in order to achieve *more* freedom, independence, satisfaction and, of course, money. Scott Estes helped launch the very successful server business at Dell. He holds a couple patents and retired from the company at a fairly young age. He hasn't slowed down since retirement, opening a music store, a home mortgage company, and other ventures too numerous to list. In fact, he wouldn't consider himself retired, just busy doing other things. I expect in 30 years he'll still be looking for some niche market to tackle.

The famous Italian Master violin maker Antonio Stradivarius handcrafted some of his finest musical instruments when he was older. Today, his violins, violas, and celli are considered the best in the world; they are played by the very best musicians and sell for more than $3,000,000, with one recently selling for more than $17,000,000.

Speaking of Italy, I met George Shafer in the town of Cortona in the fall of 2003. George had made his living selling copiers in New Jersey, and upon retiring in 1998, he became a voracious reader of travel-related books. In 1999 he picked up Frances Mayes' book, *Under the Tuscan Sun*. The story covers how Frances traveled to Cortona and entered a wondrous new world when she began restoring an abandoned villa in the Tuscan countryside. There were unexpected treasures at every turn: faded frescoes beneath the whitewashed walls in her dining room; a vineyard hidden underneath an overgrown garden, and, in the nearby hill towns, vibrant markets, delightful people, spectacular food, and all the pleasures of Italian life.

Upon completing the book George decided to make it a goal of his to spend three weeks a year in Tuscany. The first year he went with his wife, then with another couple the following year. On his fourth trip, when I met him, he was there with his wife and six other people, basking in the Italian sun while sipping wine and savoring the local fare. I mentioned that copier sales must have been good, given his ability to come to Italy each year. He replied that copier sales paid his bills and put his kids through college, but after retiring he started selling real estate on the weekends. Two days turned into five and he found he loved the interaction with clients so much it became his post-retirement career. Now he works 10 months a year, takes the other two off, and makes enough money selling real estate that he can afford to spend most of October wining and dining under the Tuscan sun. So much for retiring!

George spent the majority of his career working for others. He didn't become an entrepreneur until he was 65 years old and decided he needed to control his destiny in order to travel to the places he read about. He missed the interaction with people that a job provides. He missed getting up in the morning with concrete goals to accomplish. He missed being a super salesman and providing exemplary customer service. Age didn't stop him from becoming successful. Age certainly didn't keep him from starting a new career at age 65. And spending the majority of his life in the employ of others didn't stop him from becoming self-sufficient as an independent real estate broker, affording him world travel with friends and loved ones, while others are sitting in their rocking chairs wondering why retirement isn't more exciting.

What does all this talk of retirement have to do with you?

Perhaps you are nearing the end of your career and wondering what the next 20 years holds. Perhaps you are 30 years old and thinking you only have 35 more good earning years left. Or perhaps you are a 19 year-old high school dropout wondering how you'll ever make it to retirement age. Regardless of your situation, forget what others say about retirement. There is no reason to stop working if you love what you're doing. Ignore the naysayers when they say, "You can't do that." Challenge all the rules and define them to suit you. Keep up your enthusiasm and never let your mind stop. Life is what you make it, and proper planning, coupled with creativity and enthusiasm will guide you through years and years of fun work.

What Did You Learn?

1. There is no end to the success of an energetic, self-motivated and creative individual.
2. Many entrepreneurs follow up early successes with additional successes. Once you learn how to start a business and make it successful, it's not that difficult to repeat the same steps to turn your second venture into a success.
3. Retirement for many is an excuse to sit on the sidelines and wait for the undertaker to take you away. It need not be. Plenty of people become entrepreneurs late in life, and still enjoy a great deal of travel and leisure time.

CHAPTER 22

Yes You Can: Create A More Positive Life

Whether an employee or an entrepreneur,
success can envelope your life.

MUCH OF THE content of this book up to this point has been focused on becoming an entrepreneur and pursuing a successful business of your own. As I write this I'll bet that only 1 in 30 people who read this book will take the initiative to start their own business. For the other 29 of you, I hope to convince you to be devoted to the pursuit of excellence within a given field. Even if you spend your life in the employ of others, like George Schafer (until he started selling real estate), enthusiasm for your career (and relationships, hobbies, and all other aspects of your life) should continue so that you can keep climbing your own mountain. Money will likely motivate you, but only as a means to satisfy other more important needs. George wanted to travel and he determined that the best way to do that was to work. He started with weekends and it blossomed to a full-time job that enables him to travel overseas every year. You too can have this type of rewarding career.

Maybe you think you'll spend your life in the same job you are in now. Fine. Just make the most of it. Go to work every day knowing you're going to do your job better than anyone else can. Excel at who you are and turn your job into your career. At some point, if you feel the urge to start your own business, take the leap and do so. But if you don't, just make your existing career the best you can. We all face choices in life, and whether you work for someone else or for yourself is ultimately your choice and your choice alone.

Becoming successful incorporates many factors. But what it takes, above all else, is you. Being single-minded on reaching your goals will consume a great deal of time. This won't be easy to do but it is necessary if you are to succeed. You must realize that time is easy to give up for socializing but impossible to give up for business if you want to succeed. This does not mean that you have to become a workaholic, lose your spouse, home, and all that is pleasurable. What it does mean is that you have to realistically define your goals, dreams and lifestyle. If you commit to being the best you can be, you can plan a future for yourself that will far exceed anything in your wildest imagination.

My advice on reaching your goals is worthless if you lack the courage and dedication needed to take action. Naturally, not everyone wants to be an entrepreneur. There are plenty of risks involved and no guarantee of success. Many people reading this book, perhaps yourself included, are content to work for others, and it is my hope you will use the tips I'm sharing with you to make the best of your current and future positions and to become the best employee any employer could hope for. However, if you seek to embody the entrepreneurial spirit, even from the confines of working for others, you can be certain of a life of challenges, failures, successes, and self-worth.

Capitalism demands high production from a certain number of dedicated and daring individuals. You can be one of those people. Without creativity and enthusiasm, there is no production. Without production, there is no wealth, and the absence of wealth means an end to the whole free enterprise system and the collapse of the economy. Our economic system needs free spirits and creative individualists or else it will fail. Choosing to go this path will reward you in more ways than just money. It will give you the freedom to choose your own lifestyle and pursue whatever goals you want most. In fact, if you have spent the first part of your life as a successful entrepreneur, you will probably learn that it is most rewarding to spend the last part of your lifetime as a successful entrepreneur.

Foster Your Inner Creative Artist

You should not forget that enthusiasm for living, creativity in doing, and striving to reach your goals are things that come from within, and, like success, these qualities cannot become manifest by social status symbols or showmanship. Successful people are more apt to be loners than those seeking acceptance by the masses. They are constantly striving to improve themselves, and may be uncomfortable with the appearance of success. They are more likely to be found outside of major urban areas or exclusive social registers. A creative artist is not the one who paints a single, magnificent picture and then spends a lifetime meeting with other artists to discuss the greatness of that one work. The real creative artist is the one that continues to produce work for an entire lifetime. The reward is not being told by others how great he or she is, but in the satisfaction of striving for self-improvement. The creative artist needs to paint for the inner self and will continue to paint for that reason.

In case you might think that being creative applies only to artists, realize that the arts are not the only field where creative expression prospers. It can be found in any field or business as long as the individual strives toward excellence. Creativity in business is about finding imaginative and original ways to look at and solve problems. Ben Bassi, my partner at Lycos and YouthStream, is very creative. He can work a business deal 50 different ways in order to come up with a smart, mutually beneficial business agreement where both parties win. While many people would equate that with being smart (which Ben is), I equate it with being creative. Instead of a paintbrush, Ben uses numbers and strategic business tactics to reach his goals.

Matthew Rogers spent 15+ years with one of the leading class ring manufacturers, honing his skills to become an immensely talented marketing and brand manager. He utilizes creativity to overcome everyday obstacles like budgets, difficult customers, and aggressive competitors. He used his skills to help market Dell computers around the globe and today is helping Microsoft define and penetrate new markets.

Dean Yeck is a highly skilled manager in the telecommunications industry and has built a dedicated, effective sales team through creatively looking at business problems and solving them. Dean managed over $50 million in annual revenue for his company and he uses creativity every day in order to stay ahead of his competitors, serve his customers, and seek new ways to solve challenges.

Doug Andrews is formally trained as a Six Sigma Black Belt and is an expert in quality assurance. He uses creativity every day to come up with ideas that lead to better manufacturing and quality control processes and thus, better products.

Christopher Jensen is a human resources leader for a global semiconductor manufacturer. Chris relies on his creativity to develop programs that will attract, train, and retain the best semiconductor professionals from around the world.

Anne Akiko Meyers is one of the world's great violinists, performing more than 50 concerts a year and recording over a dozen CDs. She brings passion and excitement to music, new interpretations to the works of the great composers and exposes thousands of people every year to works by new composers, taking an active role in helping to define what classical music means for the next generation of listeners.

Joseph Curtin is a master violinmaker who handcrafts world-class violins for many of today's top performers. A luthier with research interests in nontraditional materials, nontraditional structures, and violin acoustics, Joe marries acoustic science to the art of violinmaking. His work was recognized by a MacArthur Fellows designation in 2005. The MacArthur "Genius Award," as it is often called, recognizes creativity, originality, and innovation.

These are just a few of the people I know. I'm sure you know just as many who, regardless of occupation, have found that the best way to succeed in their careers and lives is to be creative in their approach.

It is up to each one of us to separate what are truly creative endeavors from the things that are merely a means to fill in the time. When you are truly creative, your ideas have no boundaries. They can expand and flourish for years and years, continually challenging you to become better at who you are and what you do.

What Did You Learn?

1. The most important person guiding your life is you. Whether you choose to start a business or become a better employee, you and only you can choose to succeed.
2. Success must come from within. Continue to strive for personal

excellence and stay focused on your own creative energy.

3. Creativity can be used to generate new ideas, create new businesses, or make any job more rewarding. It knows no boundaries and should be used throughout one's life.

CHAPTER 23

Yes You Can: It's About Attitude

Be significant.

NOT ALL OF US are ready or even want to own our own businesses or start individual enterprises. If this is you, **do not stop reading this book.** Why? Because everything that I have said and am about to say can be applied to your life, no matter what your goals are or your hopes for the future may be. What you're about to read is useful for receptionists, government bureaucrats, janitors, salespeople, mailmen, people working at Taco Bell, and future millionaires.

Success is not something that is measured in dollar signs alone. I've said this before, but it's advice worth repeating over and over until it sinks into not just your head but into your very soul. Creativity, enthusiasm and hard work are the keys to success.

Hand-in-hand with creativity, enthusiasm and hard work is *attitude.* Attitude can mean many things to many people, but there is really only one attitude worth having and that is a *positive* attitude. No matter what your job is, become better at it. No matter what your economic situation, improve it. Become the determining factor in your life! Each day you wake up you can decide to have a negative attitude or a positive attitude. Wouldn't you rather spend the day happy and upbeat, rather than disagreeable and pessimistic?

Become the Determining Factor in Your Life

Becoming the determining factor in your life means that you take control of your decisions every waking moment. It might sound simple; maybe you believe you already make all your own decisions. But do you really? Do you decide what time to show up at work? What time to have lunch? How much money you make? Do you decide what health insurance plan you subscribe to? For example, let's say that you have to be a work at 9 a.m. Who says you can't be there at 8 a.m. and get a jump on all the other employees? If you worked one extra hour a day, what might you accomplish? A promotion? A raise? You'll never know unless you take control over your life and become the determining factor as to how you will succeed in your life and work.

Guess what? You are stuck with yourself until the day the undertaker plants you under six feet of dirt. Because of this, you are the biggest factor in your own life. Not your parents, not your spouse, not your mother-in-law (although she may want to be). You! When I say to become a determining factor in your own life I mean that you must manage creativity, attitude and control. You already know about creativity and attitude. Control means that you are the captain of your ship, the master of your universe and the molder of your destiny. As a popular comedian espoused, "I am the master of my domain." You, and only you, can make your life worthwhile. No matter what you do, no matter what your job, occupation or income, you can live a life that is significant. Otherwise you're just a mass of water and other chemicals sucking up the life-sustaining oxygen that those of us with things to do and goals to reach need to live. I don't mean that to sound harsh, but do you really want to go through life just living day to day, dragging your butt to work, waiting for the clock to reach five o'clock so you can punch out, get on the bus and arrive home in time for dinner and another night of sitting in front of the television, flipping through channels? Or would you rather go through life living to the fullest? Having fun? Getting it great? Being successful?

Flash Forward to Your Life's Story

Take a piece of paper and write down what your obituary will say. Set it aside for a week and then pick it up and read it again. Is this what your life will amount to? Would you like to see more accomplishments? Now that you've seen the synopsis of your life as you view it in the here and now, you have the ability to change it to have more impact, more success, more significance. Start changing it today.

My mother, Jacquelyn Mayer Townsend, led a charmed life. She graduated from college, sang with the popular touring musical group, Fred Waring and the Pennsylvanians, and after winning the title of Miss Ohio, won the Miss America competition in 1963. She was featured in advertisements, magazines, and television programs. She had her own record (that's "pre-CD" for you younger readers). She had a highway named after her in her home state of Ohio. She married a young, successful lawyer and had two wonderful children (her words, not mine). She was happy, content, and had reached all the goals she set forth for herself, yet she wondered what significance her life had. She was about to find out.

It was Thanksgiving night, 1970, when she awoke to the sound of my sister Kelly crying. Mom started to get out of bed but found she couldn't move. She tried to say something to Dad but she couldn't utter a single word. She was terrified. Something was seriously wrong and she had no idea what to do. At age 28, she was facing the challenge of her life.

Mom was rushed to the hospital. While being wheeled down the hallway with the fluorescent lights above her head ticking by one after another, she didn't know if she'd survive the night. My father was informed that his wife was at the completion of a massive stroke that had left her paralyzed and without speech, and the doctors wouldn't know how much more damage had been done for several hours.

Recovery was long and slow. This once vivacious, former Miss America could not even recite the ABCs. She had to learn to speak all over again. I was 5 at the time and would spend time after school teaching her to tie her shoes, something she had taught me just a few months earlier. Together we would read through my kindergarten and 1ˢᵗ grade schoolbooks so that she could relearn the alphabet.

My mother began her rehabilitation by setting goals for herself. Within weeks she had regained most of her motor skills. As her speech returned, she set a goal of being able to say the word "juxtaposition." She figured if she could properly pronounce that word, she could pronounce any word in the dictionary. Each of these goals, and many others, were used as stepping-stones to her ultimate goal of complete recovery.

Today, Mom is a professional motivational speaker who shares her story with corporate leaders, healthcare professionals, and stroke survivors. Her life now has significance and she is one of the happiest, most enthusiastic people I know. She triumphed over the obstacles placed in her path by setting goals and having dogged determination to reach those goals. In her mind, triumph is as simple as adding a little "umph" to the word "try."

Certainly, if my mother could rise above being paralyzed and unable to talk, you can figure out what it takes to make your life successful in work and play.

There are some people who are perfectly content and happy in jobs that many people might view as "menial." Janitor, bartender, grass mower, grocery store clerk, hotel maid, fast food worker and the like are jobs that many people don't hold in high esteem. Unfortunately, this is often reflected by the pay scale, so that even terrific workers don't get the money they deserve. But these jobs and the people who do them are important. They deserve respect from those of us who rely on them for the services they provide. If you don't believe me, just look at what has happened in the fast food industry in the last 10 years. Training programs have been cut, employees are not held to the high standards of yesteryear, and the educational level of many employees is the lowest it's been in decades. Service at major chains like McDonald's has gone downhill and customers are turning away. Just try ordering a meal at a McDonald's restaurant in New York City and see what kind of service you receive as compared to a McDonald's in Smalltown, USA. For a company that built its reputation on quality food and service delivered the same way regardless of location, the differences will shock you.

Why is this? Why do we get great service at one restaurant but lousy service at another? How can the same company, selling the same menu, training employees the same way, have vastly different results because of location? I think it boils down to people and the pride they have in their jobs. If Cara comes to work each day ready to do her best and enjoy the job she has, she's going to provide much better service than Chuck, who wakes up with a bad attitude dreading the 8 hours he has to give to his job.

Why do people in some areas take pride in their jobs and in other areas they do not? I believe it comes down to their surroundings: who they live with, who they interact with, what their friends think of them. I don't believe it is entirely educational as I have met many people who have high school level educations, yet understand the importance of finding significance in their lives, and thus, start each day on a positive note. I really think that you have the ability to go to work tomorrow, and with a renewed focus on being the best you can be, start to live a more successful and significant life.

If you're a bartender, janitor or fast food clerk, you might be asking why you should give a damn about striving to improve yourself when you know you'll still take home a small paycheck whether you work hard or not. The answer is, even if the monetary rewards aren't there and don't seem like they'll be there in the near future, you cannot just give up. Everything you do in your job reflects on you, not just in the eyes of others but also in how you view yourself. If you don't take control of your life, beginning right now, how will you identify it when the door to opportunity knocks?

Several years ago, I met a young woman who was working in a restaurant, barely making ends meet. When she learned I was involved in technology development for the Internet she asked me questions that only someone who was passionate about the Web would have known to ask. She had done her homework and had a goal of working in the Internet industry as a designer. She impressed me with her positive, can-do attitude, and I hired her within a few months. She started as a designer and eventually moved to New York City, where she became an art director for a major media company. Opportunity knocked for her, and instead of looking at it dumbfounded, she flung the door open and stepped right through.

I recently met a woman who was working at a hotel bar in Las

Vegas. Within minutes I knew she had the kind of positive attitude that would enable her to succeed in anything she put her mind to. I gave her my business card and suggested she consider contact me if she wanted to get out of her dead-end bar job. Within two days I received her résumé and she is now going through the interviewing process at my company to become a junior sales associate.

Every Job is Important and Makes a Difference

Attaining success and money might take some time, but that is not an excuse for not trying. Even if your friends, family or boss treats you like your job isn't important, that doesn't mean it's true. You are important, and if you don't believe that, then it's up to you and you alone to change it. No matter what your job is, you can excel at it. You can do it better, and then you will feel better about yourself. If you're a waitress, be a better waitress. If you're a cleaning person, be a better cleaning person. If you mow lawns for a living, mow them better. If you're a project manager, be the best dang project manager you can. If you're a receptionist, be the best you can be.

I tell my administrative assistants that they had one of the most important jobs in the company. They were often the first person a customer would speak to upon dialing the company. They had to manage dozens of employees calling to fill me in on successes or disappointments. They had to keep me organized so that I could work more efficiently. One administrative assistant in particular understood how important her role was to the company. She came to work every day focused and ready to tackle the world, and guess what…I noticed. Dorie DeBlasio has worked for me in three separate companies. If I could convince her to move to my city, I'd hire her tomorrow for the fourth time. The first time her role was primarily administrative and focused on managing my time and ensuring that our office stayed organized. The next two times she had additional responsibilities which she took on wholeheartedly. She excelled in these endeavors partly because she made a great effort to succeed. During her tenures with me, her salary increased four-fold. Was there a time when Dorie got a sign that she was supposed to try harder? No. She just worked hard each day, committing herself to excelling at what she did. I appreciated her efforts and hired her repeatedly because I knew she was a fighter and was controlling her own destiny. Today, Dorie has a great husband, lives in a beautiful home in a suburb of a major city, and works for a Fortune 500 company. While she didn't become an entrepreneur, she continues to be positive, strive for significance, and work hard at reaching her goals every day.

On a trip to Los Angeles I stayed at the The Peninsula Beverly Hills hotel. If you ever have the opportunity to stay there, I highly recommend it. The staff is excellent. They are personable, knowledgeable, and willing to go to any length to make your stay as comfortable and productive as possible. As I walked down the hallway one morning, I spotted the housekeeper who was taking care of the rooms on my floor. I stopped and complimented her on how nice and clean my room was and how I especially enjoyed the fresh fruit left for me. Now most people would respond by saying, "Thank you." but this woman surprised me by saying, "It's my pleasure, Mr. Townsend." She not only took my compliment and turned it around into a compliment for me, as if it was her pleasure to take care of me while I was there, but she knew my name! Talk about impressing your guests! I left a $20 tip in my room when I checked out and found myself recommending the hotel to anyone visiting Los Angeles.

I can say the same about Les Suites Taipei Da'an, a boutique hotel in Taipei, Taiwan. Months after my last stay I entered the lobby to a chorus of everyone behind the front desk saying, "Hello, Mr. Townsend" or "Welcome back, Mr. Townsend." Throughout my stay, I was always addressed when entering a room or elevator. Every request was attentively cared for. Even minor things like Maggie, the sales director, stopping at breakfast one morning to suggest I try the delicious blue cheese added to the exceptional experience I received. Would I spread the word and recommend this hotel? I just did.

How many times do you walk into a restaurant and the people there know your name? I have a favorite sushi restaurant where I walk in and they know what I want. Within a few seconds of sitting down, a cold iced tea and order of edamame is sitting in front of me. They then inform me if they have uni in stock or not. I don't even have to ask. That is providing the best service you can offer.

If I'm in New York and entertaining clients over dinner, I take them to Marchi's restaurant on the East Side of Manhattan. Marchi's is an establishment with old world Italian charm. They have served the same menu for over 70 years. You sit down and they serve you six courses over two hours. The service is impeccable. The food is delicious. And everyone from the cooks to the wait staff consistently delivers a dining experience that my business contacts remember for years to come. That is excelling at what you do.

Bonnie B's Smokin' in Pasadena, California is owned by Bonnie Henderson and Betty Miller. To ask Bonnie or Betty, about their story they would both tell you "we are here by the grace of God and a little help and love from family and friends." Upon entering their small restaurant you are immediately greeted with a friendly hello. The food is always hot and very often Bonnie will come out from the kitchen to talk to the customers and make sure everything was delicious. The enthusiasm that Bonnie and Betty have for what they do shines through in everything the restaurant stands for; and their success stems in no small part from that fact.

No matter what you do, you can be better and you know it. If you have the attitude that your job is nothing but a way to earn a paycheck, especially a paycheck that doesn't adequately compensate you for your hard work and effort, then it is likely that all you are ever going to achieve in life is a lousy way to pay your rent. If you view your job as a way to learn and progress in life, and approach it with enthusiasm and commitment, you will get noticed. Where your career goes from there is up to you.

Just about everybody will spend a great part of his or her life working at some sort of job, profession or business. If you really think about it in terms of five, eight-hour work days, fifty-two weeks each year in a working lifetime of forty-five years, you are talking about *eighty-six thousand four hundred* hours of your life. It doesn't take a computer or a degree from the Wharton School of Business to tell you that this is a heck of a lot of time. We didn't count overtime, time spent getting to and from work, or time used when paperwork is taken home from the office in the evening. That typically adds over *twenty thousand additional hours* to your lifetime tally. There are not really that many ways to avoid spending that many hours or more at work. Many of us have to work those hours to pay our bills, make our business succeed, or simply to hang onto a job. It should make sense to you that since you are going to spend this much time at work, you would be a fool not to make the best of the situation.

If you understand the *need* to strive to do your best, then you are ready to begin a process guaranteed to start you on your road to success. The process might be painful at different points in time and for different reasons. This shouldn't scare you though, because everyone I've come in contact with who has decided to become an enthusiastic employee or entrepreneur has told me that they enjoy their jobs more and get more personal satisfaction by approaching their jobs with the right mental attitude. The combination of enthusiasm for what they do and keeping a positive attitude leads most people to find the key to living a life of significance. There is no reason you can't follow the same path.

What Did You Learn?

1. There is only one kind of attitude to possess: a *positive* attitude.
2. Everything you do in your job reflects directly on you, not just in the eyes of others but also in how you view yourself.
3. 86,400 hours of your life will be spent at work. Do you want to approach those hours negatively or positively? The choice is yours.
4. Decide right here and now to live a life of significance and become the person you know you can be.

CHAPTER 24

Yes You Can: Take Note

Jot this down.

YOU WON'T FIND THIS in any of the business books. Before continuing on your journey to creating a better you, there is another piece of advice that is important for you to do at any and every step of building your own success story. Like much of what I've already told you, this advice might sound simple and certainly isn't extraordinarily difficult; but it is very important for you to pay close attention and do your very best to heed my advice.

The step I am talking about is for you to always make sure that whenever you have an idea, learn something new about yourself, or whatever, you *write it down*. Write it on anything. Buy a sixty-nine cent notepad and keep it in your pocket. Jot it down on a napkin. Scrawl notes in the margin of your newspaper. It doesn't matter what you write on, just that you record it.

Why should you right things down? Because if you don't write it down, you are probably going to forget about it. Just think about all the great ideas that people have had that never amounted to a hill of beans because they were forgotten or smothered by other thoughts or by the pressures of daily life. Good ideas can quickly slip from your mental grasp because we all have hundreds of things to do each day. Why do musicians write down music? So they won't forget it. Not all ideas can stay in your head when your brain is busy worrying about finishing a business report for your manager, taking the car to the garage for inspection, picking up little Pierce's cough medicine at the drug store, and the hundreds of other things you think about.

When Dorie DeBlasio was my executive assistant, it would drive her crazy that I had dozens of little strips of paper with notes on them littered across my desk. Each note had an idea, a task, or some other piece of information I was going to follow up on. She couldn't understand how I could keep anything straight with all these notes all over the place. Truth be told, had I not made those notes, I would have been really disorganized.

Art Fry used to put paper bookmarks in his choir hymnal. After they kept falling out he got the idea to put low-adhesive glue on the back of them. He got the glue from another guy where he worked and thus came about the invention of Post-it® Notes. Art did the hard part; you just need a couple dollars to take advantage of his creativity. Keep a package in your glove box. Keep one in your bathroom. Keep one in the kitchen. Write your ideas down on them and then stick them to a bulletin board or your desk. Then, every so often, put them into a hardbound notebook that you keep all your ideas in.

I've been tracking my notes since 1992, and now have about a dozen 160-page notebooks filled with random thoughts, concepts, inventions, complaints, lyrics, quotes, and other bits of information. Every year I go through the books and find nuggets of wisdom; a kernel of a concept for a new invention; a way to solve some problem that has been vexing me. By recording your thoughts in such a manner, you will create a paper trail of ideas – good and bad – that will become an encyclopedia you'll use over and over again.

Our lives are busy enough as it is, and no one can be expected to always remember to do everything that he or she needs to do. The simplest way to remember the important things is to take notes. This doesn't mean that you have to write in beautiful script or even that you have to write in complete sentences. Just jot down whatever it takes to jar your memory back to your brilliant ideas when you look over your notes at a later time. That way, you don't have the excuse of having "forgotten" something because the phone rang while you were thinking.

You do not necessarily have to become a note-taking lunatic, writing down every single thought that comes to your head. Some thoughts are important enough that you have either memorized them or they will repeat themselves over and over again. For instance, you might be a sales representative whose goal for the year is to earn $100,000 by selling $1,000,000 worth of product. Chances are this is the kind of goal that any good sales rep knows by heart. If earning $100,000 is important to you, you won't need notes on your refrigerator to remind you of the fact.

But if you are the same sales rep who, while driving one day between sales calls, has an idea on how to reach more customers or how to improve your product, then for heaven's sake, stop the car and write it down. You probably won't miss your next sales call if you pause for 30 seconds to take a few notes. Later, when you have more time, you can continue to think out the details of your ideas. However, chances are that if you don't at least write something down on paper, you will never return to the thoughts that might be the key to reaching your goal of earning $100,000, perhaps to exceeding your goals beyond your wildest dreams.

Taking notes is a helpful and necessary step throughout your lifetime and everything you do. Notes will help you organize your thoughts. They will serve to remind you of your plans and goals in life.

As you are well aware, opportunity does not come to he who waits. Opportunity must be created! Ideas don't just drop from the sky and neither does money. If you are really serious about wanting to succeed, you have no excuses not to take advantage of opportunities or to follow a few simple steps in making opportunities happen. If writing notes to yourself can help you achieve what you want in life, then why not do it? You have everything to gain and very little to lose by trying. Sure, some of your notes may never amount to anything more than words on paper; but one of these days, one of these pieces of paper could turn out to be just the idea you need to succeed. There is no risk involved. All you stand to lose is a little bit of your time. If you look at the habits of truly successful people, it should be apparent that the time expended in note taking is more than worth the effort if it can help you achieve your goals.

What Did You Learn?

1. If you have an idea, write it down.
2. Transpose all your notes into a hardbound notebook to create a central record that can be referred to whenever needed.
3. Even if you don't need to, go back and look through those notebooks to see if an idea you thought about long ago, but since forgot, may hold the key to a challenge you face today.

CHAPTER 25

Yes You Can: Manage Your Time

Time flies like an arrow; fruit flies like a banana.

ANOTHER IMPORTANT FUNCTION of note taking relates to our next step on your road to success. Note taking will help you organize your time. All successful people appreciate the importance of managing time. Books, seminars and television shows abound that stress time management, and their message is worth repeating. You must learn to manage your time and be smart about doing it.

Our lives are full of tasks that, though they are necessary and important, can be time-consuming and provide little long-term benefit. Sitting in line at the barbershop or at the dentist's office are examples of these sorts of necessary but time-wasting activities. You *should* attend to your dental health and you *should* try to maintain good grooming habits. To do so will provide you with multiple segments of time that, prior to reading this book, might have been wasted. Now that you've read this far you can turn this time to your advantage.

Instead of sitting in the dentist's office, absent-mindedly thumbing through a three month old copy of *US* magazine, do something constructive to pave your road to success. Read something that will help you rather than put you to sleep. Even just thinking constructive thoughts is better than staring at a picture of this year's best and worst dressed. Do a little office work or make some phone calls. Read a motivational book or a business book that you have brought with you. Sketch out product ideas. Learn about the industry the person sitting next to you works in. Do anything that benefits you, as long as you don't just sit on your duff like a zombie. I keep a couple books and trade magazines in the trunk of my car. When I find myself with spare time while waiting on an oil change or sitting at a doctor's office I grab a book and read through it.

Use Travel Time to Your Advantage

When I travel by plane I use the flight time to complete work, catch up on reading, answer e-mail, and think through complicated business strategies. (One thing I never do on an airplane is work on consulting clients' business. You never know who is looking over your shoulder. It could be a competitor.) While driving I will often listen to books on tape about subjects I'm interested in. When I lived in Manhattan and took the subway to work, I had 20 minutes each morning in which I read the Wall Street Journal. While other people looked around the car, stared at the floor, or dozed off into slumber land, I was learning what was happening in business, finance, technology, and marketing, giving myself a competitive advantage as I started the day.

Jennifer Townsend is a master of managing time. When she was Vice President at FAO Schwarz she kept immaculate, detailed records of every meeting, every project, every hour of her day. She toted her time management notebook with her everywhere she went. She was able to look up notes, appointments, and dates for everything she did. While I used to wonder how she could spend so much time writing in that notebook, I came to realize that for every five minutes she spent recording information, she'd later save ten minutes, fifteen minutes, or much more time. She is one of the best corporate managers I've ever known and her ability to manage time plays an important factor in her success.

Be Selective in How You Spend Your Free Time

In learning to manage your time, you must be cautious to avoid spreading yourself too thin. You must learn to manage yourself in everything you do. Too many commitments or involvements will mean that you are spreading yourself too thin. While involvement in the Fantasy Football League, the Girl Scouts, card clubs, sports and so on might be enjoyable and rewarding, involvement in too many activities will leave you overextended, frustrated, and without clear focus. Pick a couple of your favorite activities and make them the focus of your spare time.

Maintaining control of your life means becoming an expert in the art of prioritizing. This includes mastering the fine art of knowing how to say "no." Saying "no" isn't a bad thing. We can't be expected to do everything that is asked of us, and if we try, we're probably headed for the loony bin or an early grave. Discover what is important to you and concentrate on doing only those things related to something meaningful in your life.

Discover Hobbies That Interest You and Enrich Your Life

My hobbies include motorcycling, violins, and art. Each one is a hobby I enjoy and, not surprisingly, each relates to or supports my professional career. How?

Motorcycling keeps my physical reflexes sharp and gives me the ability to meet many people I normally would not meet in a traditional business setting. Remember my earlier remark about turning every person you meet into a possible client or link to a client? One of my favorite motorcycling partners runs a venture capital firm. Another works at Cisco. Yet another works for Dell. Since I make a good portion of my living in the tech industry, these contacts are invaluable. And because we share common interests, I am able to call upon these connections when need be, just as they can call upon me.

Playing the violin provides me a tremendously difficult challenge mastering it, one that will take my lifetime. And while I know I will never be good enough to play my favorite Bach violin concerto, attempting to get to the point where I can at least play parts of it keeps my mind sharp. By making violins I fulfill a yearning to physically build something with my hands, and by selling what I make, I increase my cash flow. Violin-making now provides cash that my family uses for trips, toys for our sons, and other things we may desire. It's our "fun money." I also donate half the violins I make to The Amati Foundation which sells them and uses the proceeds to buy violins for students who can't afford their own instruments.

Art nurtures my creativity and helps me look at things in a different light. The act of taking an image and transposing it to paper or canvas teaches you to observe. This enables me to approach business problems from multiple angles, looking and seeking for a better way to solve problems.

Although I have other interests, most of the free time I have left is reserved for my family. I used to sit on the boards of directors of a few companies, but I realized that I wanted to focus on my businesses, not others, and since attending board meetings at startups often occurs after normal business hours or on the weekend, they were eating into time I could better spend with my family. I used to golf, but after realizing that a round of golf takes four to five hours and I can only interact with a maximum of three other people during this time, it occurred to me that it was not a good use of my time. I enjoy the act of golfing, but if I am going to spend a Saturday morning away from my family, I'd rather spend it motorcycling with 20 other professionals where my odds of networking into a new project, product or company are five times greater than that found in a golf foursome.

This leads us to the topic of prioritization. You can prioritize your time, giving yourself maximum ability to focus on work, family and hobbies, by simplifying your life. Don't attend dinner parties unless they can impact your success. Take turns with a neighbor in taking the kids to baseball practice; that's what neighbors are for. Stop feeling guilty about saying "no"; you can't help or please everyone. Plan to eat dinner with your family every night; it will keep you in the loop as to what your kids are doing, while setting a very powerful example for them of what a family should be doing each evening. When hosting meetings, circulate an agenda and set a time limit for the meeting; there are few weekly management meetings that can't be completed in one hour.

Keep in mind that there are a lot of things in life you hope to accomplish, and you will never be able to succeed if you allow your time to be eaten up by insignificant events. If you do try to do everything, you will only succeed in spinning your wheels, accomplishing little, and probably ruining your mental health in the process. Don't let too many involvements result in a lifetime of failed dreams, missed opportunities and empty bank accounts. I helped one of my employees with time management, and he soon found that just by setting limits on meetings during the day he accomplished more during the week than he had previously. This let him leave work earlier, spend more time with his kids, and thus, improve his marriage. After a few months he found that his home life was happier and work life more enjoyable.

Don't Forget to Have Fun!

I don't mean to suggest that effective time management means you cannot relax and have fun. There is nothing wrong with relaxation and there is nothing wrong with fun. In fact, I believe that knowing how to relax and have fun is very important to success. If you don't do either of these things, you are headed for ulcers, heart attacks and an early trip to the mortuary. Like everything else, you should strive to be smart about how to budget time so that you can unwind in ways that you enjoy.

But be careful to avoid "forced fun"; that is, doing things like taking a cruise only because someone tells you it is "the thing to do." If a cruise isn't your thing, don't do it. If you like to golf, then golf. If you don't, then do something else. If you like lying on the beach and basking in the sun, then go get a tan. If you like looking up your family history, then do it. If you like to run, then lace up your sneakers and hit the pavement. Identify what is fun for you and be sure to make time to do it. Your life and sanity depend on it. And, if you're like me and can combine fun hobbies with your career or a means to make money, all the better! Bravo to you!

What Did You Learn?

1. Managing your time is of critical importance in creating a successful life.

2. Determine what is important in your life and stick with a few outside activities. Don't let others waste your time in meaningless meetings or activities. You must decide how you want to spend the 12 to 18 hours you're awake each day.

3. Seek out ways to interact with people who may help your career, support your business, or become mentors to you. Prioritize your activities, and don't let them overwhelm you to the point where you lose focus of the more important goal of becoming successful.

CHAPTER 26

Yes You Can: Pick Up Your Mess

Junk clutters more than your physical space,
it clutters your mental space, too.

ALONG WITH KNOWING how to budget your time is understanding how to manage your personal space. It may seem like a simple statement, but if your life is cluttered with junk, it is difficult to stay focused on your goals. Get rid of the garbage in your life. This can apply to a lot of different things, but it primarily means to eliminate those things that serve no truly useful purpose or have little utility in your life. Probably everyone has something in a basement, attic, or storage unit that they really don't want or need but have never gotten around to disposing. Call this clutter what it is: junk.

If you have things that you know qualify for the junk category, throw them away, donate them or stick them on eBay and auction the suckers off. Clear out the junk! There is no reason to complicate your life with garbage. I don't mean to suggest that you throw away things that are important to you or that you rush right out and set fire to the contents of your garage. What I'm talking about is eliminating useless stuff that serves no good purpose. Things like broken VCRs that you've been "saving" for the past five years because you might get them fixed someday. If five years have passed and you haven't fixed the VCR, then odds are you never will and this is just one useless item cluttering your life. In my household, we take one weekend each year to clear the attic, garage, closets, desks, etc. We end up with several boxes which we donate to Goodwill and the Salvation Army, a couple boxes of items we'll sell on eBay, and usually about four garbage bags filled with trash. Each time we undertake this exercise we can't believe how much we've accumulated in one year. We are astonished that we've kept certain things, like fortune cookie fortunes, broken toys, and old magazines. It's all just junk that clutters up the house. With the advent of online auction sites like eBay, or simply by holding a garage sale, you now have a profitable means to dispose of your junk. Last year a friend of ours conducted a weekend housecleaning and then sold over $14,000 worth of *junk* on ebay. $14,000! That's enough to start a business! Things they didn't want, that they would have previously thrown away, they made money from. You can too. Unclutter your life, do good by donating, and increase your equity by selling your junk to someone else.

"Junk" isn't only about things that clutter your life; it can also be about a project or activity that depletes your time and energy. I sat on the board of directors of a non-profit organization for almost two years. During that time I repeatedly heard from the executive director, in the form of weekly multi-page presentations, how the competition was doing this and accomplishing that and how his organization couldn't start to get things done because he needed more money. He viewed the competition with envy and his inability to get off his duff, pick up the phone, and make things happen became a stumbling block to making the organization successful. I realized that no matter how many good ideas I gave him or how many introductions I made for the organization, I was wasting my time if they didn't follow up on my advice. I resigned from the board because in my mind, while the concept behind the charity was worthy, the way it was being run was not. The weekly reports he provided certainly took several hours to create. The paper used to print them must have caused the death of several large trees. In fact, prior to throwing seven months of reports I decided to count the number of pages in them: 677! Six hundred seventy-seven pages of junk that was taking up my space and time. His reports were junk that didn't accomplish anything except show he knew how to use PowerPoint. His excuses were junk that I didn't have time for. And as I said earlier, the junk has to go!

Donate Your Junk and Help Someone In Need

The problem with junk is that it suffocates you. It surrounds you, annoys you and distracts you from the things that are really important to you. Furthermore, if something means nothing to you but might be enjoyed by someone else, why not be a little bit generous and share? A pair of pants in your closet that haven't fit properly for two years might clothe a homeless person. Do you really think you're going to start exercising and lose that gut so you can wear them again? Come on! Donate them! If you get rid of this kind of item by giving it to someone who really does need it, then everyone comes out a winner. The recipient gains something of value to them and you benefit by creating a more efficient management of your space. Mark my words: you will breathe easier and be more creative if you make an effort to manage both time and space.

A recent television show highlighted a $42 million lottery winner who lives in Florida. He bought a palatial spread in West Palm Beach and spent money on things like $75,000 dolphin statues, $160,000 dressers, suits of armor, 900 knives, Italian statues, and other baubles. It's all junk cluttering up his life. If he took the $18,000 a day he earns in interest and invested it into a worthwhile cause like providing a college education for a teenager from Okeechobee, Florida, I'll bet his feeling of self-worth and personal significance would be at a lifetime high. Imagine if he took the interest from one week each month and provided yearly scholarships for 84 teenagers who might not otherwise have the opportunity to attend college. Instead of being worth $42 million on paper, he'd *feel* worth $42 million. Junk clutters our lives, and if you continue to accumulate junk you're left with nothing but a really big junk pile.

Clear Out the Junk in Your Personal Finances

The third very important thing to learn to manage is your money. I am always amazed to hear people say things like, "If I could just earn $20,000 more dollars this year, then all of my money troubles would be over." Nonsense! If the person who says such a thing did earn the extra money, all they would do is spend it. The extra money would only mean that they are that much more in debt the next year.

The key to good money management is not necessarily just in earning more money; it is in knowing how to make the most of whatever money you do have. Like managing anything, the key is to prioritize. There are definitely things you spend money on that you could live without. Do you drink too much beer? Buy too many clothes? Play the lottery? Spend more than $400 a month on a car payment? Then, stop it! You might like the beer or the clothes, but do they really add quality to your life? If they don't, then you are better off without them.

I once had an employee, Brian, who asked for a 10% raise. When I asked why he wanted a raise he said he couldn't make ends meet. He was making $95,000 a year plus commissions, which added almost $30,000 to his yearly income. I asked where the money went. He replied he didn't know, but it was clear he needed to make more money to keep up with his bills. I proposed a test: Brian would keep track of all his expenses for one month. Everything he spent money on, he'd write down. Even if it was a 75 cent package of Lifesavers, he had to record it. At the end of the month we'd go through the list and if I couldn't help him cut his expenses, we'd review his request for a raise.

A month later we spent two hours after work going through his itemized listing of expenses. Now before you opine that I was the nosy boss critiquing his living expenses, let me tell you what happened. Brian came into my office and the first thing he said was, "Bill, thanks for making me do this. You will not believe what I've been wasting my money on." Brian had discovered that beyond rent, insurance, and utilities, he was letting money disappear through silly expenses. He and his wife had two newer cars, but she didn't work and he rode the subway to work each day. So two cars sat in the garage most of the time and he was paying $480 a month for the SUV and $699 a month for the German sedan. Before I could say a word, Brian told me he and his wife had decided to sell the sedan. It gets better. Brian was spending an average of $350 a month on lunches. He determined that if he brought his lunch to work two days a week, he'd save close to $100 a month. He was throwing away nearly $600 a month by going clubbing with his buddies two nights a week. Limiting going out to just Friday nights would save him $300 a month. He took the subway to work, and from the subway station took a cab to the office that cost $4.00 including tip. I suggested he consider walking the four blocks when the weather was nice, thereby saving another $80 a month. His wife was having her nails done every week at a cost of $25. She was using her weekly trip as a social event, and cutting her back to once a month saved $75. All told, Brian determined that he could save over $1,300 each month simply by eliminating expenses that didn't add to his quality of life. Month over month, that adds up to over $15,000 a year, far more than a 10% raise would have provided.

Because Brian didn't have the cash to spare, all these expenses detracted from his quality of life and added money worries that would ultimately affect his job performance. Let me tell you one other benefit of Brian's taking a hard look at his finances and acting to get them under control. He went from a salesperson that performed in the middle of the pack to one who performed in the top 5%. He did this because he wasn't worried about making money simply to cover the bills. He was focused on taking care of his customers and letting the money follow. Eliminating garbage applies to money management as well as to time or space management. Combine all three and there's no telling what you can accomplish.

If you look at Brian's example, you'll notice that I didn't sit him down and yell at him to cut his expenses. I simply gave him an idea that he then interpreted into various means to retain more cash. Just like with everything else you've been reading about, only you can make the changes required to become successful. You and you alone can make the difference in your life. Others might be able to help you or offer suggestions on how to improve yourself, but only you can act on those suggestions. No one can force you to be successful; only you can do whatever is necessary to succeed. Whatever it is you do for a living, you must learn to do better. Whatever money you waste on junk, only you can learn to budget. Sure, you can hire accountants or money managers to help you "make the most of your money" – and I agree that these professionals do serve a valuable function and can help us earn more – but the important work must be done by you and you alone. Control of your life, whether it involves your finances, work habits or personal life, is up to you.

And Brian? Seven months after adjusting his monthly budget he was on track to have the best sales quarter of his career, earning record commissions.

What Did You Learn?

1. Junk clutters your life and adds headaches you don't need on the road to becoming successful.
2. What you consider junk may be of great value to others. Donate it. Auction it. Do whatever it takes to get it out of your life and move on.
3. Managing money is an important part of managing the clutter in your life. Get rid of unnecessary expenses and simplify your finances as much as possible. The less financial headaches you have, the easier it is to maintain a positive attitude, and additional benefits will flow from that.
4. The more you focus on doing a great job, the easier it is to become successful.

CHAPTER 27

Yes You Can: Develop A Strategy To Reach Your Goals

Don't just do it. Do it right.

A S A TEENAGER I was fortunate to meet Art Rooney, the owner of the Pittsburgh Steelers,. Mr. Rooney was a man of impeccable moral fiber. I'll never forget when he told me that as I grew older, I'd succeed if I kept a focus on "God, family and business, in that order. Everything else is fluff." Since this book isn't about religion I won't delve into that topic, but since it is a book about improving yourself and reaching your goals, it is important for you to understand that activities that don't impact your beliefs, family or business are activities that take you away from reaching your goals.

I know a pastor who gives a wonderful sermon in which he described marriage as a triangle with the bride and groom on each corner of the bottom of the triangle and God at the apex. The closer each person got to God, the closer they got to each other. I often think of that analogy and apply it to other aspects of my life. If my goal is to solve a particular problem, I'll put the solution at the apex and devise two ideas that, when working together, can help me get closer to the goal. This lowers the risk of each idea while focusing on the goal. Utilizing this triangular tactic also helps me prioritize what is important in both my personal life and business.

As an example, here is what the original strategy triangle for The Amati Foundation looked like when I first sketched it on a napkin on April 4, 2000.

Goal: Assist talented young musicians in obtaining high quality instruments

Create an outreach program to convince retiring musicians to donate their instruments to the next generation.

Design a business model to efficiently acquire musical instruments to be loaned to deserving students and professionals.

The ideas themselves didn't define the strategies used to reach the apex; those came later. What the ideas did was set in place two approaches—or tactics—to reaching a goal. In the case of The Amati Foundation, both were incorporated into the organizational strategy. I also designed a public relations event known as The Amati Foundation Historical Collection, a recreation of history's most famous violins, violas, celli and basses, crafted by 34 of today's best makers from eight countries that is another tactic to promote the goals of Amati Foundation and fits nicely with the original idea shown on the bottom left of my strategy triangle.

By focusing on the concept of "efficiently acquiring musical instruments" I was able to, at a very early stage, determine that I didn't require lots of people or added costs to develop a business model that worked. Today, this model enables the foundation to place 92% of donations directly into musicians' hands, creating an unheard of level of financial efficiency (and responsibility). As the foundation evolved, I would return again and again to the strategy triangle in order to figure out how to make the organization run better. This enabled me to alter the tactics while keeping the original goal in place.

I have found that using the strategy triangle is an effective means to keep you focused on the important things in your personal and professional career. For example, while someone may come to me with a great idea for The Amati Foundation, if it doesn't fit our strategy, then it doesn't fit our organization. It's that simple. This is not to say that the idea may not have merit, but if you take on too many ideas, you simply dilute the time and energy you have to focus on reaching your goal.

Here is an example: the Amati Foundation was recently approached about opening a retail store to sell low-cost instruments to students. While the idea was interesting, it really didn't fit our strategy triangle because it didn't create huge public awareness and it didn't support musical education on a grand scale. While it certainly could have helped students afford musical instruments, there are already thousands of music stores that address this audience. The Amati Foundation didn't need to offer a "me too" solution. Because it didn't fit the strategy triangle, I had to politely say "no" to the person who brought it to me. At first I could tell he was disappointed, but once I showed him the strategy triangle and how a retail store didn't fit the bigger mission of the foundation, he understood where the foundation's priorities lay.

Remember the insurance salesman who went from earning $65,000 a year to more than $150,000? Manuel's strategy triangle began with two strategies: 1) identify and represent manufacturers seeking to enter the Hispanic market, and 2) identify customers for the goods that he would represent. He built in tactics such as providing superior service and an attractive commission structure to round out the strategy. He then posted the strategy on the wall near his desk so that he could continually focus his energies on the two paths that led to his goal. Here it is:

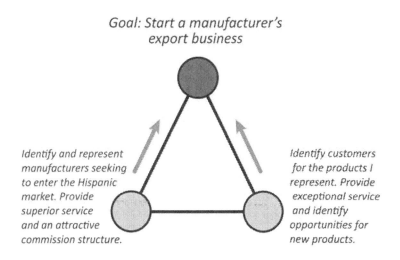

Goal: Start a manufacturer's export business

Identify and represent manufacturers seeking to enter the Hispanic market. Provide superior service and an attractive commission structure.

Identify customers for the products I represent. Provide exceptional service and identify opportunities for new products.

By utilizing a strategy triangle you can quickly visualize two separate paths—or tactics—to reach your goal. One may work and one may not. Or perhaps you'll find that both work. There is certainly no law that says you cannot strive to reach a goal by taking only one path. In fact, over the years I have had dozens of people come to me and say they've transformed the strategy triangle in to 3D models to enable them to outline multiple tactics and strategies.

But for now, let's keep things simple.

Now it is your turn. Fill in the strategy triangle below with your goal and two tactics to reach that goal. Remember to begin with your goal. Then think about two ways to reach your goal.

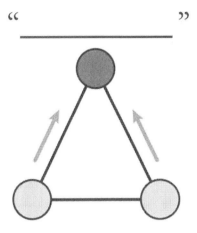

Think about your strategy and write down a few tactics that can be used to support that strategy. Don't worry about nailing down specifics right now. The idea is to jot down ideas, concepts, tactics, and then using what you know about your product and customers, figure out which tactics have the highest likelihood of supporting your strategy in order to move it closer to your goals. With practice you'll be able to use this exercise to address problems of all sizes.

What Did You Learn?

1. Focusing on a goal is the only way to reach the goal.
2. Utilizing a strategy triangle as a means to identify goals and tactics to reach those goals is an effective tool that can be help you throughout your career and life.

CHAPTER 28

Yes You Can: Pull It All Together

*Anyone who says they can't make it in America
isn't looking at what this country has to offer.*

I F YOU REALLY WANT to succeed, you must separate yourself from the rest of society that is content to live average lives. Use the strategy triangle as a means to clearly identify what you want from life and how you will reach it.

Living life with a strategy in place provides a roadmap to follow. You can build a life of significance. You can reach your goals. You can exceed your expectations. You can be successful.

You're mostly through reading this book and you're probably already thinking of a dozen ways you can make a better life.

You already know you need not fear failure. You know you need to develop a positive attitude and continually seek self-improvement. You understand that there is no reward without risk. You know that the only person on this planet who can take control of your destiny is you.

March to Your Own Drummer

When you think of yourself, think in terms of "you versus the other people." This doesn't mean that you are joining the ranks of Ted "The Unibomber" Kaczynski and are declaring war on the rest of society. Instead, this means that you can see yourself as ignoring the herd mentality and focusing instead on what makes you happy, what makes *you* content, and what will make *you* successful. Soon you will find that you've improved yourself and your life to the point where you really are apart from them. That's when you'll realize that you stand out from the crowd, not because you're weird or different, but because you've become successful in life. Now it's time for others to wish they were you. Isn't it fun how the tables can turn and life can come full circle?

As I've said before, whatever it is you do, strive to do it better. Perform well and you will be noticed. Work hard and you will be rewarded. The rewards might not come in predictable ways and may not happen just as you expect them. But since it is you who are creating your own opportunities, you can be confident that your efforts will prove worthwhile. Someone *will* notice your work. Someone *will* recognize your efforts. It may be your boss, your customers, your spouse, your parents, or even your kids. But you will get noticed.

If your boss or manager takes everything from you but never gives you back anything, then switch jobs. I don't mean to suggest that you should call your boss an inconsiderate moron and storm out the door without some sort of plan for the future. Planning is the key to being able to walk out that door with confidence and with the knowledge that you have just made a well thought out career move. Sure it's scary and it may be difficult to find a new job, but for your own sake, make the necessary changes. If you want to start your own business, go do it. But first, make sure that you have carefully thought out your plans.

Remember that new businesses often start slowly and don't necessarily show immediate profits. Sam Walton started Wal-Mart with one store. Dave Thomas started Wendy's with one restaurant. Conrad Hilton started with one hotel. What will you start with?

You must be creative in finding opportunities, making the most of them, and making sure that you are in the right place at the right time. Luck can be created. Successful people don't sit around and wait for luck to drop a pot of gold into their laps. Successful people make their own luck and reap the rewards of their self-made gold mines.

On the opposite side of good luck is bad luck. You can attempt to avoid bad luck but, just as certain as the sun will come out tomorrow, bad luck will strike. There isn't anything you can do about it, but work through it and persevere. Sometimes things happen that even the best planning or precautions couldn't prevent.

I once heard a minister's sermon talk about how we take our good fortune for granted but as soon as bad luck strikes we question God (or Buddha, Allah, Mohammed, etc.) and lash out wondering why we are being treated so unfairly. The minister said, "Do we thank God for all the good things we experience every day? If not, why not? If we do, then isn't it His choice to throw some challenges into our lives to challenge us?" Whether you are religious or not, this makes a lot of sense. If we are thankful for all the good we have, why not greet challenges, even if they are serious like cancer or loss of a job, with a positive outlook as something not to be feared, but to be challenged. To make us stronger. To be overcome. Yes You Can!

A couple of years ago, I went through nine weeks where bad luck seemed to haunt me. My car got hit. I broke my glasses. My computer's hard disk failed and I lost hundreds of files. I fell and injured my knee. The roof seal ever my back porch cracked and rain came pouring into the kitchen. To make matters worse I lost my American Express card somewhere between Boston and Austin. I was at my wit's end and cursed everything in sight. For about three weeks I was in the worst mood of my life and neither friends nor family wanted to be anywhere near me. Nobody was going to help me so I finally realized I needed to take control. You know what? You can't do anything about these situations except get up and start over. Step back and say, "Oh, well." As my former landscaper Greg would say, "The best advice I could give a person is that you've just got to start walking and stop looking back." Pastor William Hazlitt said, "Prosperity is a great teacher; adversity a greater." Perhaps Tom Cruise said it best in *Risky Business*: "Sometimes you just have to say what the ____." Well, you can fill in the rest. Try to make the most of bad situations and put the misery behind you and you will do a good job of rebuilding your life. I had to step back and take a deep breath. The simple facts were that the car could be fixed, the glasses and computer replaced, the knee would heal, the house would be repaired, and American Express would send me a new card. Sure, it was challenging at the time, but I overcame, and ultimately, everything turned out fine.

How often do you worry about being run over by an elephant? Probably not too often. How often do you worry about being bit by a mosquito? It's the little things that get you. If you learn not to let the little things bother you, then you'll eliminate most of the stress in your life. Imagine not worrying about those pesky mosquitoes. Once they're out of your periphery, you don't have anything to worry about. After all, you weren't worrying about the elephant to begin with.

When a thought pops into my mind that is something I have to do I used to worry about it. Sometimes I'd be worrying about things that were weeks into the future. It made me anxious and uptight. At times I could be a bear to be around because I'd be so wracked with worry about something that was beyond my control. Dr. Beryl Huang, a leading motivational speaker and self-improvement counselor in the American Chinese community, taught me a trick that I use daily. She said, "When something comes into your mind that you have to do, ask yourself this one question: 'What can I do about it right now?'. If the answer is nothing, then don't think about it. Don't worry about it. Deal with it when you can do something about it, but right now, if you can't, why let it eat at you?" She was absolutely right. It took me about three and a half months to be able to use this trick effectively, but thank God I did, because today it is a lifesaver. It helps me stay focused, remain calm, and keep organized and the best part is, if I can't do something about it right now, I simply do not worry about it right now. Imagine the pressure that was lifted off me.

You can live this way too! Yes You Can! Once you start living this way, you'll find that the goals you hope to reach are easier to achieve. You'll find your love life improves. You'll find you have better relationships with your family and friends. Your health may improve. Your hair may stop falling out. And you might even get along better with your mother-in-law!

Keep Reading

Anyone, not just future entrepreneurs or business owners, can use the advice in this book. I recognize that you might be happy with what you are doing. Not everybody wants to own businesses or earn millions and there is absolutely nothing wrong with that. If you're fulfilled with what you're doing, that is great news. Stick with it and keep up the good work. Take my advice and improve on the quality of your life. Make an effort to save time and money and you will be even happier than you already are.

But if you don't like your job, only you can change it. Improve your skills. Move to a different department. Change companies. If you don't like your spouse or significant other, get a new one. Quit wasting your and her time and get on with life. It's too short! If you feel that you need a college education, get one. Even if it means taking one class at a time, get started now. There are many people in their 30s, 40s, 50s, and older who are taking college classes. One of my former business acquaintances has a dark cloud of gloom hanging over his head because he didn't complete his college education. He has three choices: finish his studies and earn a degree; realize he doesn't necessarily need one and be proud of what he's accomplished to date; or keep moaning about how he doesn't have a college degree and spend the rest of his life in regret. My advice to him? Get over it! He has learned more in running his own business the past few years than he will by sitting in a classroom for four years.

Just thinking about your problems won't get you anywhere. There are no excuses. I don't care how old, fat, ugly, uneducated, or poor you are, these are only excuses and don't mean a thing when you're lying in your casket looking up at heaven. Break out of your routine and make the changes you have to make in order to succeed.

Anyone Has the Ability to Achieve Their Goals

I hear the excuses all the time. "But, I'm Black." "But my father was an alcoholic." "But I'm Hispanic and my English is no good." I don't care about the color of your skin; what socio-economic background you came from; when your Daddy left home; or what other bad things happened in your life. My mother had a stroke when I was five years old and she lay on the couch babbling incoherently while I was expecting her to teach me and help me with homework. Did her illness affect me? Absolutely! Did it hold me back? Absolutely not! In fact, I think it helped to create my own sense of empathy for people who haven't had the opportunities I have or who have faced challenges for which they had no control such as paralysis, mental retardation, and autism. But excluding these obstacles, every American child is born with the ability to go to school. Our country provides thirteen years of free education to anyone who seeks it. Our government provides myriad means to finance and gain a college education. The Small Business Administration has hundreds of programs to help fund new businesses. Social services across America can help one get training, learn a language, qualify for financial aid, provide childcare services, and so forth. If you have the will, America gives you the opportunity to create the way.

One of my lifelong friends is an attractive, smart, sophisticated woman. She also happens to be of African-American heritage. She never let the color of her skin get in the way of making her life a success. I have always admired her for that. In fact, in the 30+ years I've known her, I don't believe I've ever heard her say she couldn't do something because of her ethnicity. She has an amazingly positive attitude and is sure about her abilities and what she contributes to business. She's also smart enough to realize that if she's in the wrong department or company, she can do something about it and get back on her road to success. (I worked for her father when I was younger and he was the same way, thus I always knew where sh got her drive.)

I once had a man on one of my sales teams who came from a broken home in a bad neighborhood of New York City. His father was an alcoholic deadbeat who spent most of his time in Harlem's neighborhood bars and was never involved in his kids' lives. His brother had problems with drugs and the law. His mother raised him virtually by herself. But as he grew up he told himself he'd never lead the life of his father or brother. He strived at everything he did. He studied. He resisted the slang of the "hood" and learned to speak grammatically proper English, sometimes insisting that teachers spend time with him to delve into correct grammatical usage. He was the first person in his family to be awarded a college scholarship, followed by a college degree. He worked his butt off every day and became successful in spite of the obstacles in front of him. He once told me, "being Black means I have to work harder and be smarter than anyone else but that is OK, because I'm going to do that anyway." When I asked him who he looked up to, instead of the typical response of Kobe Bryant, Shaquille O'Neal, Eminem, Kanye West, Will.I.Am and other celebrities, he told me how his heroes were successful because of who they were and what they achieved, not because they could rap or play a sport. He believed that a person's idols should be those people whose lives mirror what your own life could be like. He looked up to former Oklahoma Congressman J.C. Watts, actor Sidney Poitier, Microsoft founders Bill Gates and Paul Allen, USA Today founder Al Neurath, and Jesus Christ.

The United States government interned thousands of Japanese during World War II. They were jailed because of where they were from. Today, the families of many of these people are wildly successful because they started businesses, worked hard, and made their dreams come true. They didn't let oppression bring them down; they rose above it. They viewed it as an obstacle along the path to success. And that's what it is really, an obstacle. An obstacle to be overcome. They did it, you can too. Yes You Can!

Let's not forget the millions of Jewish people who fled Nazi Germany and lost everything. Many came to America and built successful lives and careers. They faced obstacles greater than any most of us could imagine—Adolph Hitler and his clan of murderers attempting to extinguish an entire population—yet rose above the obstacles.

I'm not saying that there are not race issues still prevalent in our country. I know people who would avoid hiring a minority if it was the last thing they did. However, for every one of those people, I know twenty who hire based on a person's track record, ability and enthusiasm. And even if you don't have a track record, there are countless ways to develop one, which reminds me of the story of a young guy knocking on advertising agency doors who finally said, "Teach me everything you know and I'll work for free." He did it. You can too. Yes You Can!

Anyone who says they can't make it in America isn't looking at what this country has to offer. They are looking for excuses. They possess self-defeating attitudes. They will not succeed, because deep down, they don't want to succeed. Your life doesn't have to be like that. You can become whoever you want to become. The limits of your success are only bound by your willingness to achieve success.

Real success and the most fulfilling kind of happiness come from within. Some people are born into wealthy families or become wealthy through an inheritance. Let me tell you, there is nothing creative about being born into a wealthy family. I know many people like this. As a whole, they lead empty, unfulfilling lives. Many do charity work because that's what they're *supposed* to do. Many go into the family business because father and grandfather did the same. Not many strike out on their own, blaze their own trail, and end up enthusiastic about their accomplishments. If I could choose to be richly rewarded in life through my personal satisfaction in my life's accomplishments or through my great-uncle's inheritance, I'd take accomplishments 365 days of the year. Pride may not make you rich, but it will make you feel good; and that's something money alone cannot do.

Creating Success is a Way of Life

Everything you have read in these pages refers to a lifelong process. Better management of your life will not happen overnight but will take years of effort and focus. Success may not result immediately, and to be truthful, may not result at all. Don't kid yourself into believing that managing your time for one day, one week, or even one year will result in success. This just won't happen. The important changes in your life must *become your new life*. If you follow the advice I've offered, you will embark on the most important lifelong process of all: creating a future that is fuller, better, and more rewarding than anything you imagined.

Now is the time for you to begin your journey. If you are serious about getting on with your life's work, about creating a meaningful life, about becoming successful, then put down this book and make it happen. Don't close the cover and turn on the television. Grab a pencil and paper and start writing down ideas on how you are going to make your life better. Draw a strategy triangle and devise ways to reach your goals. Get ready to work hard, plan wisely and act on your intuitions. Aim for your goals and don't let anyone tell you that you can't reach them. Start every day telling yourself that you control your destiny, and today will be better than yesterday because each new day puts you one day closer to becoming successful. Become a factor in your life. Find your significance. Follow my advice as best you can, add your own ideas, and you will learn that the key to success has been staring you in the face every morning when you brush your teeth. **The key to success is you. I believe you can do it. Yes You Can!**

What Did You Learn?

1. Perform well and you will be noticed. Work hard and you will

be rewarded. Since it is you who are creating your own opportunities, you can be confident that you will succeed.

2. There are no excuses in life; only those that make excuses. Rise above your challenges and build a life that is significant.

3. The pursuit of success is a lifelong process. There are no shortcuts; no jumping to the head of the line. To be successful you must act, think, and convince yourself that you will exceed your expectations and become the person you dream about.

4. Start on your journey right here and now. Don't delay.

5. Always remember: Yes You Can!

Afterword

There Is Never Enough Time To Do All You Want,
So Make The Time

EVERY YEAR I FIND I have less and less time to do the things I want. Because of this I become more committed to accomplishing my goals and living each day to its fullest and each year to its maximum benefit.

I have goals of becoming a better partner, a better father, and a better friend.

I have goals of spending more time with my two wonderful children, Colton and Pierce, being an active participant in their lives and teaching them all I know, while encouraging them to pursue their dreams.

I have goals of getting active and creating a healthier lifestyle so I am here to see Colton and Pierce's children.

I have goals of getting to know innovative business executives that I've admired over the years, such as Barry Diller of InterActiveCorp., Eli Broad of KB Home and SunAmerica, Fox Software founder David Fulton, David Neeleman of JetBlue Airways, and Richard Branson of Virgin Atlantic.

Because of my interest in music, I want to get to know musicians like Joshua Bell, Vanessa Mae, and others, and musician/entrepreneurs such as Sammy Hagar and Ted Nugent.

When I say, "get to know," what I really mean is "learn from." As you become acquainted with a person you will invariably learn from their life experiences. Since this is the case, why shouldn't I aim high and focus on learning from the best? *(Alex Van Halen. Ritchie Sambora, Don Felder: if you're reading this, I'd really be up for a few drum and guitar lessons!)*

I have dozens of ideas for ventures and I want to pursue each of them. I want to start a T-shirt company that would provide fundraising opportunities to religious organizations. I have a concept for a screenplay I'd like to develop into a movie. Another idea I'm working on is a private equity fund that invests in rare violins, violas, and celli to make them available to professional musicians who need favorable acquisition terms in order to own the instrument of their dreams, while creating market beating returns for the fund's investors. I'm working on a project called the Institute of Stringed Instrument Studies that would create a world-class violin- and guitar-making school within the The University of Texas system. Yet another project that my business partner James Rockefeller has been leading may revolutionize the world financial markets, bringing affordable clean water, energy and education to developing nations or areas of strife and poverty. Yet another venture is a project to recreate the chemical composition of master violinmaker Antonio Stradivari's wood preparation and varnish ground, providing luthiers with an acoustically superior ground coating to be used between wood and varnish. And still another is a venture to manufacture and market state-of-the-art carbon fiber guitar picks, drum sticks and drum sets. Whew…I better get busy!

There are organizations I want to support such as The Andy

Pilgrim Foundation (http://www.andypilgrimfoundation.org/), whose mission is to educate new drivers to the dangers of driving while distracted, The Watchful Shepherd (http://www.watchful.org), which provides children and their families a voice against family violence and the abuse of children, and German Shepherd Rescue of Orange County (http://www.gsroc.org/) which is an all-volunteer organization with no paid staff focused on finding homes for abandoned German Shepherd dogs. I feel these organizations deserve my support—whether financial or through my time—and I hope you'll find organizations that warrant your attention.

Then there's The Amati Foundation, which positively impacts on school-aged children and teens while supporting orchestras, museums, professional musicians, and instrument makers around the world. Founded in 2000, Amati Foundation is one of the things I am most passionate about. I believe the programs we've created have the ability to bring lifelong joy to millions of people around the world. That alone gets me jazzed about the opportunities ahead. Are there obstacles? Of course there are. But what have we learned? Obstacles are meant to be overcome!

All these projects are above and beyond companies and projects I'm already involved with.

Here's the funny thing: the ideas just keep coming. I believe I have many more companies to start, more money to be made, more customers to serve, more people to network with, and much, much, much more success to experience.

I know I have more to learn. At age 40, I completed two years of night study to earn my Master in Business Administration (MBA) in global business at the Hankamer School of Business at Baylor University. As my background suggests, I certainly didn't need an MBA to become successful, but I chose to earn one because I wanted to improve my financial skills, and learn more about organizational behavior. I chose Baylor because it is ranked in the Top 20 universities in the world for international business, an area in which I am acutely interested. An added benefit of this experience is that I was given the distinction, through the John F. Schoen Entrepreneur-in-Residence chair, that allowed me to lecture on entrepreneurship to Baylor's students, which is a rewarding way of giving back to an institution I've come to admire.

Even after earning my MBA, I feel it is safe to reiterate that much of what is taught in an MBA course you will learn from running your own business and through books like *The Ten Day MBA*. If you make the time to continuously learn, you can stay abreast of the latest management research through publications like *Harvard Business Review* and *The McKinsey Quarterly*. If you want to learn specialized skills, there are workshops, books, and online courses that cover just about any topic imaginable. You simply have to make the decision to seek self-improvement by whatever means necessary.

To MBA or Not to MBA?

To be fair, earning an advanced degree does provide benefits. Nearly eighty percent of top executives polled in a recent survey said that earning a graduate degree in business is important for those who want to obtain top management positions in most companies. Perhaps the greatest benefit of earning an MBA is for people in mid-size and larger corporations who want to move up in their corporate hierarchy and must have a piece of sheepskin with the words "Master of Business Administration" on it in order to be considered for promotion. For those going into investment banking and venture capital who need to financially evaluate companies and require a broad spectrum of management knowledge, an MBA is now considered a necessary part of one's résumé. A recent survey of accounting/financial workers of varying skill and seniority levels found that Chief Financial Officers without a formal degree had an average salary of only $38,920; those with a bachelor's degree earned up to $88,836; while MBAs with relevant experience earned an average of $104,284. Clearly, the benefits of an MBA can be substantial. On the other hand, I know many millionaires who don't even hold a bachelor's degree, let alone a MBA. And some of the millionaires I know didn't even graduate high school. So if you can't afford to take two years to earn an MBA, don't worry, nothing can stop you from being successful if you put your heart and soul into it.

Another benefit of pursuing an advanced degree is the relationships you make through spending two years with dozens of other people. But you can build the same types of relationships by becoming active in local charities, business clubs, networking organizations, and your local church. As a small business owner it is often the case that the people within 30 miles of our business are the most important to network with. Of course, with the flattening of the world and customers now able to reach you instantly via web sites and e-mail, perhaps networking will ultimately change from face-to-face relationships to one controlled by digital messages between two or more people. For several years I have conducted business with a man in Hong Kong whom I have never met; yet via e-mail and telephone we've developed a successful professional relationship. I occasionally consult for an advertising agency halfway around the world in Lithuania, completing all our projects via e-mail. And more than 90% of The Amati Foundation work is completed online via e-mail, video conferencing, and instant messaging, giving me instant access to any of our benefactors, employees, volunteers, and suppliers.

I expect to stay busy reinventing my life and exploring new opportunities for many years to come. I hope you now see that you can too. The world is a fairly flexible place and you can make it what you want. I believe this with all my heart. I hope you take advantage of the great opportunities that lie before you. I hope you decide to pursue a life of significance. I hope you spend each day, starting today, thinking about how you can become successful. You can accomplish anything you set your mind too. If you want to send me an e-mail to let me know how you're doing, write to me at **YesYouCan@interminds.com.**

With Appreciation

*Remember To Say "Thank You" To Those
Who Have Helped You.*

MANY PEOPLE HAVE GIVEN me inspiration throughout my life. While a complete list would fill hundreds of pages, there are many important individuals that I must thank in these pages.

The importance of good parents cannot be underestimated. My parents, John and Jackie, gave me every opportunity to learn, even though I may not have realized they were doing so. The experiences I had growing up were diverse and many, and it wasn't until I reached my mid-30s that I began to realize how my parents opened the world to me. It sounds like a cliché, but they gave me the flexibility to stumble, but supported me so I wouldn't fall.

Many of my relatives opened doors for me that I am now just realizing were precious gifts. My uncle Albert Miller, founder of Meadowcroft Village in Avella, Pennsylvania, impressed upon me a love for history, paleontology, and nature. My great-grandmother, Bama, through small acts like patiently hand-painting my toy soldier set, taught me the importance of carefully completing tasks. My aunt, Aileen "Sis" Lindenbaum, instilled in me the concepts of class and graciousness and her husband, Herbert, through his daily actions, taught me the importance of clarity and calmness, and through his battle with cancer, the importance of hope and laughter. My grandparents, Al and Peg Townsend, taught me the joys of working with my hands, being creative, conservation, hunting and the outdoors, while my other grandparents, Jack and Beverly Mayer instilled in me responsibility to give back to those less fortunate and a love of music. I hope my two boys learn early in life to take advantage of every opportunity to learn from their parents and relatives.

To my teachers, all of whom touched my life in some way, I offer you my sincerest thanks and gratitude. It is unfortunate that we often wait ten, twenty, sometimes thirty years after elementary and secondary school to realize how important our teachers were in forming our lives. To Mrs. Crunnick, Ms. Fantini, Ms. Bailey, Ms. Komovic, Ms. Resick, Mr. Ferguson, Mr. Forquer, Mr. Stultz, Mr. Mumford, Mr. Makar and every other educator who took the time to impart their knowledge on me, thank you, thank you, thank you!

To Walter Zurko, professor of art at the College of Wooster, who taught me to push the limits in which I was comfortable and to not be afraid to try something new, thank you for encouraging me to look in new directions: your lessons have served me well throughout my life.

To Terry Maness, Gary Carini, John Martin, Kendall Artz, and Bill Petty, thank you for opening my eyes to the opportunities in teaching and sharing my knowledge with the students at Baylor University and the University of New Orleans. Your enthusiasm in my skills adds to my desire to share my experiences with others.

To all teachers: you work in one of the most difficult and underappreciated careers, but by far the most important outside of parenting in terms of helping establish the future directions a young person makes. Keep up the good work!

To Edward Ryan, founder of Ryan Homes, and Joseph Hardy, founder of 84 Lumber Company, you have no idea how your lives have impacted me. Mr. Ryan, your generosity and commitment to doing well and doing good at the same time is something I can only hope to achieve at a small scale compared to what you have. Your life is a model of excellence. Mr. Hardy, while you may have viewed me simply as "Maggie's fishing buddy" or "John's boy," I watched and learned from you. You are an example of how hard work and determination pays off, and more importantly, how finding a niche and working hard at being successful can lead to a prosperous career.

To the people I've worked for who have taught me what is right and wrong with management principles, thank you for showing me what is good and thank you for showing me the sometimes ugly side of management. Both have strengthened my skills.

Thanks to Bob Davis for leading by example (read Bob's book, *Speed is Life*) and Ben Bassi for years of partnership and friendship.

To Wendy Petronka, Carin Castillo, Karen Anderson, Jaime Steger, Jennifer Lee, Meng-Shih Wang, Ashley Zhang (謝謝老師。), Lin Yit, Bai Ling, Claudia Christian, Shih Shengxin, Yasuyo Ushioda, Yumi Kaneko, Kelie Plank, Kelli Lawless, Myriam Martinez, Yessenia Santos, Elizabeth Lopez, Shari Beaute Forte, Theresa Chu, Cara Marcy, Sarah Kotchen, Kristina Yao, Ronna Halbgewachs, Pat Wilson, Sandra Odle, the Schweers family, John Duke Anthony, Newt Gingrich, Rick Santorum, Jack Gardner, Jack Illare, Peter Nance, Donn Wilson, Lee Brody, Frank Federer, Randy Branch, Doug Paxton, Brian Bell, John Povich, Jeff Brodnick, Will May, Kevin Harris, Christopher Johnson, Phil Wood, Glenn Pagan, Mark Coticchia, Bruce Huang, Mel Rockefeller, Ron Burd, Esteban Felix, John Rogers, David Jansen, Fred Chang, Giggs Huang, Terry & Jenny Majamaki, Tim Slater, Mark May, Salman Bawany, Raj Sundarum, Supratik Burman, Ali Hussaini,

Dennis Guthery, Bob Skoro, John Stern, Joseph Bird, Scott Minor, Ron Slaven, Chip Dourlain, Rick Klempay, and countless others, thank you for impacting my life.

To Lucy Lui, just because. Jennifer Love Hewitt for singing in Kitson. Will Smith for making me laugh. Tom Cruise for having so much fun doing what you do. Wayne Dyer for helping me pull my own strings. Clint Eastwood for being an inspiration. Gary Sinise for your patriotism. Karla Chadimova for being so endearing. Rosario Dawson for your exceptional empathy and talent. John Cusack for leading a life that you define. Noah Wyle and Richard Rice for being such down to earth friends.

To Kevin Vest, Doug Andrews, Dean Yeck, Matt Rogers, Chris Jensen, and others at Baylor who have shared their successes, challenges, and disappointments, thank you for your friendship and for letting me experience your challenges and successes. I've gained much by knowing you.

To Dr. Steven Graff-Radford and the fine staff at Cedars-Sinai Medical Center for showing me that professionalism and commitment to serving the customer is still alive and well in America. To the staff at Les Suites Taipei Da'an for making me feel at home and exemplifying the Yes You Can! attitude.

To Nancy Todd and Bruce Todd, thank you for taking a chance on me and giving me my first ad agency job. "Nana, let's celebrate the book by eating grease at Long John Silver's." To my other Lexington friends, Lisa Davis, Brian Eastman, Skip Olson, Frank Goad, Robin McWilliams, Diane May, etc., thanks for being such positive influences on my life as a then 20-something getting his start in advertising.

To the producers and cast of *Extreme Makeover: Home Edition,* thank you for including me in your television program and exposing me to one of the most memorable and life-changing experiences of my life. Jillian, Paulie and Ed, you are artists and craftsmen. Our concert in front of 3,000 people is forever etched in my memory. What a blast! To Kylie Minogue, thanks for flying in for the concert: it was an uplifting gift to the family and all who participated in the show. Your battle with cancer proves "Yes You Can!" To Jane Marshall and her family, incredible as individuals and even more amazing as a family…I hope all your dreams come true.

To Gregg Alf, Raymond Schryer, Peter Beare, Joseph Curtin, Fan Tau, Sam Zygmuntowicz, Boris Odio de Granda, Michael Selman, and other violin industry friends, thanks for sharing your knowledge, insights, techniques, and passion. It is through your generosity in exchanging information that I have been able to improve my understanding of violin making, history, and the trade.

Thanks to Alan Jackson, Josh Groban, Eminem, Vanessa Mae, Anne Akiko Meyers, Brian Lewis, Midori, Sarah Chang, Joshua Bell, Ted Nugent, Neil Peart, and the guys in Linkin Park, Cake, and Tool for making great music that served as the backing tracks of my writing.

To Nan Ying for your enthusiasm for all things music and for teaching me the Red Violin Chaconne in an hour…I am amazed at your pedagogical abilities. I admire your "Yes You Can!" attitude and look forward to our next endeavor.

To Jim Kellahin, thank you for the inspired *"Forward,"* friendship, and shared passion in music, motion pictures, violin, and skydiving.

Thanks to Heidi LaFleche for taking the time to read my manuscript and make the suggestion to add *"What Did You Learn?"* to each chapter. As Martha Stewart would say, this is a "good thing."

To Claire Bloom, your enthusiasm for this book, invaluable insights, clarity of thought, and superb recommendations were key to getting this book written and published. Thanks for believing I had a message to tell.

To Beryl Huang who is a shining example of what positive mental attitude can do, you gave me the ability to focus on what is important, and to leave what wasn't behind. You taught that you must have hope in your heart before you can love, that every day can be whatever you believe it to be, that beauty comes from within...thank you for everything you do. I don't say it enough, but I truly appreciate you.

To my sons, Colton and Pierce, thank you for sharing your world and letting me see the simplest of life's pleasures through your eyes. Prior to your arrival, my life was career focused and I rarely took time to marvel at the numerous daily wonders that surrounded me. You have given me a newfound sense of purpose, intrigue, and love of the simplest things. Every day you are in my thoughts. To their Mom, Jennifer, thank you for being a strong, positive influence in their lives.

My sincerest gratitude to everyone I've met throughout my career. Thank you for helping me realize that success doesn't mean becoming a vice president or CEO, but instead it means making the very best of all aspects of my life from work to family and on, through every single moment of significance.

Finally, thanks to YOU, for reading this book. Go out and become what you were meant to become. Find your significance. Good luck and enjoy your life!

About the Author

Who is this guy?

BILL TOWNSEND is a serial entrepreneur who has been involved in the launch of more than a dozen companies over the past two decades. He is currently the Chairman of Amati Foundation, a nonprofit serving the education and classical music industries.

He serves on the boards of directors at Newegg.com, the #2 pure play Internet retailer and YourOffers, a leading personalized marketing provider to the retail industry. He also serves as an advisor to ANM Soft, an e-commerce platform company and New West Symphony, the outstanding orchestra based in Southern California.

His background in entrepreneurship includes being part of the founding management team and Vice President Advertising and Vice President Worldwide Ideation at Internet search engine Lycos, was one of the first Internet companies to undertake an initial public offering, doing so in a NASDAQ record of 8-months.

Bill was cofounder of YouthStream Media Networks (now Alloy), the largest publicly-held young adult marketing and media company in America. His management skills have been utilized at companies like

GeoCities (now Yahoo!), Deja News (now Google and eBay), NewsAlert (now DowJones), IntelliQuant, Really Easy Internet (now Hey, Inc.), Solidus Networks, Cyber Operations, Supermodel.com, Ocean Technology, and Interminds.

He has been a guest lecturer at Harvard University, Baylor University, Loyola Marymount University, University of Texas at Austin, University of New Orleans, Digital Hollywood, Center for Asian Americans United for Self Empowerment (CAUSE), SIMBA, Camp Internet, Violin Society of America Annual Convention, and American Institute of Attitudinal Psychology.

His numerous media appearances and interviews include *NBC Nightly News, Fortune, Wall Street Journal, People, Cosmopolitan, Baylor Magazine, The Strad, News8Austin, KDKA TV Pittsburgh, The Young and The Restless,* and ABC Television's *Extreme Makeover: Home Edition.*

He earned his MBA at Baylor University and BA at College of Wooster. He has been previously published in *Harvard Business Review* and *Hoof Beats Magazine* and is the author of the Internet's first *Children's Advertising Guidelines.* He is also the creator of Predictive Mind, a method for overcoming challenges and improving career, life, relationships, and more through pre-determination of events and reactions, and the inventor of Carbonixx musical products.

In his spare time he enjoys painting, photography, handcrafting violins, playing drums and guitar, and traveling throughout Asia.

This is his first book.

Bill can be reached at YesYouCan@Interminds.com.

13344145R00161

Made in the USA
Charleston, SC
02 July 2012